THE

(PSV)

CIRCLE

PUBLICATION G627   JUNE 2015

CURRENT FLEETS OF OPERATORS IN WEST SUSSEX

This publication is part of a series covering the Operators which appear in the PSV Circle News Sheets. It gives details of the known current fleets of operators in the County of West Sussex (WS) and is correct to News Sheet 905 (June 2015). It also includes the fleet of Stagecoach (South) (HA) which has depots in the area at Chichester and Worthing.

CONTENTS

Interpretation	1 - 2
Chassis and Body identification codes	3
West Sussex (WS) psv operators	4 - 39
West Sussex (WS) non-psv operators	39 - 60
Registration / Page number index	60 - 64
Operating names / Fleet name index	65
County code / News Sheet / Area index	66

HOW TO INTERPRET THIS BOOK

This book is presented in alphabetical order operator by operator. Each entry is split into two parts. Text in bold refers to Operator Data while ordinary text relates to Vehicle Data.

OPERATOR DATA

Each operator has a heading giving the following information:

(a) The PKxxxxxxx number at the beginning of each title is the official operator's licence number and is shown on the operator licence discs. After each number there is a code letter which represents the grade of licence held by the operator as follows:- CB = Community Bus (white); I = International (Green); N = National (blue); R = Restricted (orange) or T = Taxi. The colour of the discs is given, where applicable, in brackets.

(b) In the titles, the portion of the name and address in capital letters is that used for the operator in the PSV Circle News Sheets.

(c) The next entry (FN:) is the operator's Fleet Name(s) and these are commonly displayed on the vehicles or on the operator's publicity. If no FN: is given, the operator's fleet name is presumed to be the same as its title.

(d) Operating Centre(s) (OC:) are as reported and in some cases are subject to frequent change.

(e) Vehicles authorised (VA:) is the maximum number of vehicles that the operator is authorised to use at any one time. It does not necessarily indicate the maximum number of vehicles actually with an operator.

VEHICLE DATA

The vehicle data that follows the operator data is the recorded fleet of each operator. Data is listed in eleven columns, the first of which is often blank. These columns are explained as follows:-

(1) The first column contains the vehicle's fleet number if fleet numbers are used. It can also contain a status code letter (in lower case) where the vehicle status is other than for normal PCV use ie:- a = ancillary vehicle, tow wagon etc, p = preserved by the licenced operator; r = used for spares; t = trainer; u = unlicenced (used only in the Major Operators allocations section); w = withdrawn; x = non-PSV with the licenced operator; z = with the operator but not used, eg a store shed etc .

VEHICLE DATA (continued)

(2) The second column contains the vehicle's current registration number. Where a vehicle has previously carried other registration numbers, these are contained in a separate line underneath with the date of re-registration given adjacent to them. Individual lists are presented in vehicle registration order. Where a fleet numbering system is in consistent use that order is adopted.

(3) The third column is a code signifying the name of the chassis builder. A list of these codes is given on page 3.

(4) The fourth column is also a code and signifies the chassis model type. A list of these codes is also given on page 3

(5) The fifth column contains the vehicle's chassis number or, where known, the full 17 character VIN (Vehicle Identification Number).

(6) The sixth column contains a code and signifies the body builder or minibus converter. A list of these codes is given on page 3.

(7) The seventh column contains the body builder's body or conversion number if these numbers are allocated. Where the field is blank, no numbers are allocated.

(8) The eighth column is a complex descripter indicating the vehicle's seating capacity and certain other information. The descripter will start with one of the codes B, C, CH, DP, H, L, M or O deciphered as follows:-.

    B   indicates a single decker bus or a coach-built minibus of a bus-type style. It is followed by the number of seats and the position of the door - C (centre), D (dual, typically front and centre), F (front) or R (rear). One or more of the special fitment codes L - wheelchair accessible via a lift or T- fitted with a toilet may follow.

    C   indicates a single decker coach or a coach-built minibus to a coach style. It is also followed by the number of seats and the door position, followed by fitment codes if applicable.

    CH   indicates a double decker built to coach standards. It is followed by two numbers of seats seperated by a slash with the first being the upper deck capacity and the second being the lower deck capacity. On odd occasions, only one capacity will be given and this means that the seating split is unknown. The seating capacity is again followed by the door position and fitment codes.

    DP   indicates a dual purpose vehicle. The data that follows is similar to C.

    FH   indicates a double decker bus with a front-mounted engine but with a full front, rather than the normal half front/half bonnet. It is followed by the same information as CH. This code is rarely used.

    H   indicates a double decker bus. It is followed by the same information as CH.

    L   is also rarely used and indicates a double decker bus built to the old low bridge design. The data that follows is the same as CH.

    M   indicates a minibus typically converted from a van or crewbus design and up to and including 16 seats. It is followed by the exact number of seats where known.

    O   indicates an open top double decker. The data that follows is the same as CH.

    PO   indicates a part open / part closed top double decker. The data that follows is the same as CH.

(9) The ninth column lists the date the vehicle was new. Prior to 4/81 this date is the month of issue of the vehicle PSV licence. Since that date, where possible, this is the date of effective taxation.

(10) The tenth column contains the vehicle's previous operator where this is known, or indicates that the vehicle was new or newly converted. The previous operator's name is followed by a code signifying the area or county in which they were formerly based.

(11) The last column gives the month of issue of either the first PSV licence to the current operator (before 4/81) or of the date of arrival with the current operator. Where a precise date is not known the date is preceded by the word 'by' or 'c' (circa).

YOU CAN UPDATE THESE LISTS

You can update these lists on a monthly basis by subscribing to the PSV Circle's News Sheet 2. For details of costs and membership details, please write to the PSV Circle, Unit GK, 436 Essex Road, London, N1 3QP or visit our website www.psv-circle.org.uk

This publication was compiled by Andrew Gilmour, Paul Green and Keith Kiverstein

CHASSIS AND BODY CODES

Listed below are those codes used for space saving reasons in this and other books in the G-list series. This list is part of a more comprehensive list used by the PSV Circle in their News Sheets and other publications.

CHASSIS MAKES AND MODELS

AD	Alexander Dennis	EOS	E.O.S.	Sca	Scania
Dt	Dart	Etpr	Enterprise Engineering	Ta	Toyota
Env	Enviro 300	Fd	Ford	Tbs	Transbus
Tt	Enviro 400 / Trident	Tt	Transit	Dt	Dart
AEC	A.E.C.	Ft	Fiat	Env	Enviro
Rm	Routemaster	Do	Ducato	Jv	Javelin
Rt	Regent	Io	Iveco	Tt	Trident
Sw	Swift	Ir	Irizar	Tmsa	Temsa
As	Ayats	Ka	Setra (Kassbohrer)	VH	Van Hool
Au	Neoplan (Auwarter)	Ld	Leyland	Vo	Volvo
Ba	Bova	RT	Royal Tiger	OLY	Olympian
Bd	Bedford	LDV	L.D.V	VDL	V.D.L.
Bl	Bristol	Cy	Convoy	VW	Volkswagen
BMC	B.M.C. (Turkey)	Max	Maxus	Ce	Caravelle
Ctn	Citroen	LN	Leyland National	Crf	Crafter
Rly	Relay	MAN	M.A.N.	Tr	Transporter
DAF	D.A.F.	MB	Mercedes Benz	Vx	Vauxhall
Dr	Daimler	MCW	Metro-Cammell Weymann	Mov	Movano
Ds	Dennis	Oe	Optare	Viv	Vivaro
Dt	Dart	Pt	Peugeot	Wt	Wrightbus
Jv	Javelin	Bxr	Boxer	StLt	StreetLite
R	R series	Rt	Renault	DF	Door Forward
Tt	Trident	Mtr	Master		
Du	Duple	Tc	Trafic		

BODY CODES

ACl	Autobus/Autobus Classique	GM	G M Coachworks	PR	Park Royal
AD	Alexander Dennis	Hn	Harrington	RB	Reeve Burgess
Adn	Adamson	Ind	Indcar	RKC	Red Kite Conversions
Aqh	Asquith	Ir	Irizar	Rt	Renault
Ar	Alexander	Is	Ikarus	Sca	Scania
ArB	Alexander (Belfast)	Je	Jonckheere	SCC	SC Coachbuilders
As	Ayats	Ka	Setra (Kassbohrer)		(Caetano)
Atl	Atlas	Km	Kirkham	Srt	Short
Au	Neoplan (Auwarter)	Ks	VDL Kusters	Ssd	Sunsundegui
AVB	Advanced	KVC	Kilbeggan Vehicle	Stan	Stanford Coachworks
Ba	Bova		Conversions	Stn	Strachan
Bf	Berkhof	Lah	Lahden	Tbs	Transbus
BMC	B.M.C. (Turkey)	LCB	Leicester Carriage Builders	Tmsa	Temsa
Bs	Beulas	Ld	Leyland	Ts	Taurus
CD	Chassis Developments	LDV	L.D.V.	UNVI	U.N.V.I.
Co	Salvador Caetano	LN	Leyland National	UVG	U.V.G.
Cpt	Concept	May	Mayflower	UVM	UVModular
Csd	Courtside	MB	Mercedes Benz	UVS	U.V.S.
Cu	Cunliffe	MCC	Midland Coach Concepts	VH	Van Hool
Cym	Cymric	MCW	Metro Cammell Weymann	VW	Volkswagen
DC	Devon Conversions	Me	Mellor	Wk	Willowbrook
Do	Dormobile	MinO	Minibus Options	WMB	Walsall Motor Bodies
Du	Duple	Ml	Marshall	Wre	Whitacres
ECW	Eastern Coach Works	MM	Made to Measure	WS	Wadham Stringer
EL	East Lancs	Mpo	Marcopolo	Wt	Wright
EOS	E.O.S	NC	Northern Counties	Vx	Vauxhall
Eurm	Euromotive	Nuk	Nu-Track		
Excel	XL Conversions	O&H	Oughtred & Harrison		
Fd	Ford	Oe	Optare		
Fer	Ferqui	Pn	Plaxton		

WEST SUSSEX (WS)

PK1029219/N: A & A TRAVEL (Sussex) Limited, 16 Teign Walk, Durrington, WORTHING, BN13 3LR.
OCs: The Yard, Castle Goring, Clapham, Worthing, BN13 3UB; 16 Teign Walk, Durrington, Worthing, BN13 3LR.
VA: 4.

	DEZ 8491	MB	413CDI	WDB9046632R379090	Fer	-?-	C16F	8/02	European Travelplan, Storrington (WS) 1/1
			(ex FY 02 YHJ 5/12)						
	JEZ 8957	MB	413CDI	WDB9046632R250769	ACl	1787	M16	6/01	Moore, Constantine (CO) 6/09
			(ex Y742 OBE 7/09, 624 LAF 6/09, Y742 OBE 6/04)						
	N869 EKR	Ta	HZB50R	HZB5009000282	Co	551023	C21F	8/95	Mayday, Croydon (LN) 2/08
			(ex A 7 FWC 5/00)						
w	R148 CHT	lo	49-10	ZCFC497010D060097	Eurm	-?-	M16	6/98	Holy Family School, Patchway (YGL) by3/02
	S 8 CTD	lo	40C13	ZCFC409000D135220	Crest	IV824	M16	2/01	Holmes, Newport (SH) 5/12
			(ex X613 AVJ 3/12, B 18 TPH 7/08, X613 AVJ c2/07, K 4 ESC c11/03, X613 AVJ 10/01)						
	DA 52 YGR	MB	411CDI	WDB9046632R476138	?		M16	12/02	Warwick, Cryers Hill (BK) 3/14
			(ex H 16 AET 2/14, DA 52 YGR 10/07)						

NOTE: prior to 4/04, vehicles were licensed to PK0002927/N A C & D B Burt, Worthing.

PK0003082/R: ACCESS Car & Buses Limited, 28 Monks Close, LANCING, BN15 9DD.
OC: as address. VA: 2.

Y815 GFM	MB	411CDI	WDB9046632R274202	UVS		M14L	6/01	private owner 7/08

PK1052434/N: ACE TRAVEL (Sussex) Limited, Protran House, Boundary Road, Brighton, BN2 5TJ.
OC: The Old Cement Workshops, Shoreham Road, BEEDING, BN44 3TX. VA: 10.
PK1024379/R Clare Johnson, 39 Connell Drive, Woodingdean, Brighton, BN2 6RT.
FN: 1st Class Travel. OCs: as address; The Old Cement Workshops, Shoreham Road, Beeding, BN44 3TX. VA: 2.
PK1095087/N: Brian Williams & Clare Johnson, 32 Hartington Road, Brighton, East Sussex, BN2 3LS.
FN: Brighton Travel. OC: Old Cement Works, Beeding, BN44 3TX. VA: 6.

AEZ 1361	Sca	K124IB4	YS4K4X20001836975	lr	93319	C49FT	5/00	Countrywide, Gravesend (KT) 3/11
		(ex W342 MKY 3/05)						
NUI 5155	Sca	K93CRB	1819892	Pn	9112SEM0338	C53F	3/92	Alexcars, Cirencester (GL) 9/06
		(ex J292 NNC c12/03)						
H552 GKX	Ld	ON2R50C13Z4	ON11151	Ld	DD1111	H47/31F	1/91	Cedric Coaches, Wivenhoe (EX) 2 8/13
H 6 WTR	Sca	L94IB	1836858	lr	93642	C49FT	6/00	Goldenstand Southern, Park Royal (LN) 1/15
		(ex W264 GBV 10/06)						
J812 GGW	Ld	ON2R50C13Z4	ON20018	Ld	DD1187	H47/31F	2/92	Dorset Heritage, Holton Heath (DT) 9/11
N 3 YCL	Sca	K113CRB	1826811	lr	8791	C49FT	6/96	Dealtop, Plymouth (DN) 5/09
R 6 HLC	Sca	L94IB4	YS4L4X20001831563	lr	150204	C55F	4/98	Roots, Send (SR) 5/13
		(ex R555 ELF 3/05, R 6 HLC 11/04)						
R473 YDT	Sca	L94IB	1832416	lr	91410	C70F	6/98	Bywater, Rochdale (GM) 8/08
		(ex 98-D-41114 5/01)						
V750 DSE	Sca	K124IB4	YS4K4X20001834975	lr	92399	C49FT	10/99	Wheadon, Hereford (HW) 1/15
		(ex FXI 724 3/12, V333 ASH 11/03)						
W752 YDM	MB	413CDI	WDB9046632R106313	GM		M16	5/00	converted from a van 6/04
Y853 GDV	Sca	L94IB	YS4L4X20001839788	lr	94401	C49FT	8/01	Docherty, Auchterarder (SE) 7/12
		(ex 01-D-72094 5/05)						
SJ 51 FHV	MB	O815D	WDB6703742N096436	Sitcar	1671	C27F	10/01	Lowe, Southport (MY) 9/09
		(ex C 9 DWA 1/05, SJ 51 FHV 3/02)						
FN 02 VCC	lo	CC80.E18M/P	SBCA80D0002352507	Ind	-?-	C29F	3/02	Gilchrist, Quarrington Hill (DM) 5/06
FE 52 HFW	lo	CC95.9E.18F	SBCA80D0002352392	Ind	4.589	C29F	1/03	Gilchrist, Quarrington Hill (DM) 4/07
BU 03 UJN	MB	413CDI	WDB9046632R480948	Cym		M16	6/03	Lawson & Watson, Dover (KT) 505 7/05
WL 03 KSE	Fd	Tt	WF0EXXGBFE3E353513	Fd		M16	3/03	private owner by8/08
YX 03 FCU	Tbs	Jv	SFD741BR52GJ22429	Pn	0212GRX4795	C70F	3/03	Leicestershire County Council (XLE) YB1 11/13
GX 04 YCL	Fd	Tt	WF0EXXGBFE4B21353	Fd		M14	by8/04	-?-, -?- 4/10
		(ex -?- 4/10)						
BU 05 EEG	BMC	850	NMC850RKTRD300082	BMC		C35F	3/05	Greenwich Service Plus, Woolwich (LN) 3/12
SK 55 POJ	MB	109CDI	WDF63970523178925	MB		M8	9/05	private owner by10/10
HX 06 FOT	MB	313CDI	WDB9036632R919013	?		M16	5/06	Wiley, Bognor Regis (YWS) 1/14

ACE TRAVEL, BEEDING (continued)

x	MX 06 XSY	LDV	Max	SEYL6PFB20N207957	Cpt	M8L	8/06	H&B, Wood Green (LNx) 19	9/11
x	SJ 57 GVL	LDV	Max (ex M 9 PEY 8/13, SJ 57 GVL 4/10)	SEYL6PWA20N220276	LDV	M8	by2/08	Peyton Travel, Brynna (CC)	9/13
	GR 08 AEV	Fd	Tt	WF0DXXTTFD8K31286	Fd	M16	8/08	-?- (school), -?- (X??)	10/13
	YN 08 PKV	VW	Crf	WV1ZZZ2EZ86043362	Excel -?-	M16	7/08	Airparks Management, Callerton (ND)	2/14
	GU 58 DBV	Fd	Tt	WF0DXXTTFD8K38064	Fd	M16	9/08	Horris Hill School, Newtown (XHA)	10/13
	MX 58 AUT	VW	Crf	WV1ZZZ2EZ96009088	Excel -?-	M16	12/08	Airparks Management, Callerton (ND)	2/14
x	RX 58 GWY	VW	Tr	WV2ZZZ7HZ9H052556	Gowrings	M7	1/09	Blind Veterans UK, Brighton (XES)	7/13
x	RX 58 GXL	VW	Tr	WV2ZZZ7HZ9H055137	Gowrings	M7	2/09	Blind Veterans UK, Brighton (XES)	by1/14

NOTE: prior to 5/09 vehicles were recorded in the East Sussex section of News Sheet 2.

PK1064239/R: Abdeilah AHOUCHI, 73 Gainsborough Road, Tilgate, CRAWLEY, RH10 5LJ.
FN: A & M Transport. OC: as address. VA: 1.

No vehicles currently recorded

PK1022215/I: AIRLINKS AIRPORT Services Limited, Birmingham Coach Station, Digbeth, Birmingham, B5 6DD.
OC: [CY] Room 81, Pier 3 (airside), South Terminal, Gatwick Airport, RH6 0NP.
VA: 70. ***(National Express)***

	8563	KX 58 GUO	AD	Dt	SFD361AR28GY10803	AD	7242/5	B37F	9/08	National Express (LN) 8563	5/15
x	8600	unreg	Cobus	2700	-?-	Co	-?-	B15T	4/00	National Express Operations (LN) C1	8/04
x	8601	unreg	Cobus	2700	TAW6985301U951503	Co	965504	B15T	4/00	National Express Operations (LN) C2	8/04
x	8602	unreg	Cobus	2700	TAW6985301U951505	Co	-?-	B15T	4/00	National Express Operations (LN) C3	8/04
x	8603	unreg	Cobus	2700	-?-	Co	-?-	B15T	4/00	National Express Operations (LN) C4	8/04
x	8604	unreg	Cobus	2700	-?-	Co	-?-	B15T	4/00	National Express Operations (LN) C5	8/04
x	8605	unreg	Cobus	2700	TAW6985301U951508	Co	965509	B15T	4/00	National Express Operations (LN) C6	8/04
	8606	X831 NWX	DAF	DE02GCSB220(lpg)	XMGDE02GC0H008658	EL	35601	B29D	9/00	National Express Operations (LN) 831	8/04
	8607	X832 NWX	DAF	DE02GCSB220(lpg)	XMGDE02GC0H008659	EL	35602	B29D	9/00	National Express Operations (LN) 832	8/04
	8608	X833 NWX	DAF	DE02GCSB220(lpg)	XMGDE02GC0H008660	EL	35603	B29D	9/00	National Express Operations (LN) 833	8/04
	8610	X835 NWX	DAF	DE02GCSB220(lpg)	XMGDE02GC0H 008662	EL	35605	B29D	10/00	National Express Operations (LN) 835	8/04
	8612	X837 NWX	DAF	DE02GCSB220(lpg)	XMGDE02GC0H008664	EL	35607	B29D	11/00	National Express Operations (LN) 837	8/04
	8614	X839 NWX	DAF	DE02GCSB220(lpg)	XMGDE02GC0H008666	EL	35609	B29D	11/00	National Express Operations (LN) 839	8/04
	8615	X840 NWX	DAF	DE02GCSB220(lpg)	XMGDE02GC0H008667	EL	35610	B29D	11/00	National Express Operations (LN) 840	8/04
	8616	X841 NWX	DAF	DE02GCSB220(lpg)	XMGDE02GC0H008668	EL	35611	B29D	11/00	National Express Operations (LN) 841	8/04
	8617	X842 NWX	DAF	DE02GCSB220(lpg)	XMGDE02GC0H008669	EL	35612	B29D	11/00	National Express Operations (LN) 842	8/04
x	8641	unreg	Cobus	2700S	-?-	Co	-?-	B??T	by11/09	new	by11/09
x	8642	unreg	Cobus	2700S	-?-	Co	-?-	B??T	by11/09	new	by11/09
x	8643	unreg	Cobus	2700S	-?-	Co	-?-	B??T	by11/09	new	by11/09
x	8644	unreg	Cobus	2700S	-?-	Co	-?-	B??T	by11/09	new	by11/09
x	8645	unreg	Cobus	2700S	-?-	Co	-?-	B??T	by11/09	new	by11/09
x	8646	BK 10 EHT	MB	O530	WEB62808323120034	MB		B25D	4/10	new	4/10
x	8647	BK 10 EHU	MB	O530	WEB62808323120035	MB		B25D	4/10	new	4/10
x	8648	BK 10 EHV	MB	O530	WEB62808323120036	MB		B25D	4/10	new	4/10
x	8649	BK 10 EHW	MB	O530	WEB62808323120037	MB		B25D	4/10	new	4/10
x	8650	BK 10 EHX	MB	O530	WEB62808323120038	MB		B25D	4/10	new	4/10
x	8651	BK 10 EHY	MB	O530	WEB62808323120039	MB		B25D	4/10	new	4/10
x	8652	BK 10 EHZ	MB	O530	WEB62808323120040	MB		B25D	4/10	new	4/10

5/7 (R720/1 ODA) x3?
5 N900 LSA (*KX58EVK) MB O530 MB B22D 2009
2 KX58GUK AD Dt AD B32F 2008
3/5-7/9 FJ11 GJO/U; GKU/V/X; GLZ Vo B9R Co C48FLt 2011

AIRLINKS AIRPORT (continued)

x	8653 BK 10 EJU	MB	O530	WEB62808323120041	MB		B25D	4/10 new	4/1
x	8654 BK 10 EJV	MB	O530	WEB62808323120042	MB		B25D	4/10 new	4/1
x	8655 BK 10 EJX	MB	O530	WEB62808323120043	MB		B25D	4/10 new	4/1
x	8656 BK 10 EJY	MB	O530	WEB62808323120044	MB		B25D	4/10 new	4/1
x	8657 BK 10 EJZ	MB	O530	WEB62808323120045	MB		B25D	4/10 new	4/1
x	8658 'BU 6043'	NAW Cobus 2700	TAW6985301U951502 Co	-?-			B15T	10/99 British Airways,	
		(ex V803 DDY by9/12)						Heathrow (LNx) BU6043	9/1
x	8659 'BU6046'	NAW Cobus 2700		-?- Co	-?-		B15T	1/00 British Airways,	
								Heathrow (LNx) BU6046	9/1
x	8660 'BU6047'	NAW Cobus 2700		-?- Co	-?-		B15T	1/00 British Airways,	
								Heathrow (LNx) BU6047	9/1
x	8661 'BU6048'	NAW Cobus 2700	TAW6985301U951501 Co	-?-			B15T	1/00 British Airways,	
		(ex V804 DDY by4/05, 'BU6048' by5/03)						Heathrow (LNx) BU6048	9/1
x	8662 'BU6049'	NAW Cobus 2700		-?- Co	-?-		B15T	1/00 British Airways,	
								Heathrow (LNx) BU6049	9/1
x	8663 'BU6050'	NAW Cobus 2700		-?- Co	-?-		B15T	1/00 British Airways,	
								Heathrow (LNx) BU6050	9/1
x	8664 N470 VPJ	MB	811D	WDB6703032N039864	Wt	U404	B21F	6/96 British Airways,	
								Heathrow (LNx) CC6020	9/1
x	8665 N472 VPJ	MB	811D	WDB6703032N040668	Wt	U407	B21F	6/96 British Airways,	
								Heathrow (LNx) CC6029	9/1
x	8666 P849 BPB	MB	811D	WDB6703032N046638	Wt	W139	B21F	9/96 British Airways,	
								Heathrow (LNx) CC6030	9/1
	8684 KX 58 BHN	MAN 14.240		WMAA66ZZ68C011444	Pn 0812.2NEA7791		B31F	9/08 Airparks, Crawley (WS)	4/1
	8685 KX 58 BHO	MAN 14.240		WMAA66ZZ58C011449	Pn 0812.2NEA7792		B31F	9/08 Courtney, Finchampsted (BE)	4/1
	8683 KX 10 DVH	AD	Env	SFD191AR2AGG30446	AD 9316/3		B44F	8/10 Hulley, Baslow (DE) 14	by3/1

D= OfJ Ailinks

AIRLINKS AIRPORT - Fleet Allocation / Check List *KX 08 HOA; Cobus 613(3)18GN); ofJ501; ofJ502; ofJ505; Cobus AV11006;*

8563	o CY	8607	o CY	8641	CYx	8649	o CYx	8657	oCYx	8665	CYx
8600	o CYx	8608	o CY	8642	CYx	8650	o CYx	8658	CYx	8666	CYx
8601	o CYx	8640	w	8643	CYx	8651	o CYx	8659	o CY	KX 58 BHN	CY
8602	o CYx	8612	o CY	8644	CYx	8652	o CYx	8660	o CYx	KX 58 BHO	CY
8603	o CYx	8614	o CY	8645	CYx	8653	o CYx	8661	o CYx	KX 10 DVH	CY
8604	o CYx	8615	o CY	8646	o CYx	8654	o CYx	8662	o CYx		
8605	o CYx	8616	o CY	8647	o CYx	8655	o CYx	8663	o CYx		
8606	o CY	8617	o CY	8648	o CYx	8656	o CYx	8664	CYx		

PK0001056/N: AIRPORT PARKING & Hotels Limited, Crawley Down Garage, Snow Hill, COPTHORNE, RH10 3EQ. OC: as address. VA: 8. *YJ10 CME; YJ15 AAU; YJ66 APX, YJ66 APY;*

YJ 61 CKE	Oe	M1030SR	SABGW3AF0BL290153	Oe	B??F	11/11 new	11/1
YJ 61 CKF	Oe	M1030SR	SABGW3AF0BL290154	Oe	B24F	11/11 new	11/1
YJ 61 CKG	Oe	M1030SR	SABGW3AF0BL290155	Oe	B24F	11/11 new	11/1
YD 63 VCJ	Oe	M9600SR	SABTW3AF0DS290742	Oe	B24F	12/13 new	12/1
YD 63 VCK	Oe	M9600SR	SABTW3AF0DS290743	Oe	B24F	12/13 new	12/1
YD 63 VCL	Oe	M9600SR	SABTW3AF0DS290744	Oe	B24F	12/13 new	12/1

YJ15 AAO Oe V1080 Oe B24F 2015   YJ61 JHH Oe V1110 Oe B25F 2011
YJ15 AAU " " " "   YJ61 JHH "
YJ15 AAV " " " "

**PK1125239/N: Stephen AMES, 37 Pavilion Road, WORTHING, BN14 7EE.
FN: Route 1. OC: as address. VA: 2.**

GU 57 GXT	Fd	Tt	WF0DXXTTFD7Y04963	Fd	M16	9/07 Robertsbridge Community	
							College (XES)	6/1
AD 10 DYY	Fd	Tt	WF0DXXTTFDAT13747	Fd	M14	6/10 -?-, -?-	1/1

NOTE: this licence was granted in 1/14.

PK0003063/N: APCOA Parking (UK) Limited, Wellington House, 4-10 Cowley Road, Uxbridge, Greater London, UB8 2XW. OCs: Coach Park, South Terminal, London GATWICK Airport, West Sussex, RH6 0RN; Economy Parking Spout Lane North, Staines, Surrey. VA: 29.

No vehicles currently recorded

PK1086715/R: Nicholas James ATTWOOD, Flat 167, Howlands Court, Commonwealth Drive, Three Bridges, Crawley, RH10 1AW. OC: as address. VA: 1.

No vehicles yet recorded

PK0003171/l: Samuel James AYLING, Sailors Cross, Green Street, SHIPLEY, Horsham, West Sussex, RH13 8PB.
FN: Sussex Coaches.   OC: Rosier Farm, Coneyhurst Road, Billingshurst, RH14 9DE.   VA: 15.

Reg	Make	Model	Chassis	Body	Body No	Seats	Date	History	
JFZ 9942	Sca	N113DRB	1817360	Ar	RH78/3389/7	H45/31F	9/90	Kings Ferry,	
		(ex H208 LOM 6/12)						Gillingham (KT) B.1	2/05
JIG 9768	Sca	K114EB6	YS2K6X20001846170	Bf	4742	CH55/16CT	3/04	Siesta, Middlesbrough (CD) 17	4/12
		(ex YN 04 AHY 7/12)							
KIG 3429	DAF	DB250	XMGDE02RS0H005439	Oe	8629	H49/25F	3/99	Weaver, Newbury (BE)	2/12
		(ex T126 AUA 5/12)							
KIG 3430	MB	811D	WDB67030320917005	Oe	3505	C29F	5/89	GJ Travel, Ottershaw (SR)	5/10
		(ex F790 DWT 5/12, A 16 GJT 3/10, F790 DWT 9/93)							
MIB 927	Vo	B10M-62	YV31MA611TC060307	Pn	9612VUP5842	C57F	9/97	Impact, Carlisle (CA)	12/02
		(ex R644 XAO 7/05, SBZ 3908 by12/02)							
NIL 9248	Vo	B10M-62	YV31MA613XC061139	Pn	9912VUM0446	C57F	3/99	Shaw, Coventry (WM)	10/04
		(ex T 61 MOA 1/06)							
RHZ 4535	Vo	B10M-62	YV31M2B1X5A042622	Pn	9512VUS4134	C53F	3/95	Black Velvet Travel,	
		(ex M134 UWY 1/14, NDO 856 4/10, M134 UWY 2/05)						West End (HA)	3/15
TUI 6946	DAF	SB3000	XMGDE33WS0H009021	VH	33293	C51FT	7/01	National Express (LN) SR92	4/12
		(ex Y327 HUA 6/12)							
VIL 6773	DAF	MB230LT615	XLVDE02LT0H000113	VH	30557	C57F	3/91	Hand, Horsley (GL)	4/02
		(ex H241 AFV 11/02, B 9 AND 4/02, H241 AFV 7/00)							
CBM 12X	Ld	TRCTL11/3R	8101289	Pn	8212LTS6C006	C53F	5/82	Empress, St Leonards (ES) 45	4/98
A715 THV	MCW	DR101/18		MB7651	MCW	H41/28D	4/84	London United (LN) M1015	10/08
D150 FYM	Ld	ONLXB/1RH		ON2436	ECW 26475	H42/26D	10/86	Wells & Trent, Ipswich (P)	8/12
D113 GHY	Vo	B10M-56	YV31MGC19HA014816	Ar	10P/4086/14	DP53F	5/87	Rees, Pontyates (CW)	2/10
J137 HMT	Sca	N113DRB	YS4ND4X2B01820568	NC	4259	H41//27F	7/92	JB Tours, Watnall (NG)	11/13
K128 DAO	Ld	ON2R50G13Z4		ON20502	Ar	RL65/1192/1	H43/27F	10/92	Stagecoach (North West)	
								(CA) 14268	7/12
R175 HHK	Vo	OLY-56	YV3YNA419WC029003	NC	6000	H49/31F	6/98	United Counties (NO) 16175	9/12
R149 VPU	Vo	OLY-56	YV3YNA411VC028054	Ar	9634/6	H51/32F	8/97	Stagecoach in the Fens	
								(CM) 16049	9/12
W129 EON	Vo	B7TL	YV3S2C616YC000245	Ar	9955/17	H43/20D	3/00	London United (LN) VA95	9/12
W401 WGH	Vo	B7TL	YV3S2C616YC000472	Pn	6970	H41/19D	7/00	Western Greyhound,	
								Summercourt (CO) 461	4/15
X575 YUG	Vo	B10BLE	YV3R4A51911007187	Wt	D451	DP47F	12/00	Keighley & District (WY) 575	9/12
X576 YUG	Vo	B10BLE	YV3R4A51311007184	Wt	D452	DP47F	1/01	Keighley & District (WY) 576	9/12
SK 52 MPY	Vo	B7TL	YV3S2G5143A002363	Ar	2048/06	H45/20D	10/02	London United (LN) VA298	7/12
YN 03 AVZ	Au	N122/3	WAG3012223SS34190	Au	SS34190	CH57/22CT	4/03	Mayo, Otford (KT)	6/08
YN 54 DDO	Vo	B12B	YV3R8F8164A015300	Pn	0412TKL5616	C49FT	9/04	TGMGroup (EX)	5/12
YN 56 FEM	Sca	K380EB6	YS2K6X20001855185	Ir	103366	C57FT	11/06	new	11/06
YN 07 EXX	Sca	K470EB6	YS2K4X20001856273	Ir	103669	C57FT	3/07	Premier Connections,	
								Luton Airport (BD)	3/08

PK0001780/l: George Rutherford BELL, Church Lane, EASTERGATE, Chichester, PO20 6UZ.
FN: Rutherfords Travel.   OC: Rosier Farm, Coneyhurst Road, Billingshurst; Manor Farm, Church Lane, Eastergate,
PO20 3UZ.   VA: 10.

Reg	Make	Model	Chassis	Body	Body No	Seats	Date	History	
CCZ 6148	Ld	TRCTL11/3ARZ	TR00678	Du	8990/1104	C70F	8/89	Cheney, Banbury (OX) 127	11/03
		(ex G798 RNC by2/00, PIL 2863 by2/00, G798 RNC by2/00, NIL 8650 2/98, G798 RNC 10/97)							
w LUI 9692	Ld	TRCTL11/2RP	TR00114	Pn	8811LTP3C010	C69F	11/87	Provence, St Albans (HT)	5/07
		(ex E275 KEF 9/03)							
PUI 6623	Sca	K113CRB	1826808	Ir	8917	C49FT	5/96	PC Coaches, Lincoln (LI)	9/14
		(ex N813 DKU 3/08)							
w A129 EPA	Ld	TRCTL11/2RH	8301011	Pn	8411LTP1X537	C51F	1/84	Shearer, Mayford (SR)	10/01
A144 EPA	Ld	TRCTL11/3R	8301087	Pn	8412LTP1X542	C57F	1/84	Tramcourt, Selsey (WS)	5/00
J287 NNC	Sca	K93CRB	1819821	Pn	9112SEM0333	C53F	2/92	Burton, Fellbeck (NY)	3/11
r J 46 SNY	Ld	TRCL10/3ARZM	TR00767	Pn	9012LCJ2323	C70F	8/91	Eurotaxis,	
								Siston Common (GL)	11/10
J 28 UNY	Ld	TRCL10/3ARZM	TR00880	Pn	9012LCJ2330	C70F	1/92	Eurotaxis,	
		(ex 121 ASV 2/99, J 28 UNY 2/97)						Siston Common (GL)	12/10
L486 XOU	Ds	Jv	10SDA2120/826	WS	3839/93	DP57FA	8/93	MoD (X)	11/03
		(ex 74 KK 50 11/03, L954 KBE by11/03, 74 KK 50 by11/03)							
T373 JWA	MAN	11.220	WMA4692296G113741	Ir	9771	C35F	4/99	Bonds, Hamilton (SW)	5/11
		(ex KSU 479 5/15, T373 JWA 6/11)							
YN 05 BUH	MAN	13.220	WMAA53ZZZ5S001535	Noge	-?-	C35FT	3/05	new	3/05
YN 05 HAA	Sca	K124EB6	1850867	Ir	96429	C49FT	4/05	new	4/05

PK1080038/N: Neil Douglas BIRD, 38 Dacre Gardens, BEEDING, Steyning, BN44 3TD.
FN: Southern Transit. OC: The Old Cement Works, Shoreham Road, Beeding, BN44 3TX. VA: 8.

Reg		Chassis	Chassis no	Body	Body no	Seat	Date	History	
DAF431	W431 YBN	DAF	SB220	XMGDE02GS0H007639	Is 481V1PX1GB0135	B44F	5/00	York Pullman, York (NY) 254	5/1
			(ex W666 WMS 9/09)						
L1	A101 SYE	Ld	ONTL11/1R	ON1115	ECW 25763	H47/28D	2/84	Green Light, Copthorne (WS)	4/0
NV170	R370 LGH	Vo	OLY-50	YV3YNA413VC028377	NC 6123	CO47/24D	1/98	London General (LN) NV170	10/1
			(ex WLT 470 8/06, R370 LGH 7/98)						
RML2660	SMK 660F	AEC	Rm	RML2660	PR L5891	H40/32R	6/67	Lear, Ashbury Station (P)	10/1
RML2755	SMK 755F	AEC	Rm	RML2755	PR L5981	H40/32R	2/68	Doyle, Wembley (P)	2/1
SCANIA463	YN 03 WRL	Sca	N94UB	YS2N4X20001844404	Sca	B43F	8/03	Anglian (SK) 463	3/1
TA1	V301 KGW	Ds	Tt	SFD123BR1XGX20740	Ar 9939/1	H45/20D	2/00	Abellio (LN) 9701	9/1
TA386	Y386 NHK	Ds	Tt	SFD31BBR21GX21461	Ar 0064/28	H45/23D	6/01	East London (LN) 17386	3/1
TA400	Y514 NHK	Ds	Tt	SFD31BBR21GX21471	Ar 0068/5	H45/23D	6/01	East London (LN) 17400	7/1
TA406	Y517 NHK	Ds	Tt	SFD317BR21GX21476	Ar 0068/10	H45/23D	7/01	Selkent (LN) 17406	7/1
p	NXP 796	AEC	Rt III	O9617557	PR L2825	H30/26R	12/53	Nadin, Brighton (WSp)	6/0
w	RIL 9469	Ld	TRCTL11/3RH	8500248	Pn 8512LTH2C802	C53FT	9/86	RML2418, Wem (SH)	2/1
			(ex C201 PPE 1/00)						
	ERV 254D	Ld	PDR1/1	L43749	MCW	O43/33F	7/66	Nadin, Beeding (WS)	6/0
p	SMK 742F	AEC	Rm	RML2742	PR L5993	H40/32R	11/67	Bird, Burgess Hill (P)	6/0
a	WHE 349J	Ld	PSU3A/4R	903365	Wk CF2022	RV	10/70	Hawkins, Findon (WSp)	5/1
p	KJD 434P	Bl	LH6L	LH1274	ECW 21889	B39F	7/76	Bird, Burgess Hill (P)	6/0
p	OJD 93R	Bl	LH6L	LH1351	ECW 21943	B39F	4/77	Bird, Burgess Hill (P)	6/0
			(ex OJD 88R 4/91)						
w	CPU 125X	Ld	TRCTL11/2R	8101716	Pn 8211LTS6X514	C53F	3/82	Hedingham (EX) L270	1/0
p	YPD 101Y	Ld	TRCTL11/2R	8201042	Du 334/5236	C53F	4/83	Cooper, Thetford (P)	7/1
r	A103 SYE	Ld	ONLXB/1R	ON1117	ECW 25765	H43/28D	2/84	Griffin, Dunton Green (KT)	5/1
	B194 BLG	Ld	ONLXB/1R	ON1701	ECW 26060	H45/32F	3/85	Searle, Seaton (DN)	5/1
r	D862 GCD	Ld	ONLXB/1R	ON2459	ECW 26487	H42/26D	10/86	Renown,	
			(ex D162 FYM 2/12)					Bexhill-on-Sea (ES) 32	2/1
w	N431 FKK	Vo	YN2RC16V3	YV3YNC219TC026581	ArB D16.08	H47/27D	5/96	Universitybus, Hatfield (HT) 252	2/1
			(ex 96-D-276 12/07)						

NOTE: prior to 7/08 vehicles were licensed to PK1025676: Nadin, Beeding (WS).

PK0003479/R: BRIGHTON MINIBUS Company Limited, 17 Highclere Way, WORTHING, BN13 3RF.
FNs: Brighton Minibus; Richards Minibuses. OC: as address. VA: 2.
PK1030840/R: Richard Woolley, 17 Highclere Way, Worthing, BN13 3RF.
FNs: Brighton Minibus; Richards Minibuses. OC: as address. VA: 2.

Reg		Chassis	Chassis no	Body	Seat	Date	History	
R 11 CXA	Fd	Tt	WF0DXXTTFDAT18592	Fd	M16	7/10	-?-, -?-	1/14
			(ex BT 10 JNJ 2/14)					
HX 05 DYH	MB	311CDI	WDB9036632R709736	?	M16	3/05	-?-, -?-	8/11
OE 55 SVJ	VW	LT35	WV1ZZZ2DZ6H013145	?	M16	2/06	London Borough of Greenwich,	
							Thamesmead (XLN)	9/0
CU 57 FRK	VW	Crf	WV1ZZZ2EZ86002968	Tawe -?-	M16	12/07	Airlynx, Eastleigh (HA) 28	3/1
AJ 58 JRV	Fd	Tt	WF0DXXTTFD8L15301	Fd	M16	10/08	-?-, -?-	6/0

NOTE: prior to 2/10, this operator was recorded in the county of East Sussex, as Woolley, Brighton (ES).

PK1081336/R: John BROTHERIDGE, The Beeches, 11B Oliver Road, HORSHAM, RH12 1LH.
FN: BCD. OC: as address. VA: 1.

No vehicles yet recorded

PK0002377/I: J & M BROWN Coaches Limited, Stephenson Way, Three Bridges, CRAWLEY, RH10 1TN.
FN: Crawley Luxury Coaches. OCs: as address; Unit 13, Chartwell Road, Churchill Industrial Estate, Lancing,
BN15 8TU: The Old Cement Works, Shoreham Road, Beeding, BN44 3TX; 47 Lumley Road, Horley, RH6 7JF.
VA: 62.
PK1019302/N: Gavin & Darren Brown, 61 Arden Road, Crawley, RH10 6HL.
OC: Unit 13, Chartwell Road, Churchill Industrial Estate, Lancing, BN15 8TU. VA: 2.
PK1121401/N: David Leonard Brown, 157 Old Fort Road, Shoreham-by-Sea, BN43 5HL.
OC: Lancing Business Park, Churchill Industrial Estate, Unit 31, Chartwell Road, Lancing, BN15 8TU. VA: 4.

Reg		Chassis	Chassis no	Body	Body no	Seat	Date	History	
CL 5561	Vo	B10M-62	YV31MA6181A053475	Pn	0112VUT3592	C49FT	4/01	Voel, Dyserth (CN)	10/0
			(ex Y743 HWT 11/06, 8214 VC 6/06, Y743 HWT 5/03)						

BROWN, CRAWLEY (continued) P15cLc (9/1929/20)

Reg	B	Chassis / No	Eng / No	Body	Date	Operator	Date
9/18 CLC 145	Ka	S315GT-HD WKK62725223000216 Ka		C49FT	1/03	Bluebird, Weymouth (DT)	5/14
		(ex LW 52 AKK 6/14, Y 7 BBC 3/14, LW 52 AKK 9/12)					
9/19 DJI 654	Vo	B10M-56 009805 Pn 8511VZH2C01N		C47F	3/85	Bell, Winterslow (WI)	8/94
		(ex B190 XJD 9/94)					
3/19 HIL 7746	Vo	B10M-62 YV31MA7181A053331 Pn 0112VUL3533		C49FT	1/02	Hookways, Meeth (DN)	9/11
		(ex MF 51 MBU 1/07)					
6/14 LIW 9272	Vo	B10M-62 YV31MA6111A053334 Pn 0112VUS3118		C49FT	3/01	Humphries, Datchet (BE)	7/11
		(ex Y 27 OXF 10/13)					
12 LUO 391	Vo	B10M-62 YV31MA2B12TA045077 Pn 9612VUP5051		C53F	4/96	Stephenson, Rochford (EX) 117	12/08
		(ex A 17 SOE 3/09, N 45 ARC 6/05)					
RYY 544	Vo	B10M-62 YV31MA61XWC060973 Pn 9812VUM9494		C57F	3/00	Guideissue, Knypersley (ST) 9	7/10
		(ex W309 WRE 6/13, 1497 RU 5/10)					
1725 LJ	Vo	B10M-62 YV31MA614VA046450 Pn 9612VUP6273		C57F	2/97	Cropley, Fosdyke (LI)	2/09
		(ex P388 JJU 3/09, EAZ 5347 3/08, P388 JJU 3/03, 97-D-7810 8/02)					
6/14 52 CLC	MB	Tourismo WEB63203623000075 MB		C53F	6/09	MCH, Uxbridge (LN)	12/13
		(ex BK 09 WSX 1/14, 9 MCH by12/13, BK 09 WSX 3/10)					
171 CLC	Vo	B7R YV3R6G7265A102945 Pn 0512TLX5858		C57F	3/05	London Borough of Redbridge, Ilford (LN)	9/13
		(ex YN 05 UUR 1/14, C 3 LBR 4/13, YN 05 UUR 11/07)					
685 CLC	Vo	B10M-62 YV31MA615YA052407 Pn 0012VUL0601		C53F	10/00	Clarke, Tredegar (CS)	1/07
		(ex X663 NWY 3/07, B 10 MVO 10/06, X663 NWY 2/04)					
6/16 687 CLC	Vo	B10M-62 YV31MA7101A053596 Pn 0112VUL3962		C51FT	5/02	Clynnog & Trevor, Trefor (CN)	5/11
		(ex YS 02 YYB 6/13, KSV 361 12/09, YS 02 YYB 2/06)					
8/13 784 CLC	Vo	B10M-62 YV31MA6141A053490 Pn 0112VUT3594		C49FT	5/01	Voel, Dyserth (CN)	2/07
		(ex Y745 HWT 4/07, 1760 VC 1/07, Y745 HWT 5/03)					
8/19 789 CLC	Ka	S315GT-HD WKK62725223000217 Ka		C49FT	1/03	Bluebird, Weymouth (DT)	5/14
		(ex LW 52 AKN 5/14, T 7 BBC 3/14, LW 52 AKN 9/12)					
978 VYD	Vo	B10M-62 YV31MA7131A053222 Bf 4362		C51FT	5/01	Coachmaster, Thurmaston (LE)	7/09
		(ex Y796 HPG 1/10)					
CLC 553T	Vo	B10M-62 YV31MA61X1A053333 Pn 0112VUS3117		C53F	3/01	City of Oxford (OX) 26	12/08
		(ex CLC 145 6/14, Y956 WFC 4/09, Y 26 OXF by12/08)					
CLC 983T	Vo	B10M-62 YV31MA6161A053278 Pn 0112VUS3116		C53F	3/01	City of Oxford (OX) 25	12/08
		(ex 789 CLC 5/14, Y954 WFC 3/09, Y 25 OXF by12/08)					
HJB 635W	Bd	YMQ YMQ2DZ0KW453000 Du 050/1551		C31FT	8/80	Ron, Lancing (WS)	5/02
		(named Oliver)					
17 D 32 CLC	Vo	B10M-62 YV31MA617VC060394 VH 33006		C32FT	4/97	Tellings Golden Miller (LN)	10/11
		(ex P272 HBC 1/12, 3401 MW 1/10, P 10 TGM 11/06)					
K 2 CLC	Vo	B10M-55 YV31MGB18PA031204 Ar 26PS/3392/28		B62F	1/93	Collier, Earith (CM)	11/10
		(ex K726 DAO 3/11)					
K 3 CLC	Vo	B10M-62 YV31MA617X0061337 Pn 9912VUS1607		C49FT	3/00	Flight Delay (GM)	1/10
		(ex W676 YBN 6/10, H 12 FDS 9/09, W100 FFC 10/08)					
8/11 K 5 CLC	Vo	B10M-62 YV31MA711YA051883 Pn 0012VUS1911		C57F	3/00	Brighton & Hove (ES) 506	7/09
		(ex W606 OCD 1/10)					
9/13 L 6 CLC	Vo	B10M-62 YV31MA7161A053019 Bf 4313		C53F	3/01	Kings Ferry (KT) 5.13	10/12
		(ex L 7 KFC 10/12, Y451 TKN 10/06)					
L 9 CLC	Vo	B10M-62 YV31MA7141A053018 Bf 4312		C53F	3/01	Kings Ferry (KT) 5.10	10/12
		(ex M 2 KFC 10/12, Y449 TKN 11/06)					
6/14 N 7 CLC	Vo	B10M-62 YV31MA6191A053078 Co 043007		C51FT	3/02	Shaw, Carnforth (LA)	4/12
		(ex PN 02 SVJ 10/12, 8527 RU 3/12, PN 02 SVJ 11/06)					
N 12 CLC	Vo	B10M-62 YV31MA61A053077 Co 043006		C51FT	3/02	Shaw, Carnforth (LA)	4/12
		(ex PN 02 SVL 10/12, WX 9548 3/12, PN 02 SVL 11/06)					
N 60 CLC	Vo	B10M-62 YV31MA6141A053120 Co 043008		C51FT	3/02	Shaw, Carnforth (LA)	4/12
		(ex PN 02 SVK 10/12, 8468 RU 3/12, PN 02 SVK 11/06)					
N982 TPG	MB	811D WDB6703032N040715 Me 02344		C24F	4/96	Millennium, Warnham (WS)	10/12
P 2 CAP	Vo	B10M-62 YV31MA612TC060185 Pn 9612VUM5631		C70F	8/96	Airlinks Airport (WS) 1114	12/07
P 3 CAP	Vo	B10M-62 YV31MA614TC060186 Pn 9612VUM5632		C70F	8/96	Airlinks Airport (WS) 1115	12/07
P 14 CLC	Vo	B7R YV3R6G7144A006897 Pn 0412THX5232		C57F	3/04	London Borough of Redbridge, Ilford (LN)	12/13
		(ex EU 04 ABN 1/14, 2 LBR by12/13, EU 04 ABN 5/05)					
P 15 CLC	Vo	B7R YV3R6G7104A006802 Pn 0312THX5224		C53F	1/04	Smith, Tring (HT)	9/13
		(ex FJ 53 KZL 1/14)					
R 20 CLC	Vo	B10M-62 YV31MA610WA048908 Pn 9812VUP0416		C50FT	3/98	Wallace Arnold Coaches (WY)	8/04
		(ex R416 FWT 9/04)					
T222 ADY	MB	614D WDB6683532N079117 ACl 1632		C24F	5/99	Rambler, Hastings (ES) 15	8/13
T 16 CLC	Vo	B10M-62 YV31MA612XC061214 Pn 9912VUP0545		C51FT	4/99	Wallace Arnold Coaches (WY)	10/03
		(ex T545 EUB 10/03)					
6/14 T 17 CLC	Vo	B10M-62 YV31MA615XC061109 Pn 9912VUP0508		C55F	3/99	National Holidays Coaches (EY) 948	2/06
		(ex T508 EUB 2/06)					
6/12 T 19 CLC	Vo	B10M-62 YV31MA617XC061211 Pn 9912VUP0542		C67F	5/99	Isaac, Morriston (CW)	3/06
		(ex T542 EUB 10/06)					
9/12 T991 NOK	MB	614D WDB6683532N077694 Adn AC614V028		C24FL	5/99	Empress, St Leonards-on-Sea (ES) 93	10/14
		(ex HKZ 1066 11/14, C 6 HBG 4/14, T 7 GAE 7/05, T991 NOK by5/02)					
V 22 CLC	Vo	B10M-62 YV31MA71XYA051882 Pn 0012VUS1910		C51FT	3/00	Brighton & Hove (ES) 505	4/09
		(ex W605 OCD 5/09)					
9/12 W 30 CLC	Vo	B10M-62 YV31MA619YA052247 Pn 0012VUP0626		C51FT	6/00	Isaac, Morriston (CW)	3/06
		(ex W629 FUM 4/06)					

BROWN, CRAWLEY (continued)

Reg		Chassis	Body		Seat		Date	History	
W 40 CLC	Vo	B10M-62	YV31MA61XYA051981	Pn	0012VUP0611	C50FT	4/00	Wallace Arnold Coaches (WY)	3/0
		(ex W612 FUM 4/05 - named *Kaitlun*)							
W 44 CLC	Vo	B10M-62	YV31MA617YA051954	Pn	0012VUP0649	C51FT	3/00	Wallace Arnold Coaches (WY)	7/0
		(ex W656 FUM 2/06)							
W 55 CLC	Vo	B10M-62	YV31MA613YA051983	Pn	0012VUP0613	C50FT	4/00	Wallace Arnold Coaches(WY)	12/C
		(ex W614 FUM 2/06)							
W 66 CLC	Vo	B10M-62	YV31MA614YA052172	Pn	0012VUP0619	C51FT	4/00	Brodyr Williams,	
								Upper Tumble (CW)	12/0
		(ex W621 FUM 2/06)							
W 77 CLC	Vo	B10M-62	YV31MA616YA051878	Pn	0012VUP0642	C50FT	3/00	Swift, Great Yarmouth (NK)	11/0
		(ex W647 FUM 12/06)							
W608 FUM	Vo	B10M-62	YV31MA61XYA052399	Pn	0012VUP0608	C51FT	8/00	Frank, Hartlepool (CD)	5/0
W609 FUM	Vo	B10M-62	YV31MA612YA052400	Pn	0012VUP0609	C51FT	8/00	Taw & Torridge, Merton (DN)	5/0
X 50 CLC	Vo	B10M-62	YV31MA617YA052408	Pn	0012VUP0610	C51FT	10/00	Wallace Arnold Coaches (WY)	2/0
		(ex X661 NWY 2/05)							
OC 51 CLC	Vo	B10M-62	YV31MA7151A053352	Bf	4368	C51FT	1/02	East Yorkshire (EY) 47	3/1
		(ex YX 51 AXM 4/11, A 16 EYC 12/09, YX 51 AXM 5/03)							
VC 51 CLC	Vo	B10M-62	YV31MA6111A052779	Pn	0012VUL3127	C51FT	11/01	Berry, Taunton (SO)	3/0
		(ex YN 51 WGX 6/09)							
FK 02 CLC	Vo	B10M-62	YV31MA6141A052792	Pn	0012VUT3126	C53F	5/02	Amport & District, Thruxton (HA)	1/0
		(ex HJ 02 HXY 4/08)							
WC 02 CLC	Vo	B10M-62	YV31MA7161A053568	Pn	0112VUL3958	C51FT	5/02	Belle Vue, Heaton Chapel	
								(GM) BVM1	3/0
		(ex YS 02 YYA 4/09)							
LB 52 XHF	Fd	Tt	WF0EXXGBFE2B39999	Fd		M11	10/02	-?-, -?-	12/1
EF 03 NWU	Fd	Tt	WF0PXXBDFP3D84075	Fd		M11	5/03	Old School Bus, Woking (SR)	7/1
DS 53 OFM	MB	413CDI	WDB9046632R567471	Excel -?-		M16	12/03	Dunnachie, Craighouse (SW)	7/1
		(ex BU 53 JON 7/08)							
BU 04 EXV	Ka	S315GT-HD	WKK62725223000243	Ka		C53F	3/04	Richmond (SR) 716	2/1
DC 06 CLC	Ka	S415GT-HD	WKK63213123101018	Ka		C49FT	3/06	Ardcavan, Castlebridge (EI)	3/1
		(ex BC 06 OCF 3/15, 06-WX-900 2/15)							
NC 06 CLC	Ka	S415HD	WKK62941123000083	Ka		C49FT	1/07	Kerry, Killarney (EI)	9/1
		(ex WD 56 PPV 10/14, 07-KY-102 9/14)							
OO 60 CLC	MB	Tourismo	WEB63203623000135	MB		C53F	1/11	City Circle, Hayes (LN) 57	12/1
		(ex BD 60 XSV 3/14)							
XX 60 CLC	MB	Tourismo	WEB63203623000138	MB		C53F	1/11	City Circle, Hayes (LN) 60	12/1
		(ex BD 60 XSY 3/14)							
MC 11 CLC	MB	Tourismo	WEB63203623000148	MB		C53F	4/11	Pullmanor, Herne Hill (LN) 281	3/1
		(ex BN 11 UFS 4/15)							
BX 14 ONO	MB	Tourismo	WEB63241523000295	MB		C49FT	5/14	Chauffeurhire,	
								Chipping Sodbury (GL)	4/1

PK1102871/N: Ian Robert BROWNING, Sinnocks Nurseries Annex, Sinnocks, WEST CHILTINGTON, Pulborough, RH20 2JX.   **FN:** The Taxibus.com.   **OC:** 11 Nightingale Road, Horsham, RH12 2NW.   **VA:** 1.

Reg		Chassis	Body		Seat	Date	History	
HN 03 ZYM	Fd	Tt	WF0EXXGBFE2G36960	Fd	M8	4/03	Reliance, Ickenham (LN)	5/1

PK1029590/I: William James BUCKLAND, 14 Peerley Close, EAST WITTERING, Chichester, PO20 8PB.   **FN:** Westrings.   **OC:** Nummington Farm, Rookwood Road, West Wittering, PO20 9LZ.   **VA:** 7.

Reg		Chassis	Body		Seat	Date	History	
G 2 TSW	Fd	Tt	WF0DXXTTFD7E41616	Me	12043	M16	8/04	new	8/0
		(ex DY 57 JLO 8/10)						

PK0003035/I: David Douglas BURDITT, 30 Marlow Drive, HAYWARDS HEATH, RH16 3SH.   **FN:** Davids Travel.   **OCs:** as address; Horsted Keynes Industrial Park, Cinder Hill Lane, Horsted Keynes, RH17 7BA.   **VA:** 3.

Reg		Chassis	Body		Seat	Date	History	
WA 57 CZC	MB	O815DT	WDB6703742N122581	Sitcar	2223	C29F	9/07	new	9/07

PK1052350/R: Edward John CABLE, 114 Farhalls Crescent, HORSHAM, RH12 4BY.   **FN:** Horsham Mini Travel.   **OC:** as address.   **VA:** 1.

Reg		Chassis	Body		Seat	Date	History	
OU 53 VPJ	Fd	Tt	WF0EXXGBFE3S39524	Fd		M16	9/03	private owner	9/0

PK1109174/I: CITY OF CHICHESTER COACHES Limited, Beedingwood Farm, Forest Road, COLGATE, Horsham, RH12 4TB.   FNs; City of Chichester Coaches; The SussexBus.com   OCs: Old Cement Workshops, Shoreham Road, Beeding, BN44 3TX; Fairbridge Way, Burgess Hill, RH16 3BN; Mackley Industrial Estate, Henfield Road, Small Dole, Henfield, BN5 9XQ.   VA: 25.

See joint entry under Coach Hire, Colgate

PK0001723/I: COACH HIRE Coaches Limited, Beedingwood Farm, Forest Road, COLGATE, Horsham, RH12 4TB.   OC: Mackley Industrial Estate, Henfield Road, Small Dole, Henfield, BN5 9XQ.   VA: 18.
PK1109174/I: City Of Chichester Coaches Limited, Beedingwood Farm, Forest Road, Colgate, Horsham, RH12 4TB. FNs; City of Chichester Coaches; The SussexBus.com   OCs: Old Cement Workshops, Shoreham Road, Beeding, BN44 3TX; Fairbridge Way, Burgess Hill, RH16 3BN; Mackley Industrial Estate, Henfield Road, Small Dole, Henfield, BN5 9XQ.   VA: 25.
PK1001042/I: Sussex Commercial Services Limited, Beedingwood Farm, Forest Road, Colgate, Horsham, RH12 4TB. OC: Mackley Industrial Estate, Henfield Road, Small Dole, Henfield, BN5 9XQ.   VA: 7.
PK0002932/I: Round & About Limited, Beedingwood Farm, Forest Road, Colgate, Horsham, RH12 4TB.
OCs: as address; Albion Street Lorry Park, Southwick, Brighton BN42 4DN; Ford Industrial Estate, Burndell Road, Yapton, BN18 0HT; Western Area Office, Drayton Lane, Drayton, Chichester, PO20 2ET; Mackley Industrial Estate, Henfield Road, Small Dole, Henfield, BN5 9XQ.   VA: 12.

KV 4644	Sca	K113TRB	1826605	Ir	8751		C49FT	3/96	Durham Travel, Hetton-le-Hole (TW) 9	10/02
		(ex N 9 DTS 10/02)								
SV 9314	Vo	B12T	YV3R2EX13SA001803	VH	32019		CH57/14CT	11/95	Midland Bluebird (SE) 2211	8/02
		(ex N319 BYA 1/03)								
AIG 7944	Sca	L94IB	1835483	Ir	150452		C55F	10/99	Lewis M, Coventry (WM)	10/11
		(ex V305 EAK by7/11)								
BJZ 2804	Ld	ON3R49C18Z4	ON11773	Ar	RH82/1390/17		CH53/41F	12/90	Greater Manchester South (GM) 13626	5/08
		(ex H 41 GBD 6/08, ES 5389 (Hong Kong) 7/04)								
BNZ 3466	DAF	MB230	XMGCE02LT0H003652	VH	31903		C53F	9/94	C&S, Heathfield (ES)	by6/12
		(ex M802 RCP 3/13)								
ESV 183	Ds	Dt SLF	SFD212AR11GW15720	Pn	0110.1HJB4076		B27D	6/01	Countryliner, Uckfield (ES) DP56	10/12
		(ex Y656 NLO 10/14)								
FIL 7617	Vo	B10M-62	YV31M2F16TA045142	Pn	9612VUM4790		C51F	4/96	Fife Scottish (SE) 52285	8/11
		(ex N974 FSR 9/11, 283 URB 8/11, VLT 37 11/08, N145 XSA c2/07)								
HJI 8686	Au	N122/3	WAG301226TSP23249	Au			CH57/22CT	2/96	Pygall, Hutton Henry (DM)	12/09
		(ex N581 AWJ 2/00)								
HSV 989	Sca	K113CRB	1822858	VH	31346		C55F	3/94	Aldershot Coaches, Aldershot (HA)	6/04
		(ex L 28 ABB by4/03)								
HXN 190	Ds	Tt	SFD111BR1YGX21154	Ar	0001/36		H43/??F	10/00	Ensign, Purfleet (EX) 958	10/12
		(ex X258 NNO 12/12)								
JBZ 5056	Ld	ON3R49C18Z4	ON11830	Ar	RH82/1390/36		CH53/39FT	8/91	Greater Manchester South (GM) 13608	6/08
		(ex J734 HMY 8/08, EX 441 (Hong Kong) 2/04)								
MSV 617	Ds	Tt	SFD311BR1YGX21223	Ar	0002/57		H45/??F	1/01	East London (LN) 17317	6/12
		(ex X317 NNO 9/12)								
NIL 2458	Sca	K112CRB	1811192	EL	B21202		B53F	7/87	Yorkshire Traction (SY) 28716	6/08
		(ex D 91 ALX 2/97. Body new 2/97)								
NKK 447	Ds	Tt	SFD111BR1YGX21021	Ar	0001/10		H43/??F	9/00	Ensign, Purfleet (EX) 932	10/12
		(ex X232 NNO 12/12)								
OBY 443	Ds	Dt SLF	SFD322BR1YGW14745	Pn	0010.7HLB2511		B37F	1/01	Countryliner, Uckfield (ES) DP27	10/12
		(ex X214 ONH 10/14)								
OKF 580	Ds	Dt SLF	SFD467BR1YGW35338	Pn	0011.3HAB2780		B41F	12/00	Selkent (LN) 34225	10/12
		(ex X237 WNO 10/14)								
PSV 339	Ds	Dt SLF	SFD612BR1XGW13266	Pn	998.8GKB0602		B29F	6/99	Countryliner, Uckfield (ES) DP11	10/12
		(ex T 78 JBA 7/14)								
SJI 8128	Sca	K92CRB	1813218	VH	13527		C55F	12/88	Buddens, Romsey (HA)	1/01
		(ex F162 DET 5/95)								
r SNZ 7259	Ds	Dt SLF	SFD467BR1YGW45039	Pn	0011.3HAB3064		B41F	10/00	Galleon 2009, Roydon (EX) SPD1	9/14
		(ex X964 VAP 7/13, 404 DCD 12/11, X964 VAP 5/11)								
TFK 696	Ds	Tt	SFD311BR1YGX21220	Ar	0002/54		H45/??F	1/01	Selkent (LN) 17314	6/12
		(ex X314 NNO 9/12)								
UHE 604	Vo	B7TL	YV32C61XYA001092	EL	34402		H47/29F	11/01	Countryliner, Uckfield (ES) VEL3	10/12
		(ex FE 51 RCY 10/13)								
WTE 506	Ds	Dt SLF	SFD612BR1XGW13296	Pn	998.8GKB1127		B29F	8/99	Countryliner, Uckfield (ES) DP36	10/12
		(ex T314 SMV 3/13)								
YFV 722	Ds	Dt SLF	SFD467BR1YGW35311	Pn	0011.3HAB2777		B41F	12/00	Selkent (LN) 34234	10/12
		(ex X234 WNO 10/14)								
YSL 847	Vo	B10M-62	YV31MA7171A053515	Pn	0112VUL3947		C53F	6/01	Veolia England (LE) PJ4	10/11
		(ex Y 8 PJC 3/14)								
YYL 370	Ds	Dt SLF	SFD212AR11GW15721	Pn	0110.1HJB4078		B27D	6/01	Countryliner, Uckfield (ES) DP55	10/12
		(ex Y248 NLK 10/14)								

COACH HIRE, COLGATE (continued)

	Reg		Chassis type	Chassis no		Body no	Seating	Date	Operator	Date
	2719 DT	Sca	K113CRB	1817397	VH	30374	C49FT	3/92	Durham Travel, Hetton-le-Hole (TW) 15	10/0?
	(ex J 15 DTS 4/99)									
	3544 FH	Au	N122/3	WAG301226YSP30507	Au	1222688	CH57/20DT	4/00	Countryliner, Uckfield (ES) NSD2	6/1?
	(ex W892 MDT 8/12)									
	8957 FN	Vo	B10M-60	YV31MGD14NA028164	VH	30944	C57F	2/92	C&S, Heathfield (ES)	9/1?
	(ex J256 NNC 9/11)									
	8357 KV	Sca	K113TRB	1826604	Ir	8753	C49FT	3/96	Durham Travel, Hetton-le-Hole (TW) 8	10/0?
	(ex N 8 DTS 11/02)									
	9022 KV	Vo	B10M-60	YV31MGD10MA028159	VH	30937	C57F	2/92	C&S, Heathfield (ES)	9/1?
	(ex J248 NNC 9/11)									
	1455 MV	Vo	B10M-62	YV31MA616TC060304	Pn	9612VUP5747	C53F	4/98	C&S, Heathfield (ES)	by6/1?
	(e R 40 TGM 11/13)									
	7572 MW	Ka	S210HD	17400001035008	Ka		C35FT	9/89	Simmonds, Letchworth (HT)	10/9?
	(ex 9466 MW by8/90)									
	2851 NX	Au	N116/3	WAG30116655M22964	Au	1164509	C48FT	4/95	Embling, Guyhirn (CM)	2/0?
	(ex M 15 HMC 3/02)									
	1194 PO	Au	N122/3			88 144 93 Au		CH57/20CT	6/88	Millmans Coaches, Heathfield (DN)	12/0?
	(ex E706 CHS 6/10, MIL 2066 5/08, E706 CHS 4/01, MIL 2066, 3/00 E706 CHS 12/99, HGR 150 2/98, E706 CHS 7/97, KFK 172 5/96, E482 YWJ 10/93)									
	7855 PU	Au	N116	WAG361168WSH26754	Au		C49FT	3/98	Turner, Noak Hill (LN)	11/0?
	(ex R290 THL 11/06)									
	9041 PU	Vo	B10M-60	YV31MGD10NA028162	VH	30942	C57F	2/92	C&S, Heathfield (ES)	9/1?
	(ex J254 NNC 9/11)									
	6170 PX	Sca	K113TRB	1817651	VH	30364	C52FT	4/92	Abbott, Leeming (NY)	2/0?
	(ex J239 VVN 2/00)									
	6300 RU	Ka	S315GT-HD	WKK32600001015012	Ka		C49FT	6/99	Bawden, Townshend (CO)	3/0?
	(ex T936 YRR 3/08, MIL 2066 11/03, T936 YRR 4/00)									
	8665 UB	Au	N122/3	WAG301222PSH19915	Au		CH57/22CT	5/93	Bailey, Folkestone (KT) 30	4/0?
	(ex K921 EWG 5/03)									
	4885 UR	Au	N122/3 WAG301222WSP26895 Au 1222463					CH57/20DT	4/98	Millership, Tipton (WM)	6/0?
	(ex R542 UKO 6/07, 8686 DN 5/04, R542 YKO 12/02)									
	2941 VU	Sca	K113TRB	1817652	VH	30365	C52FT	4/92	Abbott, Leeming (NY)	9/9?
	(ex J238 VVN 9/99)									
	1521 YG	Vo	B10M-60	YV31MGD13NA028172	VH	30935	C57F	3/92	C&S, Heathfield (ES)	9/1?
	(ex J246 NNC 9/11)									
	227 BWD	Ds	Dt SLF	SFD212BR1TGW10743	Pn	9710HJZ6688	B35F	5/97	Countryliner, Uckfield (ES) DP16	10/12
	(ex P688 RWU 3/13)									
	264 CHX	Vo	B12B	YV3R8F8225A102072	Pn	0412TKL5789	C49FT	12/04	Go Northern (TW) 7091	9/13
	(ex NK 54 WMM 4/14, CU 7661 3/12)									
	331 HWD	Ld	ON3R49C18Z4	ON11755	Ar	RH82/1390/9	CH53/41F	11/90	Greater Manchester South (GM) 13604	3/08
	(ex ER 8635 (Hong Kong) 8/03)									
	869 UYB	Sca	K113CRB	1825708	VH	32150	C57F	1/96	Astons, Worcester (HW)	9/07
	(ex N282 CAK 9/07, THU 864 8/07, N282 CAK 5/06, 1533 HE 12/04, N282 CAK 8/98)									
	930 YUE	Ds	Dt SLF	SFD322BR1VGW10871	Pn	9710.6HLZ6789	B39F	7/97	Countryliner, Uckfield (ES) DP50	10/12
	(ex P282 FPK 4/13)									
	120 YUR	Ds	Dt SLF	SFD467BR1YGW35120	Pn	0011.3HAB2772	B41F	12/00	Big Lemon, Brighton (ES)	4/14
	(ex X228 WNO 10/14)									
w	J240 VVN	Sca	K113TRB	1817781	VH	30367	C51FT	4/92	Abbott, Leeming (NY)	9/9?
	(ex 1455 MV 11/13, J240 VVN 9/99)									
	M803 RCP	DAF	MB230LB615 XMGCE02LT0H003654		VH	31905	C53FT	9/94	Countryliner, Uckfield (ES) DTM803	by9/13
	P268 FPK	Ds	Dt SLF	SFD322BR1TGW10767	Pn	9710.6HLZ6650	B39F	5/97	Countryliner, Uckfield (ES) DP48	10/12
r	P686 RWU	Ds	Dt SLF	SFD212BR1TGW10740	Pn	9710HJZ6686	B35F	5/97	Countryliner, Uckfield (ES) DP15	10/12
	(ex 213 YUR 5/14, P686 RWU 3/13)									
	R511 WDC	Vo	B10M-62	YV31MA618VA046645	Pn	9712VUP6311	C49FT	4/98	C&S, Heathfield (ES)	by6/12
	T 4 HMC	Au	N116/3	WAG301166XPH28629	Au	1165352	C32FT	5/99	Chivers, Midsomer Norton (SO)	by9/12
	X601 AHE	Ds	Dt SLF	SFD322BR1XGW13366	Pn	9910.7HLB1471	B39F	9/00	Countryliner, Uckfield (ES) DP25	4/13
	X224 WNO	Ds	Dt SLF	SFD467BR1YGW35117	Pn	0011.3HAB2769	B41F	12/00	Big Lemon, Brighton (ES)	4/14
	X227 WNO	Ds	Dt SLF	SFD467BR1YGW35119	Pn	0011.3HAB2771	B41F	12/00	Selkent (LN) 34227	10/12
	X236 WNO	Ds	Dt SLF	SFD467BR1YGW35337	Pn	0011.3HAB2779	B41F	12/00	Ensign, Purfleet (EX) 810	11/12
	Y157 NLK	Ds	Dt SLF	SFD212AR11GW15730	Pn	0110.1HJB4145	B27D	7/01	Countryliner, Uckfield (ES) DP54	10/12
	KM 51 BFZ	Ds	Dt SLF	SFD3C2CR31GW16149	Ar	0155/1	B37F	2/02	Simpson, Skipton (NY) D4	9/14
	KW 02 DRO	Tbs	Env	SFD113AR12GG10109	Tbs	2018/2	B44F	8/02	CT Plus, Bristol (GL)	4/14
	(ex BN 02 EDN 2/06)									
	PJ 02 AAA	Vo	B12M	YV3R9H4141A000157	Pn	0112TJT4157	C53F	3/02	Veolia England (LE) PJ3	10/11
	KL 52 LZX	Ds	Dt SLF	SFD3CACR32GW86908	Pn	2062/14	B37F	1/03	Simpson, Skipton (NY)	7/14
	KN 52 NFM	Ds	Dt SLF	SFD3CACR32GW86890	Ar	2062/10	B37F	9/02	Simpson, Skipton (NY) D6	8/14
	KU 52 RYG	Ds	Dt SLF	SFD3CACR32GW16650	Pn	2025/3	B37F	10/02	Simpson, Skipton (NY) D8	8/14

COACH HIRE, COLGATE (continued)

Reg			Chassis/VIN		Body	Seat	Date	History
KV 03 ZFJ	Tbs	Env	SFD113AR12GG10121	Tbs 0182/9	B44F	7/03	Premiere, Nottingham (NG) 3306	10/14
KV 03 ZFK	Tbs	Env	SFD113AR12GG10120	Tbs 0182/8	B44F	5/03	Premiere, Nottingham (NG) 3322	10/14
KX 54 NKE	Tbs	Env	SFD113AR13GG10124	Tbs 3040/1	B44F	9/04	Premiere, Nottingham (NG) 3310	10/14
YK 55 ATV	Vo	B7TL	YV3S2J4276A109838	Wt K082	H41/28F	2/06	Lancashire United (LA) 408	7/14
YJ 06 LEU	VDL	SB120	XMGDE12BS0H013609	Wt K276	B39F	4/06	Kent Top Temps, Aylesford (KT) 203	8/13
YJ 06 LFA	VDL	SB120	XMGDE12BS0H013610	Wt K277	B39F	4/06	Kent Top Temps, Aylesford (KT) 201	8/13
YJ 06 LFX	VDL	SB120	XMGDE12BS0H013608	Wt K275	B39F	4/06	Kent Top Temps, Aylesford (KT) 202	8/13
SN 57 DXC	AD	Env	SFD475AR27GG30312	AD 7301/1	B45F	1/08	Lloyds Coaches, Machynlleth (CW) SDC07	9/14
			(ex LL 07 WYN 3/14, SN 57 DXC 11/10)					
SN 08 AAF	AD	Env	SFD176AR27GG30329	AD 7302/1	B45F	4/08	Lloyds Coaches, Machynlleth (CW) SDC08	9/14
PO 58 KPU	Vo	B7RLE	YV3R6M3279A129534	Oe 69701	B43F	10/08	Kent Top Temps, Aylesford (KT) 305	10/13
PO 58 KPV	Vo	B7RLE	YV3R6M3249A129538	Oe 69702	B43F	10/08	Kent Top Temps, Aylesford (KT) 306	10/13
PO 58 KPX	Vo	B7RLE	YV3R6M3259A129578	Oe 69703	B43F	10/08	Kent Top Temps, Aylesford (KT) 307	10/13
PO 58 KRD	Vo	B7RLE	YV3R6M3239A129692	Oe 69706	B43F	10/08	Kent Top Temps, Aylesford (KT) 310	10/13

NOTE: R511 WDC not yet in service.

PK0001120/I: Ian Nigel Howard COLLINS, CASTLE GORING, Worthing, BN13 3UB.
FNs: Channel Travel; ICC Tours.   OC: Newels Lane, West Ashling, Chichester, PO1 0DD.   VA: 4.

J208 KTT	MB	709D	WDB6690032P141302	RB 18606	B25F	8/91	Forward, Sampford Peverell (DN)	6/10

PK0003556/I: COMPASS Travel (Sussex) Limited, Faraday Close, Durrington, WORTHING, BN13 3RB.
OC: Faraday Close, Durrington, Worthing, BN13 3RB; Unit 16, Phoenix Industrial Estate, Lewes, BN7 2QJ; Dunsfold Aerodrome, Dunsfold Park, Cranleigh, Surrey, GU6 8TB.   VA: 70. VX05 UH5;

Reg			Chassis/VIN		Body	Seat	Date	History
YIL 4058	DAF	SB3000	XMGDE33WS0H006206	VH 32858	C53F	3/98	Cutting & Stittle, Brockley Green (SK)	9/11
			(ex R256 FBJ 6/04)					
T183 CLO	Ds	Tt	SFD111BR1XGX20406	Ar 9916/2	H45/??F	8/99	Doyle, Alfreton (DE)	2/14
T184 CLO	Ds	Tt	SFD111BR1XGX20407	Ar 9916/3	H45/??F	8/99	Doyle, Alfreton (DE)	2/14
W912 BEC	Vo	B10M-62	YV31MA613XC061304	Pn 9912VUT1363	C57F	3/00	McGowan, Neilston (SW)	1/13
			(ex B 12 WSC 1/13, W912 BEC 3/11, P300 HUW 8/10, W912 BEC 11/06, 7121 RU by2/06, W912 BEC by2/04)					
W372 RKS	DAF	SB3000	XMGDE33WS0H008093	VH 33241	C53F	5/00	Skyline, Oldbury (WM)	4/12
			(ex W200 WCM 1/00)					
Y858 LRX	Sca	L94IB	1839797	Ir 94404	C53F	8/01	Brent Community Transport, Stonebridge Park (LN)	I/10
			(ex 01-D-72093 7/05)					
WV 52 HSX	Vo	B12M	YV3R9F8172A000699	Pn 0212TJT4731	C49FT	10/02	Gibson Direct, Renfrew (SW)	10/14
			(ex M 10 MCT 6/13, WV 52 HSX 4/10)					
YD 52 JAO	Fd	Tt	WF0EXXGBFE2U30323	Fd	M16	9/02	Leeds City Council (XWY)	1/09
DF 03 NTE	Tbs	Dt SLF	SFD6BACR32GW87042	Tbs 2082/2	B29F	7/03	Huyton Travel, Huyton (MY) 28	12/07
LK 03 CEV	Tbs	Tt	SFD13GBR42GX22669	Tbs 8168	H67F	3/03	Metroline (LN) TP406	12/14
SN 53 ETK	Tbs	Dt SLF	SFD6BACR33GW87391	Tbs 3041/2	B29F	10/03	new	10/03
SN 53 ETL	Tbs	Dt SLF	SFD6BACR33GW87392	Tbs 3041/3	B29F	10/03	new	10/03
MX 54 KXR	Oe	M920	SAB19000000001368	Oe	B31F	10/04	Moffat & Williamson, St Fort (SE)	3/09
SN 54 HXG	AD	Env	SFD113AR14GG10174	AD 3092/5	B44F	1/05	Houstons, Lockerbie (SW)	1/11
GX 05 AOP	Ds	Dt SLF	SFD3CACR45GW18231	Ar 4246/7	B37F	4/05	Jenkins, Newick (ES) 124	8/11
MX 05 OTC	AD	Env	SFD113AR14GG10173	AD 3092/4	B44F	7/05	Hansons, Lye (WM)	9/10
SN 05 FHL	MB	O815D	WDB6703742N133388	Sitcar 2019	C29F	3/05	Docherty, Auchterarder (SE)	3/11
VX 05 UHS	Ds	Dt SLF	SFD6BACR45GW18195	Pn 4220/4	B29F	8/07	Astons, Worcester (HW)	
AU 55 DYO	AD	Env	SFD113AR14GG10172	AD 3092/3	B44F	10/05	Stagecoach in the Fens (CM) 27583	2/10
MX 55 NWK	AD	Env	SFD113AR14GG10171	AD 3092/2	B44F	10/05	Stagecoach in the Fens (CM) 27584	2/10
SN 55 DUU	Ds	Dt SLF	SFD6BACR45GW18294	Ar 4285/1	B29F	9/05	Irvine, Law (SW)	1/13
YJ 55 BGU	Oe	M920SL	SAB19000000002068	Oe	B31F	10/05	Holmeswood, Holmeswood (LA)	7/14
YJ 55 BGV	Oe	M920SL	SAB19000000002069	Oe	B31F	10/05	Holmeswood, Holmeswood (LA)	7/14

YJ05PXA VDLDB250 Wt H41/24F 2005
YJ05PXB "   "   "   "

Y15FT?
S44 Ds DT SLF Pn B36 1996
"?H   "   "   B343 2001
EF0 Oe M880 Oe B28F 2005
SBNK VDL DB250 Wt H43/ F 2005
55 GLV

WEST SUSSEX (WS)   G627/14

COMPASS, WORTHING (continued)

Reg		Type	Chassis			Body	Date	Operator	Date
YJ 55 YGZ	Oe	M920SL	SAB190000000002135	Oe		B31F	11/05	Holmes, Clay Cross (DE)	9/0
CN 06 BXP	Oe	M920	SAB19000000002282	Oe		B31F	6/06	Veolia Cymru (CS) 40247	11/1
MX 06 ACY	Oe	M950	SAB190000000002203	Oe		B31F	3/06	Guideissue, Biddulph (ST)	7/0
MX 56 ABZ	Oe	M950	SABFWJAE06R192577	Oe		B32F	12/06	Hansons, Lye (WM)	8/1
MX 56 NLN	AD	Dt	SFD321AR16GF10163	AD	6227/8	B38F	12/06	Guideissue, Knypersley (ST)	2/1
SN 56 AXC	AD	Dt	SFD6BACR46GW88959	AD	6226/3	B29F	10/06	Coakley Bus, Motherwell (SW)	10/0
GX 07 AVQ	AD	Dt	SFD321AR17GY10247	AD	6250/1	B38F	5/07	Jenkins, Newick (ES) 125	8/1
GX 07 BYO	AD	Dt	SFD321AR17GY10350	AD	7202/4	B37F	7/07	Jenkins, Newick (ES) 126	8/1
GX 57 AFV	AD	Dt	SFD111AR17GY10376	AD	6253/13	B29F	9/07	new	9/0
YN 08 MPX	Sca	K340EB4	YS2K4X20001860569	Ir	-?-	C49FT	8/08	Wilfreda-Beehive, Adwick-le-Street (SY)	3/1
YN 08 MPY	Sca	K340EB4	YS2K4X20001860615	Ir	131915	C49FT	8/08	Pat's Coaches, Southsea (CN)	1/1
KX 58 GUJ	AD	Dt	SFD361AR28GY10771	AD	-?-	B37F	9/08	National Express (LN) 8561	10/1
		(named *Roger Knight 1945-2014*)							
MX 58 VGP	AD	Dt	SFD151AR28GY10886	AD	8218/1	B29F	1/09	Bu-Val, Smithybridge (GM) 158	9/1
MX 58 VGR	AD	Dt	SFD151AR28GY10887	AD	8218/2	B29F	1/09	Bu-Val, Smithybridge (GM) 258	9/1
GX 09 AGO	AD	Dt	SFD151AR28GY10925	AD	8222/9	B29F	3/09	new	3/0
GX 09 AGU	AD	Dt	SFD151AR28GY10957	AD	8229/1	B29F	3/09	new	3/0
GX 09 AGV	AD	Dt	SFD151AR28GY10924	AD	8222/8	B29F	3/09	new	3/0
GX 09 AGY	AD	Dt	SFD151AR28GY10923	AD	8222/7	B29F	3/09	new	3/0
GX 09 AGZ	AD	Dt	SFD151AR28GY10958	AD	8229/2	B29F	3/09	new	3/0
MX 09 HJK	AD	Dt	SFD361AR28GY10969	AD	A8221/4	B36F	5/09	Sheffield Community, Upperthorpe (SY)	10/12
MX 09 MHN	AD	Dt	SFD361AR28GY10967	AD	A8221/2	B36F	5/09	Sheffield Community, Upperthorpe (SY)	10/12
YX 09 FNH	AD	Dt	SFD151AR28GY11018	AD	8249/1	B29F	5/09	Brunskill, Coundon (DM)	10/1
MX 60 BXE	AD	Dt	SFD361AR49GY11445	AD	9207/2	B37F	9/10	Guideissue, Knypersley (ST)	2/1
YJ 60 KHG	Oe	M950	SABFW3AFOAL193682	Oe		B31F	11/10	new	11/10
VA 61 BFN	Fd	Tt	WF0DXXTTFDBP38306	Fd		M16	2/12	Malkin, Clifford Chambers (WK)	5/1
YJ 12 PLX	Oe	M9600SR	SABTW3AC0CS290422	Oe		B36F	8/12	new	8/12
YJ 12 PLZ	Oe	M9600SR	SABTW3AC0CS290423	Oe		B36F	8/12	new	8/12
YJ 12 PMU	Oe	M9600SR	SABTW3AC0CS290424	Oe		B36F	8/12	new	8/12
YJ 12 PMV	Oe	M9600SR	SABTW3AC0CS290425	Oe		B36F	8/12	new	8/12
YJ 12 PMX	Oe	M9600SR	SABTW3AC0CS290426	Oe		B36F	8/12	new	8/12
YJ 12 PMY	Oe	M9600SR	SABTW3AC0CS290427	Oe		B36F	8/12	new	8/12
GX 62 CJO	AD	E20D	SFD1D1AR6CGY13107	AD	C226/1	B29F	9/12	new	9/12
GX 62 CJU	AD	E20D	SFD1D1AR6CGY13108	AD	C226/2	B29F	9/12	new	9/12
GX 62 CKP	AD	E20D	SFD1D1AR6CGY13125	AD	C226/4	B29F	9/12	new	9/12
GX 62 CMU	AD	E20D	SFD1D1AR6CGY13134	AD	C226/5	B29F	9/12	new	9/12
GX 62 CMY	AD	E20D	SFD1D1AR6CGY13143	AD	C226/6	B29F	9/12	new	9/12
GX 62 CNN	AD	E20D	SFD7E1AR6CGY13038	AD	C213/3	B39F	9/12	new	9/12
GX 62 COA	AD	E20D	SFD7E1AR6CGY13056	AD	C213/7	B39F	9/12	new	9/12
GX 62 CSF	AD	E20D	SFD1D1AR6CGY13419	AD	C249/6	B29F	1/13	new	1/13
MX 62 AWU	Wt	StLt	SA9DSRXXX12141119	Wt	AG079	B41F	9/12	new	9/12
MX 62 AWZ	Wt	StLt	SA9DSRXXX12141120	Wt	AG080	B41F	9/12	new	9/12
GX 13 FSL	AD	E20D	SFD1D1AR6CGY13170	AD	C234/3	B29F	7/13	new	7/13
GX 13 FSN	AD	E20D	SFD1D1AR6CGY13209	AD	C234/10	B29F	7/13	new	7/13
GX 13 FSO	AD	E20D	SFD1D1AR6CGY13197	AD	C234/5	B29F	7/13	new	7/13
GX 13 FSP	AD	E20D	SFD1D1AR6CGY13199	AD	C234/8	B29F	7/13	new	7/13
GX 13 FSS	AD	E20D	SFD1D1AR6CGY13208	AD	C234/7	B29F	7/13	new	7/13
GX 13 FSU	AD	E20D	SFD1D1AR6CGY13416	AD	C249/3	B29F	7/13	new	7/13
GX 13 FSV	AD	E20D	SFD1D1AR6CGY13418	AD	C249/5	B29F	7/13	new	7/13
MK 63 WZX	Wt	StLt DF	SA9DSRXXX12141141	Wt	AG085	B41F	9/13	new	9/13
SK 15 HBC	AD	E20D	SFD7E1AR6FGY14908	AD	-?-	B39F	4/15	new	4/15
SK 15 HBD	AD	E20D	SFD7E1AR6FGY14910	AD	-?-	B39F	4/15	new	4/15
SK 15 HBE	AD	E20D	SFD7E1AR6FGY14911	AD	-?-	B39F	4/15	new	4/15

PK1106861/R: Peter COOKSLEY, 4 Chaffinch Close, WORTHING, BN13 2TZ.
FN: Ward Air Travel.   **OC:** as address.   **VA:** 1.

LD 04 YVP	Fd	Tt	WF0EXXGBFE3P59931	Fd		M16	6/04	Albrecht, Ware (HT)	9/11

NOTE: this licence was granted in 1/12.

PK0003262/R: COTTESMORE SCHOOL Limited, Buchan Hill, PEASE POTTAGE, Crawley, RH11 9AU.
OC: as address.   **VA:** 2.

LF 52 UGL	LDV	Cy	SEYZMVSYGDN089427	LDV		M16	9/02	new	9/02

NOTE: prior to 9/08, vehicles were licenced to PK0003262/R Cottesmore School Brighton Limited.

PK0003591/I: DIAMOND TRAVEL (U K) Limited, 1 Central Avenue, BOGNOR REGIS, PO21 5HG.
OC: Unit 17B, Hooe Farm, Tye Lane, Walberton, BN10 0LU.   **VA: 7.**

S874 DPN	Ds	Jv	SFD321BR4VGJ42089	Bf	3647		C40FL	12/98	RAF Association, Storrington (XWS)	4/01
SW 02 VTT	Vo	B12M	YV3R9F8192A000350	Je	26097		C53F	3/02	Quinn, Newry (NI)	5/10
			(ex KJZ 2873 by5/10, SW 02 VTT by9/06, LSK 825 11/04)							
WF 52 ESY	Vo	B12B	YV3R8F8142A000470	Je	26259		C53F	9/02	Pewsey Vale, Pewsey (WI)	1/10
			(ex 02-G-8795 5/06)							
WA 03 HRF	Vo	B12M	YV3R9F8133A000958	VH	33722		C48FT	5/03	Westway, Raynes Park (LN)	5/12
			(ex WE 51 WAY 5/12, WA 03 HRF 12/03)							
WA 06 CDX	Vo	B12M	YV3R9F8206A109567	VH	33936		C49FT	2/06	Country Cousins, Ilfracombe (DN)	9/13
WA 56 ENK	Vo	B12M	YV3R9F8236A112687	VH	33998		C53FT	9/06	Chalfont, Southall (LN)	9/13

PK1077200/R: Peter Michael DRUMMOND, 25 Deerswood Road, West Green, CRAWLEY, RH17 7JL.
OC: as address.   **VA: 1.**

No vehicles currently recorded

PK0003508/I: EMSWORTH & DISTRICT Motor Services Limited, The Bus Garage, Clovelly Road, SOUTHBOURNE, PO10 8PE.   **OC:** as address.   **VA: 25.**

w	UOI 2679	VH	T815	YE281500A02M14272	VH	14272		C49FT	4/84	Gange, Cowes (IW)	5/12
			(ex WPT 43 3/91, A102 OYG by12/86)								
w	AML 30H	AEC	Sw	4MP2R361	MI	B4490		B46F	4/70	Musterphantom (HA)	3/88
p	MLK 708L	Fd	Tt	BC05MK66031	Stn	15671		B16F	9/72	Holmes, Gosport (HA)	2/88
w	JGV 332N	Bd	YRT	EW451890	Pn	7511TB802		B64F	5/75	Rallybeam, Debach (SK)	9/91
	OUC 45R	Ld	FE30AGR	7602359	MCW			H44/32F	11/76	West Kingsdown, West Kingsdown (KT) 45	3/99
r	VNK 595S	Fd	Tt	BD05TJ65416	Do	7239 77 910		B16F	9/77	Parmenter, Brighton (XES)	6/00
r	LUA 255V	Vo	B58-56	15126	Pn	8011VC031		C53F	3/80	Jones, Tonbridge (P)	12/07
			(ex KAO 221V, 3927 TR by9/00, SIB 2633 12/98, AJF 405A 11/95, LUA 255V 4/85)								
r	OPE 613W	Bd	YMQ	LW452773	chassis only				6/81	Jones, Oakley (HA)	10/99
	RDL 686X	Ld	ONLXB/1R	ON273	ECW	25215		CH44/30F	5/82	London Borough of Redbridge, Ilford (LN)	4/10
w	NYH 161Y	Bd	YNT	YNT3VZCT104107	Pn	8211NTS5X527		C45DL	1/83	Netley Waterside Home, Netley (XHA)	12/96
w	A889 FPM	Bd	YMT	FKFYNT3CZET102829	Pn	8411NTB1B701		B55F	3/84	Tillingbourne, Cranleigh (SR) 889	8/96
w	A829 SUL	Ld	TNLXB2RR	0889	Ld			H44/26D	8/83	Selkent (LN) T829	2/01
	A883 SUL	Ld	TNTL112RR	0943	Ld			H44/32F	11/83	Selkent (LN) T883	5/01
z	A 12 YOU	Ld	LBM6T/2RS	LBM00191	RB	17589		C37F	10/89	Avalon Tours, Cayman Islands (O)	9/00
			(ex G 93 VMM 1/99)								
w	B 29 BMC	Fd	Tt	FFAVXXBDVVEE62398	CD	-?-		M12	1/85	Castle, Clanfield (HA)	8/90
w	B999 CUS	Bd	YMP	3KFYMP2DZFT104386	Pn	858MQP2C012		C35F	6/85	Sussex Country, Brighton(ES)	10/98
			(named *Maid Marion*)								
	C 8 LEA	Fd	Tt	WF0EXXGBFE4B86395	Fd			M16	3/04	Buzzlines, Hythe (K I)	11/11
			(ex AF 04 LWK 11/11)								
w	D602 RGJ	Bd	YMT	FKFYMT3CZGT107337	Pn	8711MTD1B707		B53F	1/87	Metrobus (LN) 168	9/99
	G516 VYE	Ds	Dt	8.5SDL3003/154	Du	D9001/0050		B31F	4/90	Southern Vectis (IW) 816	3/07
z	H536 CTR	Ld	ST2R36C97A4	LBM00290	WS	3220/90		B26FL	10/90	Renown, Bexhill (ESr)	12/02
	H201 DVM	VH	T815	YE281500H01C19160	VH	19160		C53F	1/91	Boomerang, Tewkesbury (GL)	8/04
			(ex 315 ASV by8/04, H201 DVM by6/01)								
	H204 DVM	VH	T815	YE281500H01C19163	VH	19163		C49FTL	1/91	Chambers, Bures (SK)	7/02
	H532 XGK	Ds	Dt	8.5SDL3003/478	Pn	918DAR0126		B28F	5/91	Central Connect, Birmingham (WM)	6/09
			(ex WLT 532 2/01, H532 XGK 7/92)								
	J502 GCD	Ds	Dt	9.8SDL3017/731	Ar	AM88/1591/23		B41F	2/92	Southdown (WS) 32502	12/06
w	J504 GCD	Ds	Dt	9.8SDL3017/740	Ar	AM88/1591/25		B41F	3/92	Hastings & District (ES) 32504	4/04
w	J511 GCD	Ds	Dt	9.8SDL3017/747	Ar	AM88/1591/32		B41F	3/92	Southdown (WS) 32511	2/07
	J524 GCD	Ds	Dt	9.8SDL3017/789	Ar	AM88/1591/45		B41F	3/92	Southdown (WS) 32524	5/07
	J548 GCD	Ds	Dt	9.8SDL3017/864	Ar	AM92/1591/69		B40F	6/92	Hampshire Bus (HA) 32548	5/07
w	J552 GCD	Ds	Dt	9.8SDL3017/891	Ar	AM92/1591/73		B40F	6/92	Southdown (WS) 32552	6/07
	J605 XHL	Ds	Dt	9SDL3011/558	Pn	919HMN0374		B34F	9/91	Barham, Parkeston (XEX)	6/10
	K556 NHC	Ds	Dt	9.8SDL3017/964	Ar	AM92/1591/92		B40F	8/92	Southdown (WS) 32556	6/08
r	K655 NHC	Ds	Dt	9.8SDL3017/963	Ar	AM92/1591/91		B40F	8/92	Southdown (WS) 32555	2/08
	K 96 SAG	Ds	Dt	9SDL3016/1193	Pn	939HSN1268		B34F	4/93	Travel London (LN) 8896	11/09
			(ex 8325 MW 12/06, K 96 SAG 6/03)								
w	L452 UEB	Ds	Dt	9.8SDL3017/1386	MI	C27.028		B40F	9/93	Town & Around, Folkestone (KT)	9/03

EMSWORTH & DISTRICT, SOUTHBOURNE (continued)

M 8 HAT	Vo	B10M-62	YV31MA6181A052620	VH	33596	C53DL	2/01	Hillier, Foxham (WI)	9/1
		(ex X751 VWR 1/12)							
M 3 KFC	Ds	Dt SLF	SFD612BR1YGW15150	Pn	018.8GKB3757	B28F	4/01	London General (LN) LDP131	10/1
		(ex Y831 TGH 10/12)							
w M452 LLJ	Ds	Dt	9.8SDL3054/2397	EL	B13902	B40F	4/95	Bournemouth (DT) 452	6/0
M456 LLJ	Ds	Dt	9.8SDL3054/2436	EL	B13906	B40F	4/95	Bournemouth (DT) 456	8/0
N906 NAP	MB	709D	WDB6690032N038548	Ar	9526/22	B25F	1/96	Stagecoach South (HA) 40906	2/1
N731 RDD	MB	709D	WDB6690032N041688	ArB	M5816 0396	DP25F	4/96	Hampshire Bus (HA) 40731	7/0
P991 AFV	Ds	Dt SLF	SFD322BR1VGW11084	EL	22203	B40F	6/97	Bournemouth (DT) SE485	9/1
P817 REX	MB	O810D	WDB6703732N064431	Pn	977.8MWV6998	DP28F	7/97	Harrogate Coach, Green Hammerton (NY)	4/1
R475 NPR	Ds	Dt SLF	SFD212BR1WGW12224	EL	25201	B37F	6/98	Bournemouth (DT) SE475	9/1
R478 NPR	Ds	Dt SLF	SFD212BR1WGW12227	EL	25204	B37F	6/98	Bournemouth (DT) SE478	9/1
R479 NPR	Ds	Dt SLF	SFD212BR1WGW12228	EL	25205	B37F	6/98	Bournemouth (DT) SE479	9/1
R569 UOT	Ds	Jv	SFD721BR3VGJ22040	UVG	5789/97	C55DL	9/97	London Borough of Havering, Purfleet (EX) 175	1/0
R171 VLA	Ds	Dt SLF	SFD212BR1WGW12298	Pn	9810.1HJB8733	B28D	6/98	Metroline (LN) DLD71	11/0
R173 VLA	Ds	Dt SLF	SFD212BR1WGW12300	Pn	9810.1HJB8735	B28D	6/98	Metroline (LN) DLD73	11/0
R524 YRP	Ds	Dt SLF	SFD322BR1VGW11088	EL	22705	B40F	8/97	Bournemouth (DT) SE488	9/1
		(ex 97-D-63758 by8/01, R524 YRP 1/00)							
S399 HVV	Ds	Dt SLF	SFD322BR1WGW12596	EL	25108	B40F	11/98	Bournemouth (DT) SE499	9/1
T527 AOB	Ds	Dt SLF	SFD612BR1WGW13018	Pn	998.8GKB0429	B29F	3/99	Arriva North West (GM) 857	1/1
V930 EWP	Ds	Dt SLF	SFD466BR1WGW40230	Pn	9911.3HAB0392	B41F	11/99	Huyton Travel, Huyton (MY) 61	9/1
V 1 FOR	Ds	Dt SLF	SFD6B2CR31GW16225	Pn	0162/4	B29F	3/02	Castleways, Winchcombe (GL)	by2/1
		(ex VU 02 UVM 10/12)							
W195 CDN	DAF	DE33WSSB3000	XMGDE33WS0H008097	VH	33245	C48FT	5/00	Eavesway, Ashton-in-Makerfield (GM)	1/0
W681 TNV	Ds	Dt SLF	SFD322BR1WGW12897	Pn	9810.7HLB0352	B39F	5/00	Bournemouth (DT) SE492	9/1
		(ex 'CAP 10' 4/00)							
X531 UAT	Ds	Dt SLF	SFD212AR1YGW15321	Pn	0010.1HJB3364	B27D	11/00	Gard, Wallisdown (DT)	2/1
Y297 HUA	DAF	DE33WSSB3000	XMGDE33WS0H008881	VH	33259	C48FT	4/01	Eavesway, Ashton-in-Makerfield (GM)	1/0
Y432 PBD	Ds	Dt SLF	SFD322BR1WGW12080	EL	25101	B40F	3/01	Bournemouth (DT) SE495	9/1
KP 51 SYA	Ds	Dt SLF	SFD6B2CR31GW16015	Pn	0126/7	B29F	12/01	Countryliner, Uckfield (ES) DP23	3/13
KV 51 KZJ	Ds	Dt SLF	SFD6B2CR31GW16068	Pn	0156/1	B29F	11/01	Countryliner, Uckfield (ES) DP18	4/13
YJ 03 PSY	DAF	SB4000	XMGDE40XS0H010353	VH	37040	C48FT	3/03	Eavesway, Ashton-in-Makerfield (GM)	1/0
YJ 04 BJE	VH	T917	YE2917SX374M52141	VH	52141	C54FT	3/04	Eavesway, Ashton-in-Makerfield (GM)	11/1
YJ 05 PVX	VH	T917	YE2917SX327D52144	VH	52144	C54FT	3/05	Eavesway, Ashton-in-Makerfield (GM)	12/12
YJ 05 PVY	VH	T917	YE2917SX327D52145	VH	52145	C54FT	3/05	Eavesway, Ashton-in-Makerfield (GM)	11/1
SN 55 FPL	MB	1523L	WDB9702782K979323	UNVI	34004	C39FL	11/05	Holmeswood, Holmeswood (LA)	2/1

NOTE: prior to 12/00, vehicles were licenced to PK740 P R J & M J Lea, Southbourne.

PK1098623/R: Edward John EPHGRAVE, 41 Myrtle Road, LANCING, BN15 9HU.
FN: Benjamin's Travel.   OC: as address.   VA: 1.

No vehicles yet recorded

PK0003605/I: EUROPEAN TRAVELPLAN Limited, Stockbury House, Church Street, STORRINGTON, Pulborough, RH20 4LD.   OC: Chantry Industrial Estate, Chantry Lane, Storrington, Pulborough, RH20 4AD.   VA: 3.

YX 04 FYH	MB	413CDI	WDB9046632R635689	Fer	-?-	C16F	6/04	Harmer, Eastbourne (ES)	6/07

PK1133409/R: Kevin Peter FARREN, 1 Paddock Cottages, ROGATE, Petersfield, GU31 5HT.
FN: Midhurst & Rogate Cars.   OC: 8 Woods Building, The Wharf, Midhurst, GU29 9PX.   VA: 1.

No vehicles yet recorded

PK1135283/R: FORGE Mobility Services Limited, Forge Cottage, Ifield Street, Ifield, CRAWLEY, RH11 0NN.
FN: Forge Cars.   OC: as address.   VA: 2.

x	SD 06 HSY	Pt	Bxr	VF3ZCPMNC17535553	Monarch	M8	8/06 new	8/06

NOTE: prior to 2/15, vehicles were licenced to PK1061416/R Anthony John Hale, Ifield.

PK1119332/I: Anthony R FRANCIS & Lee J J GALTON, 56 Cokeham Road, Sompting, LANCING, BN15 0AG.
FN: Roadrunner Sussex.   OC: as address.   VA: 3.

SCZ 1562	Io	65C15	ZCFC65A000D195639	Nuk -?-		B24FL	6/03 Lets Go, Manselton (CW) 24	7/13
L999 RRS	MB	311CDI	WDB9036632R779071	Excel -?-		M16	6/05 Goodman, Peterborough (CM)	3/12
			(ex KM 05 OGN 10/12)					
T999 RRS	MB	413CDI	WDB9046632R408274	Onyx 558		M16	9/02 Cheetham, Northlea (DM)	7/12
			(ex N 9 NST 10/12, YR 52 OBO 1/07)					
FJ 54 MMX	Ta	BB50R	TW1FG518205500374	Co	F043071034	C26F	9/04 Southwest Minibuses,	
							Fishponds (GL)	6/14

NOTE: prior to 5/13, vehicles were licenced to PK1078054/R: Anthony Robert Francis, Lancing.

PK1095496/R: Pedro GARCIA, 57A Hawthorn Road, BOGNOR REGIS, PO21 2BS
FN: Yourstaff.   OC: 44 Manor Lane, Selsey, PO20 0NX.   VA: 1.

HV 57 TYY	Fd	Tt	WF0DXXTTFD7J53639	Fd	M16	9/07 Hendy, Chandler's Ford (YHA)	3/12
GX 58 AOV	VW	Crf	WV1ZZZ2EZ96011257	?	M16	9/08 -?-, -?-	2/13

PK1057657/N: GATWICK LINKS Limited, 11 Stace Way, Worth, CRAWLEY, RH10 7YL.
OCs: as address; 17 Furnace Drive, Crawley, RH10 6HZ; 42 Martyr Avenue, Langley Green, Crawley, RH11 7RZ; 1
Hanover Close, Crawley, RH10 5DG; 42 Langley Walk, Langley Green, Crawley, RH11 7LR.   VA: 7.

X533 AKY	Fd	Tt	WF0LXXBDVLXS44345	Fd	M16	6/00 private owner	4/07
NC 02 VSD	Fd	Tt	WF0EXXGBFE2J01487	Fd	M14	8/02 -?-, -?-	7/08
CU 03 KVH	Fd	Tt	WF0EXXGBFE3D30896	Fd	M14	6/03 Cophall Farm Parking,	
						Gatwick (YWS)	1/12
AJ 05 NHD	Fd	Tt	WF0EXXTTFE5P78650	Fd	M16	5/05 private owner	2/06
GJ 05 RJX	Fd	Tt	WF0EXXTTFE5M52336	Fd	M16	4/05 London Hire, Belvedere (XLN)	2/12
GN 55 VOB	Fd	Tt	WF0EXXTTFE5C87854	Fd	M16	1/06 new	1/06

NOTE: prior to 5/06, vehicles were licensed to PK1044242/R Mukesh Limbachia, Crawley; PK1050254/R Chandrakant Limbachia,
Crawley and PK1056077/R Manilal S Limbachia, Crawley.

PK0003328/R: GREAT BALLARD SCHOOL Limited, EARTHAM, Chichester, PO18 0LR.
OC: as address.   VA: 2.

	FV 58 LYC	Fd	Tt	WF0DXXTTFD8S45443	Fd	M16	1/09 new	1/09
	FV 58 MHO	Fd	Tt	WF0DXXTTFD8S45448	Fd	M16	1/09 new	1/09
x	AX 60 BCY	Fd	Tt	WF0BXXBDFBAG87624	Fd	M8	1/11 -?-, -?-	10/11

PK0002843/N: PC & NM HAMMER, 144 Nevill Avenue, Hove, East Sussex, BN3 7NH.
FN: Pavilion Coaches.   OC: Old Cement Workshops, Shoreham Road, BEEDING, BN44 3TX.   VA: 1.

NLE 701	Ld	7RT	524964	PR	L416	H30/26R	2/53 Purley Transport Preservation	
							Group (P)	9/03
UIL 4207	Vo	B10M-62	YV31M2B13RA041581	Pn	9512VUS2634	C53F	5/95 Smith, Leeds (WY)	6/02
		(ex M473 SBT 7/01)						

PK0003640/I: HOLT SERVICES Limited, Clayton Cottage, New Hall Lane, Small Dole, HENFIELD, BN5 9YH.
OC: as address.   VA: 2.

AE 60 DBX	Io	65C18	ZCFC65D0005738244	Ind	7055	C25F	9/10 pre-registered by dealer	4/11

PK1100761/N: HORSHAM TRAVEL Limited, Unit 1, Jubilee Estate, HORSHAM, RH13 5UE.
OCs: Abbey House, Foundry Lane, Horsham, RH13 5PX; Orchard House, Reigate Road, Hookwood, Horley, Surrey, RH6 0AR.   VA: 2.

CN 51 BKU	MB	413CDI	WDB9046122R320692	UVG 8961	B16FL	11/01 London Borough of	
						Hounslow (XLN) 7035	9/1'

PK1137063/R: Patricia HOVE, 11 Linchmere, Swanborough Drive, Whitehawk, Brighton, BN2 5QD.
FN: Door 2 Door School Bus.   OC: Logistics House, Charles Avenue, BURGESS HILL, RH15 9TQ.   VA: 1.

New application currently pending

PK1088687/R: Matthew HOWELL, 24 Harwood Avenue, Goring-by-Sea, WORTHING, BN12 6EJ.
FN: Black Tie Limo.   OC: as address.   VA: 2.

S 12 ECH	MB	411CDI	WDB9046632R198713	Koch	M16	-/00 Mostyn, Hemel Hempstead (HT) 4/14	
		(ex -?- 1/05)					

PK1008003/N: Norman Harold Stephen HUDSON, 48 Park Way, Havant, Hampshire, PO9 1HH.
FN: Normans Travel.   OC: Cut Mill, Newells Lane, BOSHAM, Chichester, PO18 8PS.   VA: 2.

z	HIL 8961	Ld	RT		RT1006	Pn	8412LRH1C01N	C47FT	4/84 Vision Travel, Cowplain (HA)	3/05
			(ex A330 XHE by7/93)							
z	IIL 4820	Fd	R1114		BCRSAL261880	Pn	8311FTP1X502	C53F	1/83 Portrest, Southam (WK)	by2/05
			(ex 609 KRA 1/93, BFH 621Y 6/86)							
w	LXI 4409	Ld	PSU3E/4R		7930191	Pn	8111LC012	C53F	11/81 Collins, Castle Goring (WS)	9/02
			(ex RDL 307X 4/92)							
w	NCZ 8070	Bd	YMT		JW454606	Pn	7911TX548	C53F	5/79 Morgan, Ingatestone (EX)	2/05
			(ex GVW 894T 1/02)							
z	644 HKX	Ld	TRCTL11/3RZ		8500622	Pn	8712LZH3C752	C53F	8/87 Solent Travel, Newport (IW)	by2/05
			(ex E664 JAV 9/89)							
w	NPX 998M	Bd	YRQ		CW453119	Du	266/218	C45F	10/73 Anstey, Haslemere (SR)	8/85
w	HPB 664N	Bd	YRQ		EW452581	Du	515/2078	C45F	6/75 Anstey, Haslemere (SR)	8/85
w	CTM 407T	Ld	PSU3E/4R		7803455	Du	933/5151	C53F	1/79 Tramcourt, Selsey (WS)	1/00
w	TTP 592T	MB	L207D		60136728063183	DC	M12	M12	3/79 Weller, Midhurst (WS)	by12/95
w	CDL 677V	Bd	YMT		YMT3DZ0JW455742	Pn	7911TC235	C53F	8/79 Traditional, Lake (IW)	8/00
w	HDL 232V	Fd	R1014		BCRSWJ377810	Pn	808FC014	C31F	2/80 Barfoot, West End (HA)	4/00
			(ex 282 GOT 3/93, CEB 137V 8/90)							
r	LVS 441V	Ld	PSU3E/4R		7930003	Pn	8011LC030	C53F	2/80 Hellyers, Fareham (HA)	by8/07
w	UNO 100W	Bd	YMT		YMT3DZ0JW456997	Pn	8011TX525	C53F	1/81 Morgan, Ingatestone (EX)	2/05
w	A113 TRP	Ld	TRCTL11/3RH		8412LTP1X533		8412LTP1X533	C57F	12/83 Buckland, West Wittering	
			(ex TAZ 3608 4/99, A113 TRP by8/98)						(WS)	by2/05
z	E749 VWT	VW	LT55		WV2ZZZ29ZJH010740	Oe	521	B25F	6/88 Flyght Travel, Cosham (HA)	2/07
w	F464 NRT	Ld	TRCTL11/3RZ		8700045	Du	8890/0678	C61F	8/88 Neilsen, Colliers Wood (LN)	1/10
w	G 67 RGG	Vo	B10M-60		YV31MGD11KA022821	Pn	9012VCB1496	C53F	3/95 Victory Travel, Havant (HA)	4/14
			(ex OAZ 5315 by9/13, G 67 RGG by7/97)							
w	H421 GPM	MB	709D		WDB6690032P039450	Do	50692 632 90	B27F	8/90 Emsworth & District,	
									Southbourne (WS)	10/07
w	J127 OBU	MB	609D		WDB6680632P177298	MM		C24F	11/91 Flyght Travel, Cosham (HA)	11/04
w	M 71 RJW	LDV	400		SEYZMYSEACN958086	WMB		M16	4/95 Lucas, South Darenth (KT)	11/05

NOTE: prior to 9/02, OLN was PH6137/I and prior to 8/00, this operator was recorded in Hampshire as Hudson, Rowlands Castle (HA).

PK0003220/R: Eileen HUNNISETT, Gorse Lane House, Gorse Lane, WORTHING, BN13 3BX.
FN: Ace Taxis (Worthing).   OC: as address.   VA: 2.

	YR 02 OAX	LDV	Cy	SEYZMVSYGDN084155	LDV	M16	4/02 National (Y)	11/10
							(via unknown operator)	
	LF 04 PJX	LDV	Cy	SEYZMVSZGDN104369	LDV	M16	6/04 -?-, -?-	10/10
x	BU 07 NUY	LDV	Max	SEYL6RXH20N216881	LDV	M8	7/07 -?-, -?-	3/11
			(carries Arun Private Hire plate 28)					
x	BU 07 RZB	LDV	Max	SEYL6RXH20N218277	LDV	M8	8/07 National Car Rental (Y)	8/09
			(carries Arun Private Hire plate 37)					
x	TN 07 SWT	VW	Tr	WV2ZZZ7HZ7H126021	VW	M8	6/07 new	6/07
			(carries Arun Private Hire plate 35)					

HUNNISETT, WORTHING (continued)

x	AE 08 BGO	LDV Max	SEYL6RXE20N223984	LDV	M8	4/08 -?-, -?-		10/10
		(carries Arun Private Hire plate 38)						
x	SA 08 RWO	VW Tr	WV2ZZZ7HZ8H062738	VW	M8	3/08 new		3/08
		(carries Arun Private Hire plate 21)						
x	SA 60 DLD	VW Tr	WV2ZZZ7HZBH061904	VW	M8	12/10 new		12/10
		(carries Arun Private Hire plate 40)						
x	SA 60 DLF	VW Tr	WV2ZZZ7HZBH062088	VW	M8	12/10 new		12/10
		(carries Arun Private Hire plate 39)						

PK0003341/R: David JELL, 5 Downs Way, EAST PRESTON, Littlehampton, BN16 1AA.
FN: DJ Services. OC: as address. VA: 1.

No vehicles yet recorded

PK1024379/R: Clare JOHNSON, 39 Connell Drive, WOODINGDEAN, Brighton, BN2 6RT.
FN: 1st Class Travel. OCs: as address; The Old Cement Workshops, Shoreham Road, Beeding, BN44 3TX. VA: 2.

See joint entry with Ace Travel, Beeding

PK1111955/R: Abdul Waheed KHAN, 35 Caburn Heights, CRAWLEY, RH11 8QX.
FN: United Hire. OC: as address. VA: 1.

YC 06 GYS	Fd Tt	WF0EXXTTFE6T49482	Fd	M16	5/06 Furlong, Kirkby (MY)	5/12

NOTE: the licence was granted in 10/12.

PK1056516/R: Andrew KIRKWOOD, Shop 1, 24 Station Road, BOGNOR REGIS, PO21 1QE.
FN: Forestburn Enterprises. OC: Motorvation, Unit 1, Durban Road Industrial Estate, Bognor Regis, PO22 9RU.
VA: 2.

No vehicles yet recorded

PK0003133/I: Robert Sydney KNIGHT, "Kingscote", Dorking Road, WARNHAM, Horsham, RH12 3RZ.
OC: Unit 1A, Lower Broad Farm, Billingshurst Road, Broadbridge Heath, Horsham, RH12 3LR. VA: 12.

J231 NNC	Vo	B10M-60	YV31MGD17MA027900	VH	30921	C70F	2/92 Lainton, Gorton (GM)	8/11
		(ex RIL 4630 2/04, J231 NNC 5/02)						
M602 ORJ	Vo	B10M-62	YV31M2B14SA043006	Je	23660	C70F	4/95 Holmeswood, Holmeswood (LA)	8/11
N 92 SKG	Vo	B10M-62	YV31M2B12TA045189	Je	24054	C70F	5/06 Holmeswood, Holmeswood (LA)	8/11
S 10 KTC	Au	N122/3	WAG301222XSP27158	Au	1222539	CH57/20CT	1/99 Mott, Aylesbury (BK)	5/11
		(ex S150 SET 8/11, 9775 MT 1/11, S150 SET 2/06, ROI 7435 by6/05, S150 SET by10/00)						
KC 55 KTC	Sca	K114IB4	YS2K4X20001851237	Ir	151667	C49FT	10/05 new	10/05
YN 57 DVC	MB	515CDI	WDB9066572S188813	KVC		C16F	9/07 Nova Bussing, Rye (ES)	12/11
		(ex FPN 259 2/10, YN 57 DVC 8/08)						
KC 08 KTC	MAN	24.440	WMAR37ZZ18C011286	Bs	08.020	C57FTL	7/08 new	7/08
YN 63 BYY	Sca	K400EB6	YS2K6X20001884417	Ir	141040	C59FT	11/13 new	11/13
YN 63 BYZ	Sca	K230IB4	YS2K4X20001884452	Ir	161283	C59D	11/13 new	11/13

PK1081402/R: David LEWIS, c/o Browns, Unit 4A, Burrell Road, Haywards Heath, RH16 1TW.
FN: Airport Shuttle. OC: Unit 4A, Burrell Road, HAYWARDS HEATH, RH16 1TW. VA: 2.

No vehicles yet recorded

PK1129919/I: LOST GENERATION 1914-18 Limited, 9 Station Road, Rawcliffe, Goole, East Yorkshire, DN14 8QP.
OC: 5-7 Spindle Way, CRAWLEY, RH10 1TG. VA: 2.

No vehicles yet recorded

PK1064258/R: Sher Afsar MALIK, 4 Hyndman Close, Broadfield, CRAWLEY, RH11 9TR.
FN: Prestige Cars. OC: as address. VA: 2.

x	GY 04 ZGA	Ft	Do	ZFA24400007177843	Ft		M8	5/04 Prestige Cars, Crawley(YWS)	12/0▮
x	HY 59 FPJ	Ft	Do	ZFA25000001651361	KFS		B16F	10/09 Oxfordshire County Council,	
								Oxford (XOX)	7/1▮

PK0003429/N: MERCURY Minibuses Limited, 34 Middleton Avenue, Hove, East Sussex, BN3 4PJ.
OC: The Granaries, Paynesfield, Henfield Road, ALBOURNE, Hassocks, BN6 9JJ. VA: 4.
PK1136499/N: MERCURY Minibuses Limited, 34 Middleton Avenue, Hove, BN3 4PJ.
OC: The Granaries, Paynesfield, Henfield Road, ALBOURNE, Hassocks, BN6 9JJ. VA: 4 (currently pending).

CU 08 EZZ	Fd	Tt	WF0DXXTTFD7P44380	Fd		M16	3/08 new		3/0▮
YX 08 ATZ	MB	O816D	WDB6703742N127682	Fer	-?-	C31F	6/08 new		6/0▮
FV 09 VYS	Fd	Tt	WF0DXXTTFD9B04698	Fd		M16	8/09 new		8/0▮
YY 63 KUB	MB	O816D	WDB6703742N147187	Pn	-?-	C29F	9/13 new		9/1▮

PK0002125/I: METROBUS Limited, Whetstone Close, Tinsley Lane North, Crawley, West Sussex, RH10 1DQ.
OC: [CY] as address.
VA: 513.

6001	BN 14 CUC	Vo	B7RLE	YV3R6R623EA164851	Wt	AJ781	B40D	3/14 new		3/1▮
6002	BN 14 CUG	Vo	B7RLE	YV3R6R622EA164873	Wt	AJ782	B40D	3/14 new		3/1▮
6003	BN 14 CUH	Vo	B7RLE	YV3R6R624EA164874	Wt	AJ783	B40D	3/14 new		3/1▮
6004	BN 14 CUJ	Vo	B7RLE	YV3R6R626EA164875	Wt	AJ784	B40D	3/14 new		3/1▮
6005	BN 14 CUK	Vo	B7RLE	YV3R6R628EA164876	Wt	AJ785	B40D	3/14 new		3/1▮
6006	BN 14 CUO	Vo	B7RLE	YV3R6R62XEA164877	Wt	AJ766	B40D	3/14 new		3/1▮
6007	BN 14 CUU	Vo	B7RLE	YV3R6R621EA164878	Wt	AJ787	B40D	3/14 new		3/1▮
6008	BN 14 CUV	Vo	B7RLE	YV3R6R628EA164912	Wt	AJ788	B40D	3/14 new		3/1▮
6009	BN 14 CUW	Vo	B7RLE	YV3R6R62XEA164913	Wt	AJ789	B40D	3/14 new		3/1▮
6010	BN 14 CUX	Vo	B7RLE	YV3R6R621EA164914	Wt	AJ790	B40D	3/14 new		3/1▮
6011	BN 14 CUY	Vo	B7RLE	YV3R6R623EA164915	Wt	AJ791	B40D	3/14 new		3/1▮
6012	BN 14 CVA	Vo	B7RLE	YV3R6R625EA164916	Wt	AJ792	B40D	4/14 new		4/1▮
6013	BN 14 CVB	Vo	B7RLE	YV3R6R627EA164917	Wt	AJ793	B40D	3/14 new		3/1▮
6014	BN 14 CVC	Vo	B7RLE	YV3R6R623EA164929	Wt	AJ794	B40D	3/14 new		3/1▮
6015	BU 14 EFS	Vo	B7RLE	YV3R6R625EA164849	Wt	AJ780	B40D	3/14 new		3/1▮
6016	BU 14 EFT	Vo	B7RLE	YV3R6R621EA164850	Wt	AJ779	B40D	3/14 new		3/1▮
6017	BU 14 EHK	Vo	B7RLE	YV3R6R621EA164847	Wt	AJ778	B40D	3/14 new		3/1▮
6018	BU 14 EHL	Vo	B7RLE	YV3R6R623EA164848	Wt	AJ777	B40D	4/14 new		4/1▮
6201	SN 03 WKU	Tbs	Dt SLF	SFD3CACR33GW97289	Tbs	3021/19	B36D	8/03 new		8/03
6202	SN 03 WKY	Tbs	Dt SLF	SFD3CACR33GW97288	Tbs	3021/18	B36D	8/03 new		8/03
6203	SN 03 WLA	Tbs	Dt SLF	SFD3CACR33GW97270	Tbs	3021/1	B36D	8/03 new		8/03
6204	SN 03 WLE	Tbs	Dt SLF	SFD3CACR33GW97271	Tbs	3021/2	B36D	8/03 new		8/03
6205	SN 03 WLF	Tbs	Dt SLF	SFD3CACR33GW97272	Tbs	3021/3	B36D	8/03 new		8/03
6206	SN 03 WLH	Tbs	Dt SLF	SFD3CACR33GW97273	Tbs	3021/4	B36D	8/03 new		8/03
6207	SN 03 WLL	Tbs	Dt SLF	SFD3CACR33GW97274	Tbs	3021/5	B36D	8/03 new		8/03
6217	SN 03 WMT	Tbs	Dt SLF	SFD3CACR33GW97285	Tbs	3021/16	B36D	8/03 new		8/03
6218	SN 03 WMV	Tbs	Dt SLF	SFD3CACR33GW97277	Tbs	3021/8	B36D	8/03 new		8/03
6287	SN 03 YCL	Tbs	Dt SLF	SFD6BACR33GW87311	Tbs	3020/17	B29F	9/03 new		9/03
6288	SN 03 YCM	Tbs	Dt SLF	SFD6BACR33GW87312	Tbs	3020/18	B29F	9/03 new		9/03
6289	SN 03 YCT	Tbs	Dt SLF	SFD6BACR33GW87313	Tbs	3020/19	B29F	9/03 new		9/03
6320	LX 03 OJP	Ds	Dt SLF	SFD3CACR32GW86889	Tbs	2062/9	B37F	5/03 new		5/03
6321	LX 03 OJN	Ds	Dt SLF	SFD3CACR32GW86906	Tbs	2062/12	B37F	5/03 new		5/03
6344	X344 YGU	Ds	Dt SLF	SFD612BR1XGW14326	Pn	008.8GKB2289	B29F	9/00 new		9/0C
6363	Y363 HMY	Ds	Dt SLF	SFD322BR1YGW14626	SCC	4139/2000	B36F	4/01 new		4/01
6365	Y365 HMY	Ds	Dt SLF	SFD322BR1YGW14681	SCC	4141/2000	B36F	4/01 new		4/01
6372	Y372 HMY	Ds	Dt SLF	SFD322BR1YGW15198	SCC	4151/2000	B36F	4/01 new		4/01
6377	Y377 HMY	Ds	Dt SLF	SFD322BR11GW15824	SCC	4201/2001	B38F	8/01 new		8/01
6378	Y378 HMY	Ds	Dt SLF	SFD322BR11GW15825	SCC	4202/2001	B38F	8/01 new		8/01
6379	Y379 HMY	Ds	Dt SLF	SFD322BR11GW15826	SCC	4203/2001	B38F	8/01 new		8/01
6469	YV 03 RBU	Sca	N94UD	YS2N4X20001845574	EL	46418	H45/29D	8/03 new		8/03
6470	YV 03 RBX	Sca	N94UD	YS2N4X20001845575	EL	46419	H45/29D	8/03 new		8/03
6471	YN 53 USG	Sca	N94UD	YS2N4X20001845576	EL	40420	H45/29D	8/03 new		8/03
			(ex YV 03 RBY 1/04)							
6472	YN 53 RYA	Sca	N94UD	YS2N4X20001846579	EL	47120	H45/29D	1/04 new		1/04
6473	YN 53 RYB	Sca	N94UD	YS2N4X20001846411	EL	47111	H45/29D	1/04 new		1/04
6474	YN 53 RYC	Sca	N94UD	YS2N4X20001846412	EL	47112	H45/29D	1/04 new		1/04
6475	YN 53 RYD	Sca	N94UD	YS2N4X20001846413	EL	47113	H45/29D	1/04 new		1/04
6476	YN 53 RYF	Sca	N94UD	YS2N4X20001846427	EL	47114	H45/29D	1/04 new		1/04
6477	YN 53 RYH	Sca	N94UD	YS2N4X20001846421	EL	47115	H45/29D	1/04 new		1/04

6019 ho BJ 15 ~~~~ Vo B7RLE Wt B40D 2015
6101 LK13 ASJ Wt SELEDF ~ B45F 2013
= 102·4

METROBUS (continued)

6478	YN 53 RYK	Sca	N94UD	YS2N4X20001846422	EL	47116	H45/29D	12/03	new	12/03
6482	YN 53 RYT	Sca	N94UD	YS2N4X20001846332	EL	47101	H45/29D	11/03	London General (LN) 482	8/12
6483	YN 53 RYV	Sca	N94UD	YS2N4X20001846340	EL	47102	H45/29D	11/03	London General (LN) 483	8/12
6484	YN 53 RYW	Sca	N94UD	YS2N4X20001846341	EL	47103	H45/29D	11/03	new	11/03
6485	YN 53 RYX	Sca	N94UD	YS2N4X20001846342	EL	47104	H45/29D	11/03	new	11/03
6486	YN 53 RYY	Sca	N94UD	YS2N4X20001846335	EL	47105	H45/29D	11/03	new	11/03
6487	YN 53 RYZ	Sca	N94UD	YS2N4X20001846336	EL	47106	H45/29D	11/03	new	11/03
6488	YN 53 RZA	Sca	N94UD	YS2N4X20001846339	EL	47107	H45/29D	11/03	new	11/03
6489	YN 53 RZB	Sca	N94UD	YS2N4X20001846408	EL	47108	H45/29D	12/03	new	12/03
6490	YN 53 RZC	Sca	N94UD	YS2N4X20001846409	EL	47109	H45/29D	1/04	new	1/04
6491	YN 53 RZD	Sca	N94UD	YS2N4X20001846410	EL	47110	H45/29D	1/04	new	1/04
6492	YN 53 RZE	Sca	N94UD	YS2N4X20001846580	EL	47121	H45/29D	1/04	new	1/04
6493	YN 53 RZF	Sca	N94UD	YS2N4X20001846581	EL	47122	H45/29D	1/04	new	1/04
6494	YN 54 AJU	Sca	N94UD	YS2N4X20001848849	EL	53601	H45/29D	2/05	new	2/05
6495	YN 54 AJV	Sca	N94UD	YS2N4X20001848926	EL	53602	H45/29D	2/05	new	2/05
6496	YN 54 AJX	Sca	N94UD	YS2N4X20001848927	EL	53603	H45/29D	2/05	new	2/05
6497	YN 54 AJY	Sca	N94UD	YS2N4X20001848928	EL	53604	H45/29D	2/05	new	2/05
6513	YP 52 CTO	Sca	N94UB	YS4N4X20001843066	Sca		B42F	10/02	new	10/02
6531	YN 03 UWU	Sca	N94UB	YS2N4X20001844410	Sca		B37D	8/03	new	8/03
6532	YN 03 UWY	Sca	N94UB	YS2N4X20001844409	Sca		B37D	8/03	new	8/03
6533	YN 03 WPM	Sca	N94UB	YS2N4X20001844406	Sca		B37D	8/03	new	8/03
6534	YN 03 WPP	Sca	N94UB	YS2N4X20001844407	Sca		B37D	8/03	new	8/03
6535	YN 03 WPR	Sca	N94UB	YS2N4X20001844408	Sca		B37D	8/03	new	8/03
6546	YN 05 HCA	Sca	N94UB	YS2N4X20001851791	Sca		B37D	7/05	new	7/05
6547	YN 05 HCC	Sca	N94UB	YS2N4X20001851792	Sca		B37D	7/05	new	7/05
6548	YN 05 HCD	Sca	N94UB	YS2N4X20001851793	Sca		B37D	7/05	new	7/05
6549	YN 05 HCE	Sca	N94UB	YS2N4X20001851794	Sca		B37D	7/05	new	7/05
6550	YN 05 HCF	Sca	N94UB	YS2N4X20001851795	Sca		B41F	7/05	new	7/05
6551	YN 05 HCG	Sca	N94UB	YS2N4X20001851796	Sca		B41F	7/05	new	7/05
6552	YN 55 PWJ	Sca	N94UB	YS2N4X20001851797	Sca		B34D	11/05	new	11/05
6553	YN 55 PWK	Sca	N94UB	YS2N4X20001852279	Sca		B34D	11/05	new	11/05
6554	YN 55 PWL	Sca	N94UB	YS2N4X20001852280	Sca		B34D	11/05	new	11/05
6555	YN 55 PWO	Sca	N94UB	YS2N4X20001852281	Sca		B34D	11/05	new	11/05
6556	YN 55 PWU	Sca	N94UB	YS2N4X20001852339	Sca		B34D	11/05	new	11/05
6557	YN 55 PWV	Sca	N94UB	YS2N4X20001852340	Sca		B34D	11/05	new	11/05
6558	YN 55 PWX	Sca	N94UB	YS2N4X20001852341	Sca		B34D	11/05	new	11/05
6559	YN 07 LKF	Sca	N230UB	SZAN4X20001857535	Sca		B40F	5/07	new	5/07
6560	YN 07 LKG	Sca	N230UB	SZAN4X20001857536	Sca		B40F	5/07	new	5/07
6582	YN 62 CLF	Sca	N230UB	SZAN4X20001879959	Sca		B35D	9/12	new	9/12
6615	YN 06 JXU	Sca	N94UB	YS2N4X20001853672	EL	C58715	B29D	3/06	new	3/06
6616	YN 06 JXV	Sca	N94UB	YS2N4X20001853673	EL	C58716	B36F	3/06	new	3/06
6617	YN 06 JXW	Sca	N94UB	YS2N4X20001853674	EL	C58717	B36F	3/06	new	3/06
6618	YN 06 JXX	Sca	N94UB	YS2N4X20001853762	EL	C58718	B36F	3/06	new	3/06
6619	YM 55 SXO	Sca	N94UB	YS2N4X20001853763	EL	C58719	B36F	2/06	new	2/06
6620	YM 55 SXP	Sca	N94UB	YS2N4X20001853764	EL	C58720	B36F	2/06	new	2/06
6621	YM 55 SXR	Sca	N94UB	YS2N4X20001853765	EL	C58721	B36F	2/06	new	2/06
6622	YN 06 JXY	Sca	N94UB	YS2N4X20001853826	EL	C58722	B36F	3/06	new	3/06
6623	YN 06 JXZ	Sca	N94UB	YS2N4X20001853827	EL	C58723	B36F	3/06	new	3/06
6624	YN 08 DFJ	Sca	N230UB	SZAN4X20001852729	Sca		B33F	3/08	new	3/08
6625	YN 08 DFK	Sca	N230UB	SZAN4X20001852787	Sca		B33F	3/08	new	3/08
6626	YN 08 DFL	Sca	N230UB	SZAN4X20001852833	Sca		B33F	3/08	new	3/08
6627	YN 08 DFO	Sca	N230UB	SZAN4X20001852834	Sca		B33F	3/08	new	3/08
6628	YN 08 DFP	Sca	N230UB	SZAN4X20001852835	Sca		B33F	3/08	new	3/08
6629	YN 08 DFU	Sca	N230UB	SZAN4X20001852894	Sca		B33F	3/08	new	3/08
6630	YN 08 DFV	Sca	N230UB	SZAN4X20001852895	Sca		B33F	3/08	new	3/08
6631	YN 08 DFX	Sca	N230UB	SZAN4X20001852896	Sca		B33F	3/08	new	3/08
6632	YN 08 DFY	Sca	N230UB	SZAN4X20001852897	Sca		B33F	3/08	new	3/08
6633	YN 08 DFZ	Sca	N230UB	SZAN4X20001852898	Sca		B33F	3/08	new	3/08
6725	GN 07 AVR	AD	Dt	SFD511AR17GY10301	AD	6256/1	B36F	6/07	Arriva Guildford & West Surrey (SR) 3976	10/09
6726	GN 07 AVT	AD	Dt	SFD511AR17GY10302	AD	6256/2	B36F	6/07	Arriva Guildford & West Surrey (SR) 3977	10/09
6727	GN 07 AVU	AD	Dt	SFD511AR17GY10303	AD	6256/3	B36F	6/07	Arriva Guildford & West Surrey (SR) 3978	10/09
6728	GN 07 AVV	AD	Dt	SFD511AR17GY10304	AD	6256/4	B36F	6/07	Arriva Guildford & West Surrey (SR) 3979	10/09
6729	GN 07 AVW	AD	Dt	SFD511AR17GY10310	AD	6256/5	B36F	6/07	Arriva Guildford & West Surrey (SR) 3980	10/09
6730	GN 07 AVY	AD	Dt	SFD511AR17GY10311	AD	6256/6	B36F	6/07	Arriva Guildford & West Surrey (SR) 3981	10/09
6734	SN 12 AAE	AD	E20D	SFD7E1AR6BGY12783	AD	B249/1	B38F	3/12	new	3/12
6735	SN 12 AAF	AD	E20D	SFD7E1AR6BGY12778	AD	B249/2	B38F	3/12	new	3/12
6736	SN 12 AAJ	AD	E20D	SFD7E1AR6BGY12779	AD	B249/3	B38F	3/12	new	3/12
6737	SN 12 AAK	AD	E20D	SFD7E1AR6BGY12781	AD	B249/4	B38F	3/12	new	3/12

6955-9 YP09 HWB/A/C/D/J, Sca N270UD4, Sca H45/31F 2009

WEST SUSSEX (WS) **G627/22**

METROBUS (continued)

6738	SN 12 AAO	AD	E20D	SFD7E1AR6BGY12782	AD	B249/5	B38F	3/12	new	3/12
6739	SN 12 AAU	AD	E20D	SFD7E1AR6BGY12786	AD	B249/6	B38F	3/12	new	3/12
6763	YX 63 ZWW	AD	E20D	SFD7E1AR6DGY14064	AD	D244/1	B38F	12/13	new	12/13
6764	YX 63 ZWY	AD	E20D	SFD7E1AR6DGY14065	AD	D244/2	B38F	12/13	new	12/13
6765	YX 63 ZWZ	AD	E20D	SFD7E1AR6DGY14077	AD	D244/3	B38F	12/13	new	12/13
6766	YX 63 ZXA	AD	E20D	SFD7E1AR6DGY14078	AD	D244/4	B38F	12/13	new	12/13
6767	YX 63 ZXB	AD	E20D	SFD7E1AR6DGY14079	AD	D244/5	B38F	12/13	new	12/13
6768	YX 63 ZXC	AD	E20D	SFD7E1AR6DGY14080	AD	D244/6	B38F	12/13	new	12/13
6769	YX 63 ZXD	AD	E20D	SFD7E1AR6DGY14081	AD	D244/7	B38F	12/13	new	12/13
6770	YX 63 ZXE	AD	E20D	SFD7E1AR6DGY14082	AD	D244/8	B38F	12/13	new	12/13
6771	YX 63 ZXF	AD	E20D	SFD7E1AR6DGY14083	AD	D244/9	B38F	12/13	new	12/13
6772	YX 63 ZXG	AD	E20D	SFD7E1AR6DGY14084	AD	D244/10	B38F	12/13	new	12/13
6773	YY 15 GBZ	AD	E20D	SFD7LBAR7EGY74756	AD	E265/1	B37F	3/15	new	3/15
6774	YY 15 GCF	AD	E20D	SFD7LBAR7EGY74757	AD	E265/2	B37F	3/15	new	3/15
6775	YY 15 GCK	AD	E20D	SFD7LBAR7EGY74758	AD	E265/3	B37F	3/15	new	3/15
6776	YY 15 GCO	AD	E20D	SFD7LBAR7EGY74759	AD	E265/4	B37F	3/15	new	3/15
6777	YY 15 GCU	AD	E20D	SFD7LBAR7EGY74760	AD	E265/5	B37F	3/15	new	3/15
6778	YY 15 GCV	AD	E20D	SFD7LBAR7EGY74761	AD	E265/6	B37F	3/15	new	3/15
6779	YY 15 GCX	AD	E20D	SFD7LBAR7EGY74762	AD	E265/7	B37F	3/15	new	3/15
6780	YY 15 GCZ	AD	E20D	SFD7LBAR7EGY74763	AD	E265/8	B37F	3/15	new	3/15
6781	YY 15 GDA	AD	E20D	SFD7LBAR7EGY74771	AD	E265/9	B37F	3/15	new	3/15
6782	YY 15 GDE	AD	E20D	SFD7LBAR7EGY74772	AD	E265/10	B37F	3/15	new	3/15
6938	YN 56 FDO	Sca	N94UD	YS2N4X20001855090	EL	C62111	H45/31F	10/06	new	10/06
6939	YN 56 FDP	Sca	N94UD	YS2N4X20001855091	EL	C62112	H45/31F	10/06	new	10/06
6953	YN 08 OBP	Sca	N230UD	SZAN4X20001860616	Sca		H47/31F	7/08	new	7/08
6954	YN 08 OBR	Sca	N230UD	SZAN4X20001860678	Sca		H47/31F	7/08	new	7/08
7208	SN 03 WLP	Tbs	Dt SLF	SFD3CACR33GW97275	Tbs	3021/6	B36D	8/03	new	8/03
7209	SN 03 WLU	Tbs	Dt SLF	SFD3CACR33GW97276	Tbs	3021/7	B36D	8/03	new	8/03
7380	LK 51 JYJ	Ds	Dt SLF	SFD2B2CR31GW15949	MI	C39.750	B14D	10/01	CentreWest (LN) DML41411-3	12/07
7381	LK 51 JYL	Ds	Dt SLF	SFD2B2CR31GW15950	MI	C39.751	B14D	10/01	CentreWest (LN) DML41411-3	12/07
7382	LK 51 JYN	Ds	Dt SLF	SFD2B2CR31GW15952	MI	C39.752	B14D	10/01	CentreWest (LN) DML41411-3	12/07
8043	LX 59 BCF	Rt	Tc	VF1JLAHAHAV360223	Rt		M7	9/09	new	9/09
8044	LX 59 BCO	Rt	Tc	VF1JLAHAHAV360222	Rt		M7	9/09	new	9/09
8070	RE 13 CJZ	MB	113CDI	WDF63970123813744	MB		M8	5/13	new	5/13

METROBUS – Fleet allocation / Check list 6019-22; 6101-27; LV61 EYF (ex ...); 8102 (SJ17 HLW ...); 6701/2/83; 8031 (D...

6019
6020
6101
6955
6956
6957
6958
6959

6001	CY	6218	CY	6485	CY	6553	CY	6632	CY	6775	CY
6002	CY	6287	CY	6486	CY	6554	CY	6633	CY	6776	CY
6003	CY	6288	CY	6487	CY	6555	CY	6725	CY	6777	CY
6004	CY	6289	CY	6488	CY	6556	CY	6726	CY	6778	CY
6005	CY	6320	CY	6489	CY	6557	CY	6727	CY	6779	CY
6006	CY	6321	CY	6490	CY	6558	CY	6728	CY	6780	CY
6007	CY	6344	CY	6491	CY	6559	CY	6729	CY	6781	CY
6008	CY	6363	CY	6492	CY	6560	CY	6730	CY	6782	CY
6009	CY	6365	CY	6493	CY	6582	CY	6734	CY	6938	CY
6010	CY	6372	CY	6494	CY	6615	CY	6735	CY	6939	CY
6011	CY	6377	CY	6495	CY	6616	CY	6736	CY	6953	CY
6012	CY	6378	CY	6496	CY	6617	CY	6737	CY	6954	CY
6013	CY	6379	CY	6497	CY	6618	CY	6738	CY	7208	CYt
6014	CY	6469	CY	6513	CY	6619	CY	6739	CY	7209	CYt
6015	CY	6470	CY	6531	CY	6620	CY	6763	CY	7380	CYt
6016	CY	6471	CY	6532	CY	6621	CY	6764	CY	7381	CYt
6017	CY	6472	CY	6533	CY	6622	CY	6765	CY	7382	CYt
6018	CY	6473	CY	6534	CY	6623	CY	6766	CY	8043	CYa
6201	CY	6474	CY	6535	CY	6624	CY	6767	CY	8044	CYa
6202	CY	6475	CY	6546	CY	6625	CY	6768	CY	8070	CYa
6203	CY	6476	CY	6547	CY	6626	CY	6769	CY		
6204	CY	6477	CY	6548	CY	6627	CY	6770	CY		
6205	CY	6478	CY	6549	CY	6628	CY	6771	CY		
6206	CY	6482	CY	6550	CY	6629	CY	6772	CY		
6207	CY	6483	CY	6551	CY	6630	CY	6773	CY		
6217	CY	6484	CY	6552	CY	6631	CY	6774	CY		

NOTE: prior to 7/14, this operator was recorded in the Greater London area as Metrobus (LN).

PK1133455/N: MIDDLE EARTH Minibus Company LLP, 18 Roman Lane, SOUTHWATER, Horsham, RH13 9AG.
OC: Unit 53A, Rosier Commercial Centre, Coneyhurst Road, Billingshurst, RH14 9DE. VA: 1.

No vehicles yet recorded

Trans Als 917

WIDE LANE, SOUTHAMPTON AIRPORT.
COACHPARK, SOUTH TERMINAL, LGW; AIRSIDE LGW + LCY.
OFJ CONNECTIONS LTD: UNIT 2, RUNWAY PARK, CHURCH ROAD, LOWFIELD HEATH, CRAWLEY;

CSU908 (*YN07 OOX) Vo B12B Pn CS3F 2007	BP08 WNF MB 0530 MB B18D 2008	
CSU909 (*YN07 OOY) " " " "	BP08 WNG " " " "	
OFJ S80 Cobus 2700s Co B D+ 2004	BP08 WNH " " " /	
OFJ S81 " " " " " "	BP08 WNJ " " " " /	
OFJ S82 " " " " " "	BP08 WNL " " " "	
TUI 4766 (*FJ06 ZKL) Vo B12B Bf CS5FE 2006	BP08 WNM " " " /	
TUI 4852 (*YN06 CJZ) Sca K114EB4 Ir CS3F	KX08 ONG " 0816D Pn C29F "	
TUI 4853 (*YN07 LGW) " K340 EB4 " 2007	SN15 LNF AD E20D AD B23D 2015	
BX04 MYK MB 0530G MB AB T 2004	SN15 LNG " " " " "	
LW04 4ZG (*630D4E LX04 LBZ) MB 0530G MB AB49 T Pay	SN15 LNH " " "	
LX04 KZG MB 0530G MB AB49T 2004	YN05 GWZ Scw K114B4 Ir CS7F 2005	
LX04 KZL " " " " "		
LX04 KZV " " " " "		
LX04 LBJ " " " " "		
LX04 LBK " " " " "		
LX04 LBP " " " " "		
LX04 LBY " " " " "		
LX04 LCG " " " " "		
LX04 LCJ " " " " "		
LX04 LCN " " " "		
LX04 LCU " " " " "		
LX04 LCW (*VLT240 LX04 LCW) " "		
YN04 AHG Sca N94UB4 Sca B36F+ " /		
YN04 AHJ " " " " "		
YN04 AHK " " " " "		
YN04 AHL " " " " "		
YN04 AHP " " " " "		
BX54 UDB MB 0530G MB AB49T "		
HT05 4CZ Vx Viv Vx M8 2005 /		
RA05 XEC VW Tc Vw " "		
BD08 DZN MB 0530 MB B23D 2008		
BD08 DZO " " " " "		
BD08 DZP " " " " "		
BD08 DZS " " " " "		
BD08 DZT " " " " "		
BD08 DZU " " " " "		
BP08 WNC " " " " "		
BP08 WND " " " " /		
BP08 WNE " " " " /		

PK1060533/N: MILLENNIUM Coaches Limited, 17 Leith Grove, Beare Green, Dorking, Surrey, RH5 4RF.
OCs: The Goods Yard, Warnham Station, WARNHAM, Horsham, RH12 3SR; Norlet Farm, Horsham Road, Cranleigh, Surrey, GU6 8EH. **VA: 5.**

MIL 1850	Vo	B10M-62	YV31MA6101A052885	VH	33610	C46FT	3/01 Shearings (CH) 310		8/09
		(ex Y387 KNB 9/09)							
MIL 1851	MB	O814D	WDB6703742N074037	Pn	988.5MZE9607	C25F	5/00 Brown, Builth Wells (CW)		8/07
		(ex W214 UFO 9/07)							
MIL 1852	MB	1223L	WDB9702582K729509	Fer		C35F	9/02 Frost, Woodbridge (SK)		10/11
		(ex NL 52 VKR 5/12)							
MIL 8322	Vo	B10M-62	YV31MA61XVA046064	VH	32643	C53F	2/97 Shearings (CH) 817		11/05
		(ex P817 GBA 12/05)							
MIL 9337	MB	O814D	WDB6703742N113135	Pn	048.5MAE5412	C33F	6/04 Staines, Little Warley (EX)		9/12
		(ex YN 04 WSV 2/13)							

NOTE: prior to 8/06, vehicles were licensed to PK0003452/I Christopher B Bowler, Warnham.

PK0001130/I: Hugo MILLER, 71 Curzon Avenue, HORSHAM, RH12 2LA.
FN: Arun Coaches.   **OC:** The Transport Depot, Mercer Road, Warnham, Horsham, RH12 3HL.   **VA: 3.**

r ACY 178A	Du	425	SDA1510/059	Du	8785/0576	C70F	3/88 Smiths Coaches, Liskeard (CO)	6/13
ARU 99A	Du	425	SDA1512/107	Du	8885/0844	C55F	3/89 Clowes & Barks, Longnor (ST)	5/14
		(ex FNZ 6990 3/15, F 68 AWM 4/08)						
ARU 100A	Du	425	SDA1504/016	Du	8485/0559	C59F	7/86 Snell, Newton Abbot (DN)	11/92
		(ex ARU 499A 1/03, C302 JNS 11/92)						
ARU 500A	Du	425	SDA1512/063	Du	8785/0505	C45FT	4/88 Spirit of London,
							Hounslow (LN)	12/94
		(ex A 4 SOL 6/95, E747 YSU 12/91)						

PK1119111/I: MOUNTAIN MOMENTS Limited, Unit C, Ote Hall Farm Business Units, Janes Lane, BURGESS HILL, RH15 0SR. **OC:** as address. **VA: 2.**

DG 53 EHK	MB	313CDI	WDB9036632R559094	MinO		M14	10/03 National Blood Transfusion
							Service (X)	7/13

PK1112961/I: MR CLIVE Travel Limited, 40 Lincoln Road, Portslade, BN41 1LL.
OC: The Old Cement Works, Shoreham Road, BEEDING, BN44 3TX. **VA: 3.**

FY 52 GUJ	MB	O814D	WDB6703742N106132	ACI	1821	C29F	10/02 Hillier, Foxham (WI)	11/09
		(ex RED 57 5/07, FY 52 GUJ 6/06)						
AE 04 FUV	As	A14-9.6/PT	VS928VN213A031001	As	30043	C37F	4/04 Don, Great Dunmow (EX)	4/13

NOTE: prior to 11/12, vehicles were licenced to PK1006605/N Clive V Wilson, Beeding

PK1013257/N: OVERLAND TRAVEL (Sussex) Limited, Farrowfield, Roundstone Lane, ANGMERING, BN16 4AT.
OC: as address. **VA: 6.**

KJD 530P	LN	10351A/2R		03589	LN	DP42F	7/76 Turner, Reading (P)		7/11
BYW 382V	LN	10351A/2R		06424	LN	B44F	11/79 Arriva Midlands North (ST) 33	11/10
J617 CEV	Vo	B10M-60	YV31MGD11NA028669	VH	30753	C49FT	3/92 Citibus, Hong Kong (O) 1271	4/06
		(ex FB 9806 (Hong Kong) 4/06)						
L250 JBV	Vo	B10M-62	YV31M2B13RA041144	Je	23461	C49FT	4/94 Holdsworth,
							Great Harwood (LA) 250	6/04
N 65 FWU	EOS	E180Z	YA9CF2H22TB128175	EOS		C49FT	5/96 Lever, Motcombe (DT)	5/05

PK1075201/R: PEARL HOTEL (Gatwick) Limited, Crabbet Park, Turners Hill Road, Worth, CRAWLEY, RH10 4ST.
FN: Gatwick Worth Hotel. **OC:** as address. **VA: 1.**

No vehicles currently recorded

PK0002752/N: Ian Frank PULLEN, 6 Pentland Road, WORTHING, BN13 2PP.
FN: I C P Travel.   OC: as address.   VA: 2.

x	48 WT	VW	Tr	WV1ZZZ70Z2H042744	VW		M8	9/01	private owner	11/04
			(ex CU 51 NBP 3/13)							
	K 60 TCC	Ka	S215HD	VS9215HD0N1001052	Ka		C49FT	4/93	Solus, Tamworth (ST)	by5/14
			(ex K126 OCT 4/94)							

PK0001549/I: RICHARDSON Travel Limited, Coach Depot, Pitsham Lane, MIDHURST, GU29 9RA.
OC: as address.   VA: 17.

1	P514 UUG	Vo	B10B-58	YV3R1A515VA003023	Wt	W373	DP47F	1/97	Yorkshire Traction (SY) 21026	9/08
2	M461 VCW	Vo	B10M-55	YV31M2F10SA042929	Ar	29PS/9412/11	DP48F	3/95	Southdown (WS) 20461	4/09
4	L635 TDY	Vo	B10M-55	YV31M2F13RA041462	Ar	29PS/1993/30	B61F	6/94	Hampshire Bus (HA) 20635	6/10
5	M589 OSO	Vo	B10M-55	YV31M2F16RA041732	Ar	29PS/1993/51	DP48F	9/94	Southdown (WS) 20189	12/10
291	YN 57 PYJ	MB	O816D	WDB6703742N127917	Pn	078.5MBE7166	C29F	1/08	new	1/08
292	YU 04 XJV	MB	O814D	WDB6703742N113974	Pn	048.5MAE5459	C29F	8/04	Heffernan, Perivale (LN)	2/10
496	YN 60 BZY	Vo	B9R	YV3S5P722AA136721	Pn	0912.6TSA8392	C49FT	9/10	new	9/10
533	YN 07 NUF	Vo	B12M	YV3R9K8257A120140	Pn	0712.8TXL7124	C53FT	4/07	new	4/07
534	YN 09 DXR	Vo	B12M	YV3R9M9299A132949	Pn	0912.8TXT8265	C53F	4/09	new	4/09
576	YN 57 BWE	Vo	B12M	YV3R9L2207A119427	Pn	0712TXT7245	C57F	9/07	new	9/07
577	YN 58 NDG	Vo	B7R	YV3R6K6228A129357	Pn	0812TWX7987	C57F	1/09	new	1/09
578	YN 09 DXY	Vo	B12M	YV3R9M9259A132950	Pn	0912.8TXT8266	C57F	3/09	new	3/09
701	PK 02 PUJ	Ds	R410	SFD112BR11GC10153	Pn	0212GWT4661	C70F	5/02	Sleaford Taxi, Sleaford (LI)	7/12
			(ex UJL 270 10/11, PK 02 PUJ 2/10)							
791	PN 05 SYF	Vo	B7TL	YV3S2G6235A105043	EL	53901	CH47/32F	3/05	new	3/05
792	SN 62 APY	AD	E40D	SFD4DSBRFCGXD6980	AD	0404/1	H79F	10/12	new	10/12
801	PN 52 XBP	Vo	B7TL	YV3S2G6113A002285	EL	43101	CH47/33F	9/02	new	9/02
	WLZ 3488	Vo	OLY-56	YV3YNA414WC028731	EL	B19813	H51/32F	2/98	York Pullman, York (NY) 225	11/11
			(ex R372 DJN 9/08)							
	R789 DHB	Vo	B10M-55	YV31MA510WC060661	Ar	9731/25	B48F	3/98	Red & White (CS) 20389	3/15
	X104 UAO	Vo	B7TL	YV3S2C618YA001025	Ar	0029/7	H49/27F	9/00	Dublin Bus (EI) AV7	8/14
			(ex 00-D-40007 11/13)							
x	MW 04 TGJ	VW	Tr	WV2ZZZ7HZ4X034114	VW		M7	6/04	new	6/04

PK1007507/R: John M D ROADLEY, 1 Potters Croft, HORSHAM, RH13 5LR.
FN: First Choice Taxis.   OC: as address.   VA: 2.

WL 53 FYV	Fd	Tt	WF0EXXGBFE3J67402	Fd		M16	11/03	Brewer & Hampton, Falmouth (CO)	12/11

PK0002856/N: ROADMARK Travel Limited, Stockbury House, Church Street, STORRINGTON, RH20 4LD.
OC: Leech Auto Service, Slaughter Bridge, Coolham, Horsham, RH13 8GT.   VA: 3.

401 DCD	Ld	PD3/4	L02939	NC	6013	FCO39/30F	5/64	Southdown Historic,Worthing (WS)	11/05
		(ex PRX 206B 7/06, 401 DCD 11/87)							
BF 61 HBH	MB	Tourismo	WEB63203623000171	MB		C49FT	9/11	Evobus, Coventry (Qd)	2/12
YN 14 NRE	Ir	i6	VS916AD00D1016199	Ir	-?-	C??FT	4/14	new	4/14

PK0002932/I: ROUND & ABOUT Limited, Beedingwood Farm, Forest Road, COLGATE, Horsham, RH12 4TB.
OCs: as address; Albion Street Lorry Park, Southwick, Brighton BN42 4DN; Ford Industrial Estate, Burndell Road, Yapton, BN18 0HT; Western Area Office, Drayton Lane, Drayton, Chichester, PO20 2ET; Mackley Industrial Estate, Henfield Road, Small Dole, Henfield, BN5 9XQ.   VA: 12.

See joint entry under Coach Hire, Colgate

PK1008249/N: ROUNDABOUT BUSES, 25 Oldfield Road, Bexleyheath, DA7 4DX.
OC: Unit 3, Silverwood, Snow Hill, COPTHORNE, RH10 3EN.   VA: 3.

No vehicles currently recorded

PK0003009/I: Peter David & Rosemary Ann SILVERTON, 109 South Street, Tarring, WEST WORTHING, BN14 7ND.
FN: Tarring Coaches.   **OC:** Farrowfield, Roundstone Lane, Angmering, BN16 4AT.   **VA:** 2.

No vehicles currently recorded

PK0003583/R: Colin SLACK, 13 Sylvan Road, Sompting, LANCING, BN15 0BT.
FN: Breaks-A-Way Travel.   **OC:** as address.   **VA:** 1.

No vehicles currently recorded

PK1116894/R: SMILE HOLIDAYS Limited, Churchills, The Cotswolds, SOUTHWICK, Brighton, BN42 4GH.
OC: as address.   **VA:** 2.

MV 06 KUA	Fd	Tt	WF0EXXTTFE5E60082	Fd	M16	3/06 Winks, Runcorn (CH)	2/10

NOTE: prior to 1/13, vehicles were licenced to PK1056770/R Jone Eugene Turnbull, Hove (ES).

PK0003438/I: SOUTHCOAST MOTOR Services Limited, P O Box 1029, Croydon, Greater London, CR9 6AA.
OC: Unit 1, Warehead Farm, Halnaker, CHICHESTER, PO18 0NF.   **VA:** 6.

2722 CD	Ld	L2	610431	Hn	2492	C41F	6/61 Baker, West Hoathley (P)	12/99
954 CUF	Ld	PD3/4	L02484	NC	6001	FH39/30F	6/64 Elliott & Burtenshaw, Chichester (P)	by6/08
406 DCD	Ld	PD3/4	L03147	NC	6024	FCO39/30F	6/64 Elliott & Baker, Crawley (P)	12/99
		(ex WRU 702B 3/04, 406 DCD 2/85)						
HCD 350E	Ld	PD3/4	L63987	NC	6484	FH39/30F	7/67 Elliott & Burtenshaw, Crawley (P)	12/99

PK1006483/N: SOUTHDOWN HISTORIC Vehicles Limited, 73 Cuckfield Crescent, WORTHING, BN13 2EB.
OCs: Stagecoach, Worthing Garage, Library Place, Worthing, BN11 0XX; Chaffolds Farm, Rusper, Horsham, RH12 9AA.
VA: 3.

412 DCD	Ld	PD3/4	L03366	NC	6007	FCO39/30F	3/64 Southdown 412 Group, Worthing (P)	6/02
		(ex AOR 158B 9/07, 412 DCD 7/86)						
416 DCD	Ld	PD3/4	L03398	NC	6003	FCO39/30F	3/64 Pearce, Worthing (P)	6/02
		(ex PRX 190B 3/04, 416 DCD 11/87)						
KMW 175P	Dr	CRG6LX	68733	ECW	20850	O43/31F	3/76 Blair, Eastleigh (P)	1/06

PK1007823/N. SOUTHDOWN PSV Limited, Unit 3, Silverwood, Snow Hill, COPTHORNE, RH10 3EN.
OC: as address.   **VA:** 35.

101	GX 57 BXG	AD	Dt	SFD321AR16GY10155	AD	6423/1	B37F	1/08 new	1/08
105	SN 53 LWL	Tbs	Dt SLF	SFD3CACR43GW87516	Tbs	3057/4	B42F	1/04 Cushing & Littlewood, Acle(NK)	6/08
106	GX 06 AOE	Vo	B7L	YV3S2G5285A106740	EL	56001	H45/27F	4/06 Centrebus East (LE) 924	9/13
108	YX 59 BZB	AD	Dt	SFD361AR28GY10962	AD	8230/1	B37F	9/09 new	9/09
109	YX 59 BZC	AD	Dt	SFD361AR28GY10965	AD	8230/4	B37F	9/09 new	9/09
110	YX 59 BZD	AD	Dt	SFD361AR28GY10966	AD	8230/5	B37F	9/09 new	9/09
111	LK 55 ACV	AD	Dt SLF	SFD4DBER35GW38501	EL	57508	B40F	12/05 First Beeline (BE) 43918	8/10
112	LK 55 ADX	AD	Dt SLF	SFD4DBER35GW38493	EL	57505	B40F	12/05 First Beeline (BE) 43915	8/10
113	LK 55 ADZ	AD	Dt SLF	SFD4DBER35GW38499	EL	57506	B40F	1/06 First Beeline (BE) 43916	8/10
114	LK 55 AEA	AD	Dt SLF	SFD4DBER35GW38507	EL	57507	B40F	1/06 First Beeline (BE) 43917	8/10
115	F 1 LGW	Ds	Dt SLF	SFD322AR1YGW25026	Pn	0010.7HLB3202	B25D	9/00 London United (LN) DP506	7/11
			(ex X606 QKH 7/11)						
116	F 2 LGW	Ds	Dt SLF	SFD322AR1YGW24989	Pn	0010.7HLB3196	B25D	9/00 London United (LN) DP500	7/11
			(ex X611 OKH 7/11)						
117	E 3 LGW	Ds	Dt SLF	SFD322BR1YGW14891	Pn	0110.7HLB3774	B25D	3/01 London General (LN) LDP137	7/11
			(ex Y837 TGH 7/11)						
132	T132 AUA	DAF	DE02RSDB250	XMGDE02RS0H007002	Pn	6357	H45/19D	3/99 Buzzlines, Hythe (KT)	4/06
133	PM 03 EHV	DAF	DB250	XMGDE02PS0H010909	EL	45807	H47/27F	5/03 Isle of Man (IM) 2	8/14
			(ex GMN 613E 8/14)						
134	PG 53 YCT	DAF	DB250	XMGDE02PS0H010912	EL	45810	H47/27F	5/03 Isle of Man (IM) 6	8/14
			(ex GMN 616E 7/14)						

WEST SUSSEX (WS)   G627/26

SOUTHDOWN PSV, COPTHORNE (continued) 4X71OHN; 4X71OHL;

135	PM 03 EHW	DAF	DB250	XMGDE02PS0H010680	EL	45801	H47/27F	6/03	Isle of Man (IM) 5	8/1
				(ex GMN 70E 8/14)						
136	LF 52 URM	DAF	DB250	XMGDE02PS0H010185	Pn	8060	H45/19D	1/03	Arriva London North	
									(LN) DLP106	12/1
139	T139 AUA	DAF	DB250	XMGDE02RS0H007011	Pn	6364	H45/19D	6/99	Buzzlines, Hythe (KT)	4/0
341	W341 VGX	Ds	Dt SLF	SFD612BR1XGW14344	Pn	008.8GKB2276	B29F	3/00	Compass, Worthing (WS)	10/1
343	W343 VGX	Ds	Dt SLF	SFD612BR1XGW14353	Pn	008.8GKB2288	B29F	4/00	Huyton Travel, Huyton (MY) 79	6/1
380	V380 SVV	Ds	Dt SLF	SFD322BR1XGW13707	Pn	9910.7HLB1462	B36F	9/99	Q-Park & Fly,	
									Manchester Airport (GM)	4/0
463	W463 BCW	Vo	B7TL	YV3S2C616YC000276	Pn	6901	H41/19D	5/00	London United (LN) VP116	9/1
464	W464 BCW	Vo	B7TL	YV3S2C611YC000279	Pn	6902	H41/19D	4/00	London United (LN) VP117	9/1
465	W465 BCW	Vo	B7TL	YV3S2C61XYC000278	Pn	6903	H41/21D	5/00	London United (LN) VP118	3/1
834	Y834 TGH	Ds	Dt SLF	SFD322BR1YGW14760	Pn	0110.7HLB3771	B38F	3/01	London General (LN) LDP134	3/1
839	Y839 TGH	Ds	Dt SLF	SFD322BR1YGW14793	Pn	0110.7HLB3776	B38F	3/01	London General (LN) LDP134	3/1
840	Y840 TGH	Ds	Dt SLF	SFD322BR1YGW14916	Pn	0110.7HLB3777	B38F	3/01	London General (LN) LDP134	3/1
841	Y841 TGH	Ds	Dt SLF	SFD322BR1YGW14956	Pn	0110.7HLB3778	B38F	3/01	London General (LN) LDP134	3/1

PH0005857/I: STAGECOACH (SOUTH) Limited, Bus Station, Southgate, Chichester, West Sussex, PO19 8DG.
PK0002571/I: STAGECOACH (SOUTH) Limited, Bus Station, Southgate, Chichester, West Sussex, PO19 8DG.
FNs: Stagecoach in Hants & Surrey: Goldline.
OCs:
    [AR] 83-84 Livingstone Road, Walworth Industrial Estate, Andover, SP10 5NS.
    [AT] Halimote Road, Aldershot, GU11 1NJ; Bus Station, Station Road, Aldershot, GU1 1HN.
    [BE] Rankine Road, Basingstoke, RG24 8PH: Bus Station, New Market Square, Basingstoke.
    [CR] Basin Road, Chichester, PO19 8DG.
    [GD] Unit 7, Riverway Industrial Estate, Peasmarsh, Guildford, GU3 1LZ.
    [PM] Walton Road, Farlington, Portsmouth, PO6 1TU;
    [WI] Bar End Industrial Estate, Bar End Road, Winchester, SO23 9NT; Bus Station, 161-162 High Street, Winchester, SO23 9BA. {outstations at Farringdon Business Park, Lower Farringdon, Alton, GU34 3DZ and Unit 41S, Bottings Industrial Estate, Hillsons Road, Curdridge, Southampton, SO30 2DY}
    [WG] Library Place, Worthing, BN11 3PT {outstations at Lower Station Road, Henfield and Hobbs Farm, Grevatts Lane, Climping}.
    [res] reserve fleet.
VA: 378 [PH0005857]: 204 [PK0002571].   *(Stagecoach)*

10001	GX 12 DXM	AD	E40D	SFD4DTBRFCGXD6630	AD	B444/1	H47/32F	4/12	Southdown (WS) 10001	6/14
10008	GX 12 DXP	AD	E40D	SFD4DTBRFCGXD6631	AD	B444/2	H47/32F	4/12	Southdown (WS) 10008	6/14
10009	GX 12 DXR	AD	E40D	SFD4DTBRFCGXD6632	AD	B444/3	H47/32F	4/12	Southdown (WS) 10009	6/14
15585	GX 59 JYS	Sca	N230UD	SZAN4X20001866535	AD	9420/1	H47/29F	12/09	Hampshire Bus (HA) 15585	10/14
15586	404 DCD	Sca	N230UD	SZAN4X20001866536	AD	9420/2	H47/29F	12/09	Southdown (WS) 15586	6/14
				(ex GX 59 JYT 4/15)						
15588	GX 10 HAA	Sca	N230UD	SZAN4X20001866538	AD	9420/4	H47/29F	3/10	Southdown (WS) 15588	6/14
15589	GX 10 HAE	Sca	N230UD	SZAN4X20001866539	AD	9420/5	H47/29F	3/10	Southdown (WS) 15589	6/14
15590	GX 10 HAO	Sca	N230UD	SZAN4X20001866540	AD	9420/6	H47/29F	3/10	Southdown (WS) 15590	6/14
15591	GX 10 HAU	Sca	N230UD	SZAN4X20001866541	AD	9420/7	H47/29F	3/10	Southdown (WS) 15591	6/14
15592	GX 10 HBA	Sca	N230UD	SZAN4X20001866542	AD	9420/8	H47/29F	3/10	Southdown (WS) 15592	6/14
15593	GX 10 HBB	Sca	N230UD	SZAN4X20001866543	AD	9420/9	H47/29F	3/10	Southdown (WS) 15593	6/14
15594	GX 10 HBC	Sca	N230UD	SZAN4X20001866770	AD	9420/10	H47/29F	3/10	Southdown (WS) 15594	6/14
15595	GX 10 HBD	Sca	N230UD	SZAN4X20001866771	AD	9420/11	H47/29F	3/10	Southdown (WS) 15595	6/14
15596	GX 10 HBE	Sca	N230UD	SZAN4X20001866772	AD	9420/12	H47/29F	3/10	Southdown (WS) 15596	6/14
15597	GX 10 HBF	Sca	N230UD	SZAN4X20001866773	AD	9420/13	H47/29F	3/10	Southdown (WS) 15597	6/14
15598	GX 10 HBG	Sca	N230UD	SZAN4X20001866902	AD	9420/14	H47/29F	3/10	Southdown (WS) 15598	10/14
15599	GX 10 HBH	Sca	N230UD	SZAN4X20001866903	AD	9420/15	H47/29F	3/10	Southdown (WS) 15599	10/14
15600	GX 10 HBJ	Sca	N230UD	SZAN4X20001866904	AD	9420/16	H47/29F	3/10	Southdown (WS) 15600	10/14
15601	GX 10 HBK	Sca	N230UD	SZAN4X20001866905	AD	9420/17	H47/29F	3/10	Southdown (WS) 15601	10/14
15602	GX 10 HBL	Sca	N230UD	SZAN4X20001866906	AD	9420/18	H47/29F	3/10	Southdown (WS) 15602	6/14
15603	GX 10 HBN	Sca	N230UD	SZAN4X20001867018	AD	9420/19	H47/29F	3/10	Southdown (WS) 15603	10/14
15604	GX 10 HBO	Sca	N230UD	SZAN4X20001867019	AD	9420/20	H47/29F	3/10	Southdown (WS) 15604	10/14
15605	GX 10 HBP	Sca	N230UD	SZAN4X20001867020	AD	9420/21	H47/29F	3/10	Southdown (WS) 15605	10/14
15804	GX 12 DXS	Sca	N230UD	SZAN4X20001877761	AD	B433/1	H47/28F	3/12	Hampshire Bus (HA) 15804	10/14
15805	GX 12 DXT	Sca	N230UD	SZAN4X20001877762	AD	B433/2	H47/28F	3/12	Hampshire Bus (HA) 15805	10/14
15806	GX 12 DXU	Sca	N230UD	SZAN4X20001877763	AD	B433/3	H47/28F	3/12	Hampshire Bus (HA) 15806	10/14
15982	YN 64 XSJ	Sca	N230UD	YS2N4X20001887060	AD	E408/1	H47/28F	9/14	new	9/14
15983	YN 64 XSK	Sca	N230UD	YS2N4X20001887061	AD	E408/2	H47/28F	9/14	new	9/14
15984	YN 64 XSL	Sca	N230UD	YS2N4X20001887062	AD	E408/3	H47/28F	9/14	new	9/14
15985	YN 64 XSM	Sca	N230UD	YS2N4X20001887163	AD	E408/4	H47/28F	9/14	new	9/14
15986	YN 64 XSO	Sca	N230UD	YS2N4X20001887164	AD	E408/5	H47/28F	9/14	Southdown (WS) 15986	10/14
15987	YN 64 XSP	Sca	N230UD	YS2N4X20001887165	AD	E408/6	H47/28F	9/14	Southdown (WS) 15987	10/14
15988	YN 64 XSR	Sca	N230UD	YS2N4X20001887166	AD	E408/7	H47/28F	9/14	Southdown (WS) 15988	10/14
15989	YN 64 XST	Sca	N230UD	YS2N4X20001887167	AD	E408/8	H47/28F	9/14	Southdown (WS) 15989	10/14

86 | MX55 KRG; KS|C| AD Tt AD A47/28F 2006
VU06 JCV
P527 EFL Vo YN2RV18V3 NC P049/33F 1996
VX04 GHH Tbs Tt Tbs H47/28F 2004

STAGECOACH (SOUTH) (HA) (continued) 716504 716279

15990	YN 64 XSU	Sca	N230UD	YS2N4X20001887168	AD	E408/9	H47/28F	9/14	Southdown (WS) 15990	10/14
15991	YN 64 XSV	Sca	N230UD	YS2N4X20001887169	AD	E408/10	H47/28F	9/14	Southdown (WS) 15991	10/14
15992	YN 64 XSW	Sca	N230UD	YS2N4X20001887278	AD	E408/11	H47/28F	9/14	Southdown (WS) 15992	10/14
15993	YN 64 XSX	Sca	N230UD	YS2N4X20001887279	AD	E408/12	H47/28F	9/14	Southdown (WS) 15993	10/14
16129	R129 EVX	Vo	OLY-56	YV3YNA417WC028741	Ar	9712/8	H51/34F	3/98	Cheltenham & Gloucester (GL) 16129	4/13
16261	P261 WPN	Vo	OLY-56	YV3YNA416VC027417	Ar	9418/65	H51/32F	2/97	Fleet Buzz (HA) 16261	10/14
16262	P262 WPN	Vo	OLY-56	YV3YNA417VC027426	Ar	9418/69	H51/32F	3/97	Hampshire Bus (HA) 16262	10/14
16263	P263 WPN	Vo	OLY-56	YV3YNA410VC027428	Ar	9418/70	H51/32F	3/97	Hampshire Bus (HA) 16263	10/14
16268	P268 VPN	Vo	OLY-56	YV3YNA416VC027269	Ar	9418/46	H51/36F	1/97	Hampshire Bus (HA) 16268	10/14
16269	P269 VPN	Vo	OLY-56	YV3YNA411VC027289	Ar	9418/46	H51/36F	12/96	Southdown (WS) 16269	6/14
16278	P278 VPN	Vo	OLY-56	YV3YNA416VC027336	Ar	9418/55	H51/36F	2/97	Southdown (WS) 16278	6/14
16282	P282 VPN	Vo	OLY-56	YV3YNA411VC027342	Ar	9418/58	H51/36F	1/97	Fleet Buzz (HA) 16282	10/14
16291	R291 HCD	Vo	OLY-56	YV3YNA419WC028630	ArB	9730/170198	H51/36F	2/98	Hampshire Bus (HA) 16291	9/14
16292	YLJ 332 (ex R292 HCD 5/11)	Vo	OLY-56	YV3YNA410WC028631	Ar	9730/18	H51/30F	2/98	Hampshire Bus (HA) 16292	10/14
16293	R293 HCD	Vo	OLY-56	YV3YNA412WC028632	Ar	9730/19	H51/36F	2/98	Hampshire Bus (HA) 16293	10/14
16295	R295 HCD	Vo	OLY-56	YV3YNA411WC028637	ArB	9730/210298	H51/36F	2/98	Hampshire Bus (HA) 16295	9/14
16302	S302 CCD	Vo	OLY-56	YV3YNA410WC029326	Ar	9745/22	H51/36F	9/98	Lincolnshire (LI) 16302	8/12
16303	S303 CCD	Vo	OLY-56	YV3YNA414WC029328	Ar	9745/23	H51/36F	9/98	Hampshire Bus (HA) 16303	10/14
16304	S304 CCD	Vo	OLY-56	YV3YNA412WC029330	Ar	9745/24	H51/36F	9/98	Hampshire Bus (HA) 16304	10/14
16305	S305 CCD	Vo	OLY-56	YV3YNA418WC029333	Ar	9745/25	H51/36F	9/98	Southdown (WS) 16305	9/03
16312	S312 CCD	Vo	OLY-56	YV3YNA415WC029371	Ar	9745/43	CH47/32F	12/98	Southdown (WS) 16312	6/14
16502	NDZ 3020 (ex R502 UWL 5/11)	Vo	OLY-56	YV3YNA415VC028297	Ar	9711/2	H51/30F	9/97	Hampshire Bus (HA) 16502	10/14
16523	R423 XFC	Vo	OLY-56	YV3YNA419WC028594	Ar	9729/10	H51/36F	1/98	Hampshire Bus (HA) 16523	10/14
16524	R424 XFC	Vo	OLY-56	YV3YNA416WC028598	Ar	9729/11	H51/36F	1/98	Hampshire Bus (HA) 16524	10/14
16525	R425 XFC	Vo	OLY-56	YV3YNA414WC028602	Ar	9729/12	H51/36F	1/98	Hampshire Bus (HA) 16525	10/14
16590	S590 BCE	Vo	OLY-56	YV3YNA419XC029438	Ar	9811/20	H47/32F	11/98	Hampshire Bus (HA) 16590	10/14
16591	S591 BCE	Vo	OLY-56	YV3YNA410XC029439	Ar	9811/21	CH47/32F	11/98	Hampshire Bus (HA) 16591	10/14
16624	P224 VCK	Vo	YN2RV18V3	YV3YNA413TC026920	NC	5382	H49/33F	10/96	Stagecoach (North West) (CA) 16624	5/04
16625	P225 VCK	Vo	YN2RV18V3	YV3YNA414TC026814	NC	5383	H49/33F	10/96	Stagecoach (North West) (CA) 16625	5/04
16627	P227 VCK	Vo	YN2RV18V3	YV3YNA415TC026966	NC	5385	H49/33F	10/96	Stagecoach (North West) (CA) 16627	7/04
16628	P228 VCK	Vo	YN2RV18V3	YV3YNA419TC026968	NC	5386	H49/33F	10/96	Stagecoach (North West) (CA) 16628	6/04
16629	P229 VCK	Vo	YN2RV18V3	YV3YNA413TC026903	NC	5387	H49/33F	10/96	Ribble (LA) 16629	4/04
16631	P231 VCK	Vo	YN2RV18V3	YV3YNA416TC026927	NC	5389	H49/33F	10/96	Lincolnshire (LI) 16631	8/12
16632	P232 VCK	Vo	YN2RV18V3	YV3YNA418TC026928	NC	5390	H49/33F	10/96	Lincolnshire (LI) 16632	8/12
16633	P233 VCK	Vo	YN2RV18V3	YV3YNA410TC026857	NC	5391	H49/33F	10/96	Hampshire Bus (HA) 16633	8/12
16748	R748 DRJ	Vo	OLY-56	YV3YNA418WC029008	Ar	9743/5	H51/36F	6/98	Hampshire Bus (HA) 16748	9/12
16752	R752 DRJ	Vo	OLY-56	YV3YNA41XWC029012	Ar	9743/8	H51/36F	6/98	Southdown (WS) 16752	6/14
16756	R756 DRJ	Vo	OLY-56	YV3YNA412WC029053	Ar	9743/12	H51/36F	6/98	Southdown (WS) 16756	3/10
16767	CSU 978 (ex S767 SVU 7/11)	Vo	OLY-56	YV3YNA410WC029147	Ar	9745/1	H51/30F	8/98	Hampshire Bus (HA) 16767	10/14
16769	S769 RVU	Vo	OLY-56	YV3YNA413WC029143	Ar	9745/3	H51/36F	8/98	Hampshire Bus (HA) 16769	10/14
16787	WVT 618 (ex P717 GND 8/11)	Vo	YN2RV18V3	YV3YNA418TC027061	Ar	9418/2	H51/30F	10/96	Hampshire Bus (HA) 16787	10/14
16797	P727 GND	Vo	YN2RV18V3	YV3YNA414TC027123	Ar	9418/12	H51/36F	10/96	Greater Manchester South (GM) 16797	2/15
16798	P728 GND	Vo	YN2RV18V3	YV3YNA418TC027125	Ar	9418/13	H51/36F	10/96	Greater Manchester South (GM) 16798	2/15
16799	P729 GND	Vo	YN2RV18V3	YV3YNA411TC027127	Ar	9418/14	H51/36F	10/96	Greater Manchester South (GM) 16799	2/15
17425	LX 51 FJY	Ds	Tt	SFD317BR21GX21497	Ar	0068/30	H45/29F	9/01	East London (LN) 17425	1/15
17672	V172 DFT	Ds	Tt	SFD311BR1XGX20593	Ar	9914/49	H51/28F	11/99	Southdown (WS) 17672	10/14
17740	LY 52 ZDX	Ds	Tt	SFD33GBR32GX42490	Ar	2070/01	H45/29F	12/02	Western Buses (SW) 17740	12/14
18184	MX 54 LPK	Ds	Tt	SFD33GBR64GX53535	Ar	4404/6	H47/28F	10/04	Hampshire Bus (HA) 18184	10/14
18185	MX 54 LPL	Ds	Tt	SFD33GBR64GX53536	Ar	4404/7	H47/28F	10/04	Hampshire Bus (HA) 18185	10/14
18186	MX 54 LPN	Ds	Tt	SFD33GBR64GX53537	Ar	4404/8	H47/28F	10/04	Hampshire Bus (HA) 18186	10/14
18187	MX 54 LPO	Ds	Tt	SFD33GBR64GX53538	Ar	4404/9	H47/28F	10/04	Hampshire Bus (HA) 18187	10/14
18188	MX 54 LPP	Ds	Tt	SFD33GBR64GX53539	Ar	4404/10	H47/28F	10/04	Hampshire Bus (HA) 18188	10/14
18191	MX 54 LPY	Ds	Tt	SFD33GBR64GX53548	Ar	4404/13	H47/28F	10/04	Hampshire Bus (HA) 18191	10/14
18193	MX 54 LRA	Ds	Tt	SFD33GBR64GX53550	Ar	4404/15	H47/28F	10/04	Hampshire Bus (HA) 18193	10/14
18194	MX 54 LRE	Tbs	Tt	SFD33GBR64GX53551	Tbs	4404/16	H47/28F	10/04	Hampshire Bus (HA) 18194	10/14
18310	KX 54 TWG	Ds	Tt	SFD33GBR64GX53643	Ar	5402/10	H47/28F	6/05	Hampshire Bus (HA) 18310	10/14
18311	KX 54 TWJ	Ds	Tt	SFD33GBR64GX53644	Ar	5402/11	H47/28F	6/05	Hampshire Bus (HA) 18311	10/14
18502	KX 06 LYU	AD	Tt	SFD33GBR65GX53884	AD	5422/2	H47/28F	4/06	Hampshire Bus (HA) 18502	10/14
18503	KX 06 LYV	AD	Tt	SFD33GBR65GX53885	AD	5422/3	H47/28F	4/06	Hampshire Bus (HA) 18503	10/14
18504	KX 06 LYW	AD	Tt	SFD33GBR65GX53886	AD	5422/4	H47/28F	4/06	Hampshire Bus (HA) 18504	10/14
18505	KX 06 LYY	AD	Tt	SFD33GBR66GX53893	AD	5422/5	H47/28F	4/06	Hampshire Bus (HA) 18505	10/14
18510	GX 06 DXH	AD	Tt	SFD33GBR66GX53901	AD	5422/10	H47/28F	5/06	Hampshire Bus (HA) 18510	10/14

STAGECOACH (SOUTH) (HA) (continued) ˙20830 ˙20834 ˙20436

18511	GX 06 DXJ	AD	Tt	SFD33GBR66GX53902	AD	5422/11	H47/28F	5/06	Hampshire Bus (HA) 18511	10/14
18512	XSU 612	AD	Tt	SFD33GBR66GX53903	AD	5422/12	H47/28F	5/06	Hampshire Bus (HA) 18512	10/14
	GX06GXK			(ex GX 06 DXK 2/13)						
18513	GX 06 DXL	AD	Tt	SFD33GBR66GX53905	AD	5422/13	H47/28F	5/06	Hampshire Bus (HA) 18513	10/14
18514	GX 06 DXM	AD	Tt	SFD33GBR66GX53906	AD	5422/14	H47/28F	5/06	Hampshire Bus (HA) 18514	10/14
18515	GX 06 DXO	AD	Tt	SFD33GBR66GX53907	AD	5422/15	H47/28F	5/06	Hampshire Bus (HA) 18515	10/14
18516	GX 06 DXP	AD	Tt	SFD33GBR66GX53908	AD	5422/16	H47/28F	5/06	Hampshire Bus (HA) 18516	10/14
18517	NDZ 3017	AD	Tt	SFD33GBR66GX53911	AD	5422/17	H47/28F	5/06	Southdown (WS) 18517	10/14
				(ex GX 06 DXR 2/13)						
18518	NDZ 3018	AD	Tt	SFD33GBR66GX53912	AD	5422/18	H47/28F	5/06	Southdown (WS) 18518	10/14
				(ex GX 06 DXS 2/13)						
18519	NDZ 3019	AD	Tt	SFD33GBR66GX53913	AD	5422/19	H47/28F	5/06	Hampshire Bus (HA) 18519	10/14
				(ex GX 06 DXT 2/13)						
18520	GX 06 DXU	AD	Tt	SFD33GBR66GX53914	AD	5422/20	H47/28F	5/06	Hampshire Bus (HA) 18520	10/14
18521	GX 06 DXV	AD	Tt	SFD33GBR66GX53915	AD	5422/21	H47/28F	5/06	Hampshire Bus (HA) 18521	10/14
18522	XSU 682	AD	Tt	SFD33GBR66GX53916	AD	5422/22	H47/28F	5/06	Hampshire Bus (HA) 18522	10/14
				(ex GX 06 DXW 2/13)						
18523	GX 06 DXY	AD	Tt	SFD33GBR66GX53917	AD	5422/23	H47/28F	5/06	Hampshire Bus (HA) 18523	10/14
18524	GX 06 DXZ	AD	Tt	SFD33GBR66GX53918	AD	5422/24	H47/28F	5/06	Hampshire Bus (HA) 18524	10/14
18525	GX 06 DYA	AD	Tt	SFD33GBR65GX53877	AD	5422/25	H47/28F	5/06	Hampshire Bus (HA) 18525	10/14
18526	GX 06 DYB	AD	Tt	SFD33GBR65GX53878	AD	5422/26	H47/28F	5/06	Hampshire Bus (HA) 18526	10/14
18527	GX 06 DYC	AD	Tt	SFD33GBR65GX53879	AD	5422/27	H47/28F	5/06	Hampshire Bus (HA) 18527	10/14
19055	MX 56 FSE	AD	Tt	SFD43GBRA6GXD4010	AD	5423/20	H47/33F	9/06	Hampshire Bus (HA) 19055	10/14
19063	MX 56 FSP	AD	Tt	SFD43GBRA6GXD4017	AD	5425/6	H47/33F	9/06	Southdown (WS) 19063	10/14
19069	MX 56 FTA	AD	Tt	SFD43GBRA6GXD4023	AD	5425/12	H47/33F	9/06	Yorkshire Traction (SY) 19069	5/15
19071	MX 56 FTD	AD	Tt	SFD43GBRA6GXD4025	AD	5425/14	H47/33F	9/06	Southdown (WS) 19071	10/14
19077	MX 56 FTP	AD	Tt	SFD43GBRA6GXD4031	AD	6404/2	H47/33F	10/06	Southdown (WS) 19077	10/14
19078	MX 56 FTT	AD	Tt	SFD43GBRA6GXD4032	AD	6404/3	H47/33F	10/06	Southdown (WS) 19078	10/14
19079	MX 56 FTU	AD	Tt	SFD43GBRA6GXD4033	AD	6404/4	H47/33F	10/06	Hampshire Bus (HA) 19079	10/14
19081	MX 56 FTY	AD	Tt	SFD43GBRA6GXD4035	AD	6404/6	H47/33F	10/06	Yorkshire Traction (SY) 19081	11/14
19090	MX 56 FUM	AD	Tt	SFD43GBRA6GXD4044	AD	6404/15	H47/33F	11/06	Southdown (WS) 19090	10/14
19096	MX 07 HLP	AD	Tt	SFD43GBRA6GXD4050	AD	6402/6	H47/33F	3/07	Hampshire Bus (HA) 19096	10/14
19097	MX 07 HLR	AD	Tt	SFD43GBRA6GXD4051	AD	6402/7	H47/33F	3/07	Yorkshire Traction (SY) 19097	10/14
19099	MX 07 HLV	AD	Tt	SFD43GBRA6GXD4053	AD	6402/9	H47/33F	3/07	Hampshire Bus (HA) 19099	10/14
19881	GX 11 AKF	AD	Tt	SFD4DTBRGBGXD5969	AD	B402/1	H47/33F	5/11	Southdown (WS) 19881	6/14
19882	GX 11 AKG	AD	Tt	SFD4DTBRGBGXD5970	AD	B402/2	H47/33F	5/11	Southdown (WS) 19882	6/14
19883	GX 11 AKJ	AD	Tt	SFD4DTBRGBGXD5985	AD	B402/3	H47/33F	6/11	Southdown (WS) 19883	6/14
19884	GX 11 AKK	AD	Tt	SFD4DTBRGBGXD5986	AD	B402/4	H47/33F	6/11	Southdown (WS) 19884	6/14
19885	GX 11 AKN	AD	Tt	SFD4DTBRGBGXD5992	AD	B402/5	H47/33F	6/11	Southdown (WS) 19885	6/14
19886	GX 11 AKO	AD	Tt	SFD4DTBRGBGXD5993	AD	B402/6	H47/33F	6/11	Southdown (WS) 19886	6/14
19887	GX 11 AKP	AD	Tt	SFD4DTBRGBGXD5994	AD	B402/7	H47/33F	6/11	Southdown (WS) 19887	6/14
19900	SF 11 LBE	AD	Tt	SFD4DTBRGBGXD6061	AD	B401/13	H47/33F	7/11	Southdown (WS) 19900	6/14
19909	409 DCD	Ld	PD3/4		L03225	NC	6025	FCO39/30F	6/64	(Southdown (WS) 19909	6/14
19913	UF 4813	Ld	TD1		170477	Brush		O27/24RO	6/29	Southdown (WS) 19913	6/14
19945	CD 7045	Ld	G7		12347	Srt		27/24RO	6/22	Southdown (WS) 19945	6/14
20228	R228 CRW	Vo	B10M-55	YV31MA517WC060804	Ar	9731/9	B49F	2/98	Hampshire Bus (HA) 20228	10/14
20937	R937 XVM	Vo	B10M-55	YV31MA519VC060561	Ar	9633/77	B49F	10/97	Hampshire Bus (HA) 20937	10/14
22741	GX 58 MVE	MAN	18.240	WMAA69ZZ09C012754	AD	8305/1	DP41F	1/09	new	1/09
22742	GX 58 MVF	MAN	18.240	WMAA69ZZ39C012750	AD	8305/2	DP41F	1/09	new	1/09
22743	GX 58 MVG	MAN	18.240	WMAA69ZZ49C012756	AD	8305/3	DP41F	1/09	new	1/09
22744	GX 58 MVH	MAN	18.240	WMAA69ZZ89C012758	AD	8305/4	DP41F	2/09	new	2/09
22745	GX 58 MVJ	MAN	18.240	WMAA69ZZ89C012856	AD	8305/5	DP41F	2/09	new	2/09
22746	GX 58 MVK	MAN	18.240	WMAA69ZZ19C012729	AD	8305/6	DP41F	2/09	new	2/09
22747	GX 58 MVL	MAN	18.240	WMAA69ZZ39C012764	AD	8305/7	DP41F	2/09	new	2/09
22748	GX 58 MVM	MAN	18.240	WMAA69ZZ99C012963	AD	8305/8	DP41F	2/09	new	2/09
22749	GX 58 MVN	MAN	18.240	WMAA69ZZ79C012752	AD	8305/9	DP41F	2/09	new	2/09
22750	GX 58 MVO	MAN	18.240	WMAA69ZZ49C012966	AD	8305/10	DP41F	2/09	new	2/09
22751	GX 58 MVP	MAN	18.240	WMAA69ZZ59C012913	AD	8305/11	DP41F	2/09	new	2/09
22752	GX 58 MVR	MAN	18.240	WMAA69ZZ79C012976	AD	8305/12	DP41F	2/09	new	2/09
22753	GX 58 MVS	MAN	18.240	WMAA69ZZX9C012955	AD	8305/13	DP41F	2/09	new	2/09
22754	GX 58 MVT	MAN	18.240	WMAA69ZZ09C012866	AD	8305/14	DP41F	2/09	new	2/09
27511	GX 06 DZF	AD	Env	SFD125AR26GG10243	AD	6301/1	B44F	8/06	Southdown (WS) 27511	6/14
27512	GX 06 DZG	AD	Env	SFD125AR26GG10244	AD	6301/2	B44F	8/06	Southdown (WS) 27512	6/14
27513	GX 06 DZH	AD	Env	SFD125AR26GG10245	AD	6301/3	B44F	8/06	Southdown (WS) 27513	6/14
27514	GX 06 DZJ	AD	Env	SFD125AR26GG10246	AD	6301/4	B44F	8/06	Southdown (WS) 27514	6/14
27515	GX 06 DZK	AD	Env	SFD125AR26GG10247	AD	6301/5	B44F	8/06	Southdown (WS) 27515	6/14
27553	GX 58 GME	AD	Env	SFD185AR28GG30352	AD	8303/1	B44F	10/08	Southdown (WS) 27553	10/14
27554	GX 58 GMF	AD	Env	SFD185AR28GG30353	AD	8303/2	B44F	10/08	Southdown (WS) 27554	10/14
27555	GX 58 GMG	AD	Env	SFD185AR28GG30354	AD	8303/3	B44F	11/08	Southdown (WS) 27555	10/14
27556	GX 58 GMO	AD	Env	SFD185AR28GG30355	AD	8303/4	B44F	11/08	Southdown (WS) 27556	10/14
27557	GX 58 GMU	AD	Env	SFD185AR28GG30350	AD	8303/5	B44F	11/08	Southdown (WS) 27557	10/14
27558	GX 58 GMV	AD	Env	SFD185AR28GG30351	AD	8303/6	B44F	11/08	Southdown (WS) 27558	10/14
27559	GX 58 GMY	AD	Env	SFD185AR28GG30333	AD	8303/7	B44F	11/08	Southdown (WS) 27559	10/14
27560	GX 58 GMZ	AD	Env	SFD185AR28GG30334	AD	8303/8	B44F	11/08	Southdown (WS) 27560	10/14

STAGECOACH (SOUTH) (HA) (continued)

27561	GX 58 GNF	AD	Env	SFD185AR28GG30335	AD 8303/9	B44F	11/08 Southdown (WS) 27561	10/14
27562	GX 58 GNJ	AD	Env	SFD185AR28GG30336	AD 8303/10	B44F	11/08 Southdown (WS) 27562	10/14
27563	GX 58 GNK	AD	Env	SFD185AR28GG30337	AD 8303/11	B44F	11/08 Southdown (WS) 27563	10/14
27564	GX 58 GNN	AD	Env	SFD185AR28GG30338	AD 8303/12	B44F	11/08 Southdown (WS) 27564	10/14
27565	GX 58 GNO	AD	Env	SFD185AR28GG30339	AD 8303/13	B44F	11/08 Southdown (WS) 27565	10/14
27566	GX 58 GNP	AD	Env	SFD185AR28GG30340	AD 8303/14	B44F	11/08 Southdown (WS) 27566	10/14
27567	GX 58 GNU	AD	Env	SFD185AR28GG30356	AD 8303/15	B44F	11/08 Southdown (WS) 27567	10/14
27568	GX 58 GNV	AD	Env	SFD185AR28GG30357	AD 8303/16	B44F	11/08 Southdown (WS) 27568	10/14
27569	GX 58 GNY	AD	Env	SFD185AR28GG30358	AD 8303/17	B44F	11/08 Southdown (WS) 27569	10/14
27570	GX 58 GNZ	AD	Env	SFD185AR28GG30359	AD 8303/18	B44F	11/08 Southdown (WS) 27570	10/14
27616	GX 10 HCD	AD	Env	SFD1A5AR2AGG30437	AD 9311/1	B45F	4/10 Hampshire Bus (HA) 27616	10/14
27617	GX 10 HCE	AD	Env	SFD1A5AR2AGG30438	AD 9311/2	B45F	4/10 Hampshire Bus (HA) 27617	10/14
27618	GX 10 HCF	AD	Env	SFD1A5AR2AGG30439	AD 9311/3	B45F	4/10 Hampshire Bus (HA) 27618	10/14
27619	GX 10 HCG	AD	Env	SFD1A5AR2AGG30440	AD 9311/4	B45F	4/10 Hampshire Bus (HA) 27619	10/14
27620	GX 10 HCH	AD	Env	SFD1A5AR2AGG30441	AD 9311/5	B45F	4/10 Hampshire Bus (HA) 27620	10/14
27621	GX 10 HCJ	AD	Env	SFD1A5AR2AGG30442	AD 9311/6	B45F	4/10 Hampshire Bus (HA) 27621	10/14
27622	GX 10 HCK	AD	Env	SFD1A5AR2AGG30443	AD 9311/7	B45F	4/10 Hampshire Bus (HA) 27622	10/14
27642	GX 10 HBU	AD	Env	SFD1A5AR2AGG30460	AD 9315/1	B42F	6/10 Southdown (WS) 27642	6/14
27643	GX 10 HBY	AD	Env	SFD1A5AR2AGG30461	AD 9315/2	B42F	6/10 Southdown (WS) 27643	6/14
27644	GX 10 HBZ	AD	Env	SFD1A5AR2AGG30462	AD 9315/3	B42F	6/10 Southdown (WS) 27644	6/14
27648	GX 10 KZA	AD	Env	SFD1A5AR2AGG30466	AD 9315/7	B42F	6/10 Southdown (WS) 27648	6/14
27649	GX 10 KZB	AD	Env	SFD1A5AR2AGG30468	AD 9315/8	B42F	6/10 Southdown (WS) 27649	6/14
27650	GX 10 KZC	AD	Env	SFD1A5AR2AGG30469	AD 9315/9	B42F	6/10 Southdown (WS) 27650	6/14
27651	403 DCD	AD	Env	SFD1A5AR2AGG30470	AD 9315/10	B42F	6/10 Southdown (WS) 27651	10/14
			(ex GX 10 KZD 5/15)					
27652	GX 10 KZE	AD	Env	SFD1A5AR2AGG30471	AD 9315/11	B42F	6/10 Southdown (WS) 27652	6/14
27653	GX 10 KZF	AD	Env	SFD1A5AR2AGG30472	AD 9315/12	B42F	7/10 Southdown (WS) 27653	6/14
27654	GX 10 KZG	AD	Env	SFD1A5AR2AGG30473	AD 9315/13	B42F	6/10 Southdown (WS) 27654	6/14
27655	GX 10 KZH	AD	Env	SFD1A5AR2AGG30474	AD 9315/14	B42F	6/10 Southdown (WS) 27655	6/14
27656	GX 10 KZJ	AD	Env	SFD1A5AR2AGG30475	AD 9315/15	B42F	7/10 Southdown (WS) 27656	6/14
27657	GX 10 KZK	AD	Env	SFD1A5AR2AGG30476	AD 9315/16	B42F	7/10 Southdown (WS) 27657	6/14
27658	GX 10 KZL	AD	Env	SFD1A5AR2AGG30477	AD 9315/17	B42F	7/10 Southdown (WS) 27658	6/14
27659	GX 10 KZM	AD	Env	SFD1A5AR2AGG30478	AD 9315/18	B42F	7/10 Southdown (WS) 27659	6/14
27660	GX 10 KZN	AD	Env	SFD1A5AR2AGG30479	AD 9315/19	B42F	7/10 Southdown (WS) 27660	6/14
27661	GX 10 KZO	AD	Env	SFD1A5AR2AGG30480	AD 9315/20	B42F	7/10 Southdown (WS) 27661	6/14
27662	GX 10 KZP	AD	Env	SFD1A5AR2AGG30481	AD 9315/21	B42F	7/10 Southdown (WS) 27662	6/14
27663	GX 10 KZR	AD	Env	SFD1A5AR2AGG30467	AD 9315/22	B42F	7/10 Southdown (WS) 27663	6/14
27664	GX 10 KZS	AD	Env	SFD1A5AR2AGG30483	AD A300/1	B42F	8/10 Southdown (WS) 27664	6/14
27665	GX 10 KZT	AD	Env	SFD1A5AR2AGG30484	AD A300/2	B42F	8/10 Southdown (WS) 27665	6/14
27666	GX 10 KZU	AD	Env	SFD1A5AR2AGG30485	AD A300/3	B42F	8/10 Southdown (WS) 27666	6/14
27667	GX 10 KZV	AD	Env	SFD1A5AR2AGG30486	AD A300/4	B42F	8/10 Southdown (WS) 27667	6/14
27668	GX 10 KZW	AD	Env	SFD1A5AR2AGG30487	AD A300/5	B42F	8/10 Southdown (WS) 27668	6/14
27669	GX 10 KZY	AD	Env	SFD1A5AR2AGG30488	AD A300/6	B42F	8/10 Southdown (WS) 27669	6/14
27670	GX 60 PBY	AD	Env	SFD1A5AR2AGG30489	AD A300/7	B42F	9/10 Southdown (WS) 27670	6/14
27671	GX 60 PBZ	AD	Env	SFD1A5AR2AGG30490	AD A300/8	B42F	9/10 Southdown (WS) 27671	6/14
27672	GX 60 PCV	AD	Env	SFD1A5AR2AGG30491	AD A300/9	B42F	9/10 Southdown (WS) 27672	6/14
27673	GX 60 PCY	AD	Env	SFD1A5AR2AGG30492	AD A300/10	B42F	9/10 Southdown (WS) 27673	6/14
27674	GX 60 PCZ	AD	Env	SFD1A5AR2AGG30493	AD A300/11	B42F	9/10 Southdown (WS) 27674	6/14
27675	GX 60 PDK	AD	Env	SFD1A5AR2AGG30494	AD A300/12	B42F	9/10 Southdown (WS) 27675	6/14
27676	GX 60 PDO	AD	Env	SFD1A5AR2AGG30482	AD A300/13	B42F	9/10 Southdown (WS) 27676	6/14
27677	GX 60 PDU	AD	Env	SFD1A5AR2AGG30495	AD A300/14	B42F	9/10 Southdown (WS) 27677	6/14
27678	GX 60 PDV	AD	Env	SFD1A5AR2AGG30496	AD A300/15	B42F	9/10 Southdown (WS) 27678	6/14
27679	GX 60 PDY	AD	Env	SFD1A5AR2AGG30497	AD A300/16	B42F	9/10 Southdown (WS) 27679	6/14
27680	GX 60 PDZ	AD	Env	SFD1A5AR2AGG30498	AD A300/17	B42F	9/10 Southdown (WS) 27680	6/14
27741	GX 11 AKU	AD	Env	SFD1C5AR2BGG30570	AD A306/1	B42F	5/11 Southdown (WS) 27741	6/14
27742	GX 11 AKV	AD	Env	SFD1C5AR2BGG30571	AD A306/2	B42F	5/11 Southdown (WS) 27742	6/14
27755	GX 11 AKY	AD	Env	SFD1C5AR2BGG30584	AD B303/1	B43F	8/11 Stagecoach UK Events (LN) 27755	9/12
27756	GX 11 AKZ	AD	Env	SFD1C5AR2BGG30585	AD B303/2	B43F	8/11 Stagecoach UK Events (LN) 27756	9/12
27828	GX 62 BPV	AD	E30D	SFD1C5AR2CGG30708	AD C304/1	B41F	1/13 Hampshire Bus (HA) 27828	10/14
27829	GX 62 BPZ	AD	E30D	SFD1C5AR2CGG30709	AD C304/2	B41F	1/13 Hampshire Bus (HA) 27829	10/14
27830	GX 62 BTV	AD	E30D	SFD1C5AR2CGG30710	AD C304/3	B41F	1/13 Hampshire Bus (HA) 27830	10/14
27831	GX 62 BUJ	AD	E30D	SFD1C5AR2CGG30712	AD C304/4	B41F	1/13 Hampshire Bus (HA) 27831	10/14
27832	GX 62 BUU	AD	E30D	SFD1C5AR2CGG30713	AD C304/5	B41F	1/13 Hampshire Bus (HA) 27832	10/14
27833	GX 62 BUV	AD	E30D	SFD1C5AR2CGG30711	AD C304/6	B41F	1/13 Hampshire Bus (HA) 27833	10/14
27834	GX 62 BVA	AD	E30D	SFD1C5AR2CGG30714	AD C304/7	B41F	1/13 Hampshire Bus (HA) 27834	10/14
27835	GX 62 BVV	AD	E30D	SFD1C5AR2CGG30715	AD C304/8	B41F	1/13 Hampshire Bus (HA) 27835	10/14
27836	GX 62 BVW	AD	E30D	SFD1C5AR2CGG30716	AD C304/9	B41F	1/13 Hampshire Bus (HA) 27836	10/14
27837	GX 62 BWJ	AD	E30D	SFD1C5AR2CGG30717	AD C304/10	B41F	1/13 Hampshire Bus (HA) 27837	9/13
27838	GX 13 AOA	AD	E30D	SFD1C5AR2CGG30718	AD C305/1	DP39F	3/13 Southdown (WS) 27838	6/14
27839	GX 13 AOB	AD	E30D	SFD1C5AR2CGG30719	AD C305/2	DP39F	3/13 Southdown (WS) 27839	6/14
27840	GX 13 AOC	AD	E30D	SFD1C5AR2CGG30720	AD C305/3	DP39F	3/13 Southdown (WS) 27840	6/14
27841	GX 13 AOD	AD	E30D	SFD1C5AR2CGG30721	AD C305/4	DP39F	3/13 Southdown (WS) 27841	6/14

WEST SUSSEX (WS)   G627/30

STAGECOACH (SOUTH) (HA) (continued)

Fleet	Reg			Chassis		Body	Type	Date	Previous owner	Date
27842	GX 13 AOE	AD	E30D	SFD1C5AR2CGG30722	AD	C305/5	DP39F	3/13	Southdown (WS) 27842	6/14
27843	GX 13 AOF	AD	E30D	SFD1C5AR2CGG30723	AD	C305/6	DP39F	3/13	Southdown (WS) 27843	6/14
27844	GX 13 AOG	AD	E30D	SFD1C5AR2CGG30724	AD	C305/7	DP39F	3/13	Southdown (WS) 27844	6/14
27861	GX 13 ANU	AD	E30D	SFD1C5AR2DGG30839	AD	D304/1	B41F	7/13	Southdown (WS) 27861	10/14
27862	GX 13 ANV	AD	E30D	SFD1C5AR2DGG30840	AD	D304/2	B41F	7/13	Southdown (WS) 27862	10/14
27863	GX 13 AOH	AD	E30D	SFD1C5AR2DGG30841	AD	D304/3	B41F	7/13	Southdown (WS) 27863	10/14
27864	GX 13 AOJ	AD	E30D	SFD1C5AR2DGG30842	AD	D304/4	B41F	7/13	Southdown (WS) 27864	10/14
27865	GX 13 AOK	AD	E30D	SFD1C5AR2DGG30843	AD	D304/5	B41F	7/13	Southdown (WS) 27865	10/14
27866	GX 13 AOL	AD	E30D	SFD1C5AR2DGG30844	AD	D304/6	B41F	7/13	Southdown (WS) 27866	10/14
27867	GX 13 AOM	AD	E30D	SFD1C5AR2DGG30848	AD	D304/7	B41F	7/13	Southdown (WS) 27867	10/14
27868	GX 13 AON	AD	E30D	SFD1C5AR2DGG30850	AD	D304/8	B41F	7/13	Southdown (WS) 27868	10/14
27869	GX 13 AOO	AD	E30D	SFD1C5AR2DGG30845	AD	D304/9	B41F	8/13	Southdown (WS) 27869	10/14
27870	GX 13 AOP	AD	E30D	SFD1C5AR2DGG30846	AD	D304/10	B41F	8/13	Southdown (WS) 27870	10/14
27871	GX 13 AOR	AD	E30D	SFD1C5AR2DGG30849	AD	D304/11	B41F	8/13	Southdown (WS) 27871	10/14
27872	GX 13 AOS	AD	E30D	SFD1C5AR2DGG30847	AD	D304/12	B41F	8/13	Southdown (WS) 27872	10/14
27873	GX 13 AOT	AD	E30D	SFD1C5AR2DGG30853	AD	D304/13	B41F	8/13	Southdown (WS) 27873	10/14
27874	GX 13 AOU	AD	E30D	SFD1C5AR2DGG30854	AD	D304/14	B41F	8/13	Southdown (WS) 27874	10/14
27875	GX 13 AOV	AD	E30D	SFD1C5AR2DGG30861	AD	D304/15	B41F	8/13	Southdown (WS) 27875	10/14
27876	GX 13 AOW	AD	E30D	SFD1C5AR2DGG30862	AD	D304/16	B41F	8/13	Southdown (WS) 27876	10/14
27877	GX 13 AOY	AD	E30D	SFD1C5AR2DGG30863	AD	D304/17	B41F	8/13	Southdown (WS) 27877	10/14
27878	GX 13 AOZ	AD	E30D	SFD1C5AR2DGG30864	AD	D304/18	B41F	8/13	Southdown (WS) 27878	10/14
27918	SN 63 YPU	AD	E30D		AD	D309/1	B39F	10/13	new	10/13
32501	J501 GCD	Ds	Dt	9.8SDL3017/655	Ar	AM88/1591/1	B41F	12/91	Southdown (WS) 32501	8/14
33020	T593 CGT	Ds	Dt SLF	SFD322BR1WGW12876	Pn	9810.7HLB0345	B39F	3/99	new	8/99
33156	LK 55 KZZ	AD	Dt SLF	SFD3CACR45GW18386	AD	5220/4	B37F	1/06	Southdown (WS) 33156	10/14
33189	LK 06 BWB	AD	Dt SLF	SFD4DBER35GW38502	EL	C59001	B40F	5/06	Safeguard, Guildford (SR)	9/13
33190	LK 07 CBO	AD	Dt SLF	SFD4DBER36GW39040	EL	C62408	B40F	4/07	Safeguard, Guildford (SR)	9/13
33191	LK 07 CBU	AD	Dt SLF	SFD4DBER35GW39041	EL	C62409	B40F	4/07	Safeguard, Guildford (SR)	9/13
33306	AE 51 VFV	Ds	Dt SLF	SFD322BR11GW15827	Pn	0110.7HLB3842	B37F	9/01	Fleet Buzz (HA) 33306	10/14
33381	T927 PNV	Ds	Dt SLF	SFD322BR1WGW12562	Pn	9810.7HLB8582	B35F	3/99	Southdown (WS) 33381	6/14
			(ex T 5 BUS 4/05)							
33443	X613 JCS	Ds	Dt SLF	SFD322BR1YGW65492	Ar	0004/25	B38F	2/01	Southdown (WS) 33443	3/13
33444	X614 JCS	Ds	Dt SLF	SFD322BR1YGW65486	Ar	0004/26	B38F	2/01	Southdown (WS) 33444	3/13
33446	X616 JCS	Ds	Dt SLF	SFD322BR1YGW15203	Ar	0004/28	B38F	2/01	Southdown (WS) 33446	3/13
33447	X617 JCS	Ds	Dt SLF	SFD322BR1YGW15217	Ar	0004/29	B38F	2/01	Southdown (WS) 33447	3/13
34414	GX 53 MWE	Tbs	Dt SLF	SFD3CACR33GW87207	Tbs	3033/14	B38F	11/03	Southdown (WS) 34414	6/14
34415	GX 53 MWF	Tbs	Dt SLF	SFD3CACR33GW87208	Tbs	3033/15	B38F	11/03	Southdown (WS) 34415	6/14
34416	GX 53 MWG	Tbs	Dt SLF	SFD3CACR33GW87209	Tbs	3033/16	B38F	11/03	Southdown (WS) 34416	6/14
34417	GX 53 MWJ	Tbs	Dt SLF	SFD3CACR33GW87210	Tbs	3033/17	B38F	11/03	Southdown (WS) 34417	6/14
34418	GX 53 MWK	Tbs	Dt SLF	SFD3CACR33GW87211	Tbs	3033/18	B38F	11/03	Hampshire Bus (HA) 34418	10/14
34445	GX 53 MWL	Tbs	Dt SLF	SFD3CACR33GW87346	Tbs	3033/45	B38F	1/04	Southdown (WS) 34445	10/14
34446	GX 53 MWM	Tbs	Dt SLF	SFD3CACR33GW87347	Tbs	3033/46	B38F	1/04	Southdown (WS) 34446	10/14
34447	GX 53 MWN	Tbs	Dt SLF	SFD3CACR33GW87348	Tbs	3033/47	B38F	1/04	Southdown (WS) 34447	10/14
34448	GX 53 MWO	Tbs	Dt SLF	SFD3CACR33GW87349	Tbs	3033/48	B38F	1/04	Southdown (WS) 34448	10/14
34449	GX 53 MWP	Tbs	Dt SLF	SFD3CACR33GW87350	Tbs	3033/49	B38F	1/04	Southdown (WS) 34449	10/14
34450	GX 53 MWU	Tbs	Dt SLF	SFD3CACR33GW87351	Tbs	3033/50	B38F	1/04	Hampshire Bus (HA) 34450	10/14
34451	GX 53 MWV	Tbs	Dt SLF	SFD3CACR33GW87352	Tbs	3033/51	B38F	1/04	Hampshire Bus (HA) 34451	10/14
34452	GX 53 MWW	Tbs	Dt SLF	SFD3CACR33GW87353	Tbs	3033/52	B38F	1/04	Hampshire Bus (HA) 34452	10/14
34453	GX 53 MWY	Tbs	Dt SLF	SFD3CACR33GW87354	Tbs	3033/53	B38F	1/04	Hampshire Bus (HA) 34453	10/14
34454	GX 53 MWZ	Tbs	Dt SLF	SFD3CACR33GW87355	Tbs	3033/54	B38F	1/04	Hampshire Bus (HA) 34454	10/14
34514	GX 04 EXH	Tbs	Dt SLF	SFD3CACR44GW87658	Tbs	3050/14	B38F	3/04	Southdown (WS) 34514	7/10
34515	GX 04 EXJ	Tbs	Dt SLF	SFD3CACR44GW87659	Tbs	3050/15	B38F	3/04	Southdown (WS) 34515	7/10
34516	GX 04 EXK	Tbs	Dt SLF	SFD3CACR44GW87660	Tbs	3050/16	B38F	3/04	Southdown (WS) 34516	7/10
34517	GX 04 EXL	Tbs	Dt SLF	SFD3CACR44GW87661	Tbs	3050/17	B38F	3/04	Southdown (WS) 34517	6/14
34518	GX 04 EXM	Tbs	Dt SLF	SFD3CACR44GW87662	Tbs	3050/18	B38F	3/04	Southdown (WS) 34518	7/10
34519	GX 04 EXN	Tbs	Dt SLF	SFD3CACR44GW87663	Tbs	3050/19	B38F	3/04	Southdown (WS) 34519	11/10
34520	GX 04 EXP	Tbs	Dt SLF	SFD3CACR44GW87664	Tbs	3050/20	B38F	3/04	Southdown (WS) 34520	7/13
34521	GX 04 EXR	Tbs	Dt SLF	SFD3CACR44GW87665	Tbs	3050/21	B38F	3/04	Southdown (WS) 34521	8/13
34522	GX 04 EXS	Tbs	Dt SLF	SFD3CACR44GW87666	Tbs	3050/22	B38F	3/04	Southdown (WS) 34522	6/14
34523	GX 04 EXT	Tbs	Dt SLF	SFD3CACR44GW87667	Tbs	3050/23	B38F	3/04	Southdown (WS) 34523	6/14
34524	GX 04 EXU	Tbs	Dt SLF	SFD3CACR44GW87681	Tbs	3050/24	B38F	3/04	Southdown (WS) 34524	6/14
34527	GX 04 EXZ	Tbs	Dt SLF	SFD3CACR44GW87684	Tbs	3050/27	B38F	3/04	Southdown (WS) 34527	6/14
34528	GX 04 EYA	Tbs	Dt SLF	SFD3CACR44GW87683	Tbs	3050/28	B38F	3/04	Southdown (WS) 34528	6/14
34529	GX 04 EYB	Tbs	Dt SLF	SFD3CACR44GW87686	Tbs	3050/29	B38F	3/04	Southdown (WS) 34529	6/14
34531	GX 04 EYD	Tbs	Dt SLF	SFD3CACR44GW87698	Tbs	3050/31	B38F	3/04	Southdown (WS) 34531	6/14
34629	GX 54 DVW	Ds	Dt SLF	SFD3CACR44GW17878	Ar	4205/9	B38F	9/04	Southdown (WS) 34629	8/10
34631	GX 54 DVZ	Ds	Dt SLF	SFD3CACR44GW17879	Ar	4205/11	B38F	9/04	Hampshire Bus (HA) 34631	10/14
34632	GX 54 DWA	Ds	Dt SLF	SFD3CACR44GW17881	Ar	4205/12	B38F	9/04	Hampshire Bus (HA) 34632	10/14
34633	GX 54 DWC	Ds	Dt SLF	SFD3CACR44GW17882	Ar	4205/13	B38F	9/04	Hampshire Bus (HA) 34633	11/14
34634	GX 54 DWD	Ds	Dt SLF	SFD3CACR44GW17883	Ar	4205/14	B38F	9/04	Hampshire Bus (HA) 34634	11/14
34635	GX 54 DWE	Ds	Dt SLF	SFD3CACR44GW17877	Ar	4205/15	B38F	9/04	Hampshire Bus (HA) 34635	10/14
34636	GX 54 DWF	Ds	Dt SLF	SFD3CACR44GW17884	Ar	4205/16	B38F	9/04	Hampshire Bus (HA) 34636	10/14
34637	GX 54 DWG	Ds	Dt SLF	SFD3CACR44GW17885	Ar	4205/17	B38F	9/04	Hampshire Bus (HA) 34637	10/14
34638	GX 54 DWJ	Ds	Dt SLF	SFD3CACR44GW17886	Ar	4205/18	B38F	9/04	new	9/04

STAGECOACH (SOUTH) (HA) (continued)

34684	PX 05 EKT	Ds	Dt SLF	SFD3CACR45GW18279	Ar	5204/4	B38F	5/05	Southdown (WS) 34684	6/14
34686	PX 05 EKV	Ds	Dt SLF	SFD3CACR45GW18281	Ar	5204/6	B38F	5/05	Southdown (WS) 34686	6/14
34689	PX 05 EKZ	Ds	Dt SLF	SFD3CACR45GW18284	Ar	5204/9	B38F	6/05	Southdown (WS) 34689	6/14
34690	PX 05 ELC	Ds	Dt SLF	SFD3CACR45GW18285	Ar	5204/10	B38F	6/05	Southdown (WS) 34690	6/14
34852	GX 06 DXA	AD	Dt SLF	SFD3CACR45GW88604	AD	5215/51	B38F	3/06	new	3/06
34853	GX 06 DXB	AD	Dt SLF	SFD3CACR45GW88636	AD	5215/52	B38F	3/06	new	3/06
34854	GX 06 DXC	AD	Dt SLF	SFD3CACR45GW88642	AD	5215/53	B38F	3/06	new	3/06
34855	GX 06 DXD	AD	Dt SLF	SFD3CACR45GW88644	AD	5215/54	B38F	3/06	new	3/06
34856	GX 06 DXE	AD	Dt SLF	SFD3CACR45GW88675	AD	5215/55	B38F	3/06	new	3/06
34857	GX 06 DXF	AD	Dt SLF	SFD3CACR45GW88678	AD	5215/56	B38F	3/06	new	3/06
34858	GX 06 DXG	AD	Dt SLF	SFD3CACR45GW88591	AD	5215/57	B38F	3/06	new	3/06
35117	GX 06 AZG	AD	Dt SLF	SFD3CACR46GW88733	AD	5244/17	B38F	7/06	Southdown (WS) 35117	6/14
35118	GX 56 KVU	AD	Dt SLF	SFD3CACR46GW88734	AD	5244/18	B38F	9/06	Southdown (WS) 35118	6/14
35119	GX 56 KVV	AD	Dt SLF	SFD3CACR46GW88735	AD	5244/19	B38F	9/06	Southdown (WS) 35119	6/14
35120	GX 56 KVW	AD	Dt SLF	SFD3CACR46GW88736	AD	5244/20	B38F	9/06	Southdown (WS) 35120	6/14
35121	GX 56 KVY	AD	Dt SLF	SFD3CACR46GW88753	AD	5245/1	B38F	9/06	Southdown (WS) 35121	6/14
35122	GX 56 KVZ	AD	Dt SLF	SFD3CACR46GW88754	AD	5245/2	B38F	9/06	Southdown (WS) 35122	6/14
35123	GX 56 KWA	AD	Dt SLF	SFD3CACR46GW88755	AD	5245/3	B38F	9/06	Southdown (WS) 35123	6/14
35124	GX 56 KWB	AD	Dt SLF	SFD3CACR46GW88756	AD	5245/4	B38F	9/06	Southdown (WS) 35124	6/14
35125	GX 56 KWC	AD	Dt SLF	SFD3CACR46GW88757	AD	5245/5	B38F	9/06	Southdown (WS) 35125	6/14
35126	GX 56 KWD	AD	Dt SLF	SFD3CACR46GW88758	AD	5245/6	B38F	9/06	Southdown (WS) 35126	6/14
35127	GX 56 KWE	AD	Dt SLF	SFD3CACR46GW88759	AD	5245/7	B38F	9/06	Southdown (WS) 35127	6/14
35151	GX 56 KWF	AD	Dt SLF	SFD3CACR46GW88814	AD	5245/31	B38F	9/06	Hampshire Bus (HA) 35151	8/07
35152	GX 56 KWG	AD	Dt SLF	SFD3CACR46GW88815	AD	5245/32	B38F	9/06	Hampshire Bus (HA) 35152	8/07
35210	GX 56 KWH	AD	Dt SLF	SFD3CACR46GW88977	AD	6214/25	B38F	11/06	Hampshire Bus (HA) 35210	10/14
35211	GX 56 KWJ	AD	Dt SLF	SFD3CACR46GW88978	AD	6214/26	B38F	10/06	Hampshire Bus (HA) 35211	10/14
35212	GX 56 KWK	AD	Dt SLF	SFD3CACR46GW88979	AD	6214/27	B38F	10/06	Hampshire Bus (HA) 35212	10/14
35213	GX 56 KWL	AD	Dt SLF	SFD3CACR46GW88980	AD	6214/28	B38F	10/06	Hampshire Bus (HA) 35213	10/14
35214	GX 56 KWM	AD	Dt SLF	SFD3CACR46GW88981	AD	6214/29	B38F	12/06	Hampshire Bus (HA) 35214	10/14
35215	GX 56 KWN	AD	Dt SLF	SFD3CACR46GW88983	AD	6214/30	B38F	12/06	Hampshire Bus (HA) 35215	10/14
35216	GX 56 KWO	AD	Dt SLF	SFD3CACR46GW88984	AD	6214/31	B38F	12/06	Hampshire Bus (HA) 35216	10/14
35217	GX 56 KWP	AD	Dt SLF	SFD3CACR46GW88985	AD	6214/32	B38F	12/06	Hampshire Bus (HA) 35217	10/14
35250	GX 56 OGA	AD	Dt SLF	SFD3CACR46GW89015	AD	6237/27	B38F	12/06	Southdown (WS) 35250	6/14
35251	GX 56 OGB	AD	Dt SLF	SFD3CACR46GW89016	AD	6237/28	B38F	12/06	Southdown (WS) 35251	6/14
35252	GX 56 OGC	AD	Dt SLF	SFD3CACR46GW89017	AD	6237/29	B38F	12/06	Southdown (WS) 35252	6/14
35253	GX 56 OGD	AD	Dt SLF	SFD3CACR46GW89018	AD	6237/30	B38F	12/06	Southdown (WS) 35253	8/10
35254	GX 56 OGE	AD	Dt SLF	SFD3CACR46GW89019	AD	6237/31	B38F	12/06	Hampshire Bus (HA) 35254	10/14
35255	GX 56 OGF	AD	Dt SLF	SFD3CACR46GW89020	AD	6215/1	B38F	12/06	Hampshire Bus (HA) 35255	10/14
35256	GX 56 OGG	AD	Dt SLF	SFD3CACR46GW89021	AD	6215/2	B38F	12/06	Hampshire Bus (HA) 35256	10/14
35257	GX 56 OGH	AD	Dt SLF	SFD3CACR46GW89022	AD	6215/3	B38F	12/06	Hampshire Bus (HA) 35257	10/14
35258	GX 56 OGJ	AD	Dt SLF	SFD3CACR46GW89023	AD	6215/4	B38F	12/06	Hampshire Bus (HA) 35258	10/14
35259	GX 56 OGK	AD	Dt SLF	SFD3CACR46GW89024	AD	6215/5	B38F	12/06	Hampshire Bus (HA) 35259	10/14
35260	GX 56 OGL	AD	Dt SLF	SFD3CACR46GW89025	AD	6215/6	B38F	12/06	Hampshire Bus (HA) 35260	10/14
36014	414 DCD	AD	Dt SLF	SFD321AR17GY10399	AD	7204/4	B38F	7/07	Hampshire Bus (HA) 36014	10/14
	(ex GX 07 FXB 3/13)									
36015	GX 07 FXC	AD	Dt SLF	SFD321AR17GY10400	AD	7204/5	B38F	7/07	Hampshire Bus (HA) 36015	10/14
36016	GX 07 FXD	AD	Dt SLF	SFD321AR17GY10401	AD	7204/6	B38F	7/07	Hampshire Bus (HA) 36016	10/14
36017	417 DCD	AD	Dt SLF	SFD321AR17GY10402	AD	7204/7	B38F	7/07	Hampshire Bus (HA) 36017	10/14
	(ex GX 07 FXE 3/13)									
36018	418 DCD	AD	Dt SLF	SFD321AR17GY10403	AD	7204/8	B38F	7/07	Hampshire Bus (HA) 36018	10/14
	(ex GX 07 FXF 3/13)									
36019	GX 07 FXG	AD	Dt SLF	SFD321AR17GY10404	AD	7204/9	B38F	7/07	Hampshire Bus (HA) 36019	10/14
36020	420 DCD	AD	Dt SLF	SFD321AR17GY10405	AD	7204/10	B38F	7/07	Hampshire Bus (HA) 36020	10/14
	(ex GX 07 FXH 3/13)									
36021	421 DCD	AD	Dt SLF	SFD321AR17GY10406	AD	7204/11	B38F	7/07	Hampshire Bus (HA) 36021	10/14
	(ex GX 07 FXJ 1/13)									
36022	402 DCD	AD	Dt SLF	SFD321AR17GY10407	AD	7204/12	B38F	7/07	Hampshire Bus (HA) 36022	10/14
	(ex GX 07 FXK 4/13)									
36023	GX 07 HUJ	AD	Dt SLF	SFD321AR17GY10408	AD	7204/13	B38F	7/07	Hampshire Bus (HA) 36023	10/14
	(ex 403 DCD 5/15, GX 07 HUJ 1/13)									
36024	GX 07 HUK	AD	Dt SLF	SFD321AR17GY10409	AD	7204/14	B38F	7/07	Hampshire Bus (HA) 36024	10/14
	(ex YEL 4T 10/14, GX 07 HUK 1/13)									
36025	GX 07 HUO	AD	Dt SLF	SFD321AR17GY10410	AD	7204/15	B38F	7/07	Hampshire Bus (HA) 36025	10/14
36026	GX 07 HUP	AD	Dt SLF	SFD321AR17GY10421	AD	7204/16	B38F	7/07	Hampshire Bus (HA) 36026	10/14
36027	407 DCD	AD	Dt SLF	SFD321AR17GY10422	AD	7204/17	B38F	7/07	Hampshire Bus (HA) 36027	10/14
	(ex GX 07 HUU)									
36028	408 DCD	AD	Dt SLF	SFD321AR17GY10423	AD	7204/18	B38F	7/07	Hampshire Bus (HA) 36028	10/14
	(ex GX 07 HUV 1/13)									
36029	GX 07 HUY	AD	Dt SLF	SFD321AR17GY10424	AD	7204/19	B38F	7/07	Hampshire Bus (HA) 36029	10/14
36030	GX 07 HUZ	AD	Dt SLF	SFD321AR17GY10425	AD	7204/20	B38F	7/07	Hampshire Bus (HA) 36030	10/14
36036	GX 57 BHZ	AD	Dt SLF	SFD321AR17GY10478	AD	7219/1	B38F	11/07	Hampshire Bus (HA) 36036	10/14
36051	GX 58 GKZ	AD	Dt SLF	SFD361AR28GY10840	AD	8224/1	B38F	12/08	Hampshire Bus (HA) 36051	10/14
36052	GX 58 GLF	AD	Dt SLF	SFD361AR28GY10841	AD	8224/2	B38F	12/08	Hampshire Bus (HA) 36052	10/14
36053	GX 58 GLJ	AD	Dt SLF	SFD361AR28GY10842	AD	8224/3	B38F	12/08	Hampshire Bus (HA) 36053	10/14

STAGECOACH (SOUTH) (HA) (continued)

36054	GX 58 GLK	AD	Dt SLF	SFD361AR28GY10843	AD	8224/4	B38F	12/08	Hampshire Bus (HA) 36054	10/14
36055	GX 58 GLV	AD	Dt SLF	SFD361AR28GY10844	AD	8224/5	B38F	12/08	Hampshire Bus (HA) 36055	10/14
36056	GX 58 GLY	AD	Dt SLF	SFD361AR28GY10845	AD	8224/6	B38F	12/08	Hampshire Bus (HA) 36056	10/14
36057	GX 58 GLZ	AD	Dt SLF	SFD361AR28GY10846	AD	8224/7	B38F	12/08	Hampshire Bus (HA) 36057	10/14
36431	GX 61 AYJ	AD	Dt	SFD7H7AR6BGY12548	AD	B226/1	B37F	11/11	Southdown (WS) 36431	9/12
36432	GX 61 AYL	AD	Dt	SFD7H7AR6BGY12549	AD	B226/2	B37F	11/11	Southdown (WS) 36432	9/12
36433	GX 61 AYM	AD	Dt	SFD7H7AR6BGY12550	AD	B226/3	B37F	11/11	Southdown (WS) 36433	9/12
36434	GX 61 AYN	AD	Dt	SFD7H7AR6BGY12560	AD	B226/4	B37F	11/11	Southdown (WS) 36434	9/12
36435	GX 61 AYO	AD	Dt	SFD7H7AR6BGY12561	AD	B226/5	B37F	11/11	Southdown (WS) 36435	9/12
36436	GX 61 AYP	AD	Dt SLF	SFD7H7AR6BGY12562	AD	B226/6	B37F	11/11	Hampshire Bus (HA) 36436	10/14
36437	GX 61 AYS	AD	Dt SLF	SFD7H7AR6BGY12551	AD	B226/7	B37F	11/11	Hampshire Bus (HA) 36437	10/14
36438	GX 61 AYT	AD	Dt SLF	SFD7H7AR6BGY12552	AD	B226/8	B37F	11/11	Hampshire Bus (HA) 36438	10/14
36439	GX 61 AYU	AD	Dt SLF	SFD7H7AR6BGY12563	AD	B226/9	B37F	11/11	Hampshire Bus (HA) 36439	10/14
36440	GX 61 AYV	AD	Dt SLF	SFD7H7AR6BGY12564	AD	B226/10	B37F	11/11	Hampshire Bus (HA) 36440	10/14
36441	GX 61 AYW	AD	Dt SLF	SFD7H7AR6BGY12568	AD	B226/11	B37F	11/11	Hampshire Bus (HA) 36441	10/14
36442	GX 61 AYY	AD	Dt SLF	SFD7H7AR6BGY12569	AD	B226/12	B37F	11/11	Hampshire Bus (HA) 36442	10/14
36443	GX 61 AYZ	AD	Dt SLF	SFD7H7AR6BGY12570	AD	B226/13	B37F	11/11	Hampshire Bus (HA) 36443	10/14
36823	GX 62 BAO	AD	E20D	SFD7H7AR6CGY13410	AD	C225/1	B37F	1/13	Southdown (WS) 36823	10/14
36824	GX 62 BAV	AD	E20D	SFD7H7AR6CGY13424	AD	C225/2	B37F	1/13	Southdown (WS) 36824	10/14
36825	GX 62 BBK	AD	E20D	SFD7H7AR6CGY13425	AD	C225/3	B37F	1/13	Southdown (WS) 36825	10/14
36826	GX 62 BBN	AD	E20D	SFD7H7AR6CGY13426	AD	C225/4	B37F	1/13	Southdown (WS) 36826	10/14
36827	GX 62 BBU	AD	E20D	SFD7H7AR6CGY13427	AD	C225/5	B37F	1/13	Southdown (WS) 36827	10/14
36828	GX 62 BCU	AD	E20D	SFD7H7AR6CGY13428	AD	C225/6	B37F	1/13	Southdown (WS) 36828	10/14
36829	GX 62 BDV	AD	E20D	SFD7H7AR6CGY13429	AD	C225/7	B37F	1/13	Southdown (WS) 36829	10/14
36830	GX 62 BDZ	AD	E20D	SFD7H7AR6CGY13423	AD	C225/8	B37F	1/13	Southdown (WS) 36830	10/14
36831	GX 62 BFK	AD	E20D	SFD7H9BR6CGY13289	AD	C228/1	B37F	2/13	Southdown (WS) 36831	10/14
36832	GX 62 BFV	AD	E20D	SFD7H9BR6CGY13443	AD	C228/2	B37F	2/13	Southdown (WS) 36832	10/14
36833	GX 62 BGE	AD	E20D	SFD7H9BR6CGY13445	AD	C228/3	B37F	2/13	Southdown (WS) 36833	10/14
36834	GX 62 BGF	AD	E20D	SFD7H9BR6CGY13444	AD	C228/4	B37F	2/13	Hampshire Bus (HA) 36834	10/14
36835	GX 62 BHL	AD	E20D	SFD7H9BR6CGY13446	AD	C228/5	B37F	2/13	Hampshire Bus (HA) 36835	10/14
36836	GX 62 BHZ	AD	E20D	SFD7H9BR6CGY13447	AD	C228/6	B37F	2/13	Hampshire Bus (HA) 36836	10/14
36837	GX 62 BKG	AD	E20D	SFD7H9BR6CGY13448	AD	C228/7	B37F	2/13	Hampshire Bus (HA) 36837	10/14
36838	GX 62 BMZ	AD	E20D	SFD7H9BR6CGY13449	AD	C228/8	B37F	2/13	Hampshire Bus (HA) 36838	10/14
36839	GX 62 BNL	AD	E20D	SFD7H9BR6CGY13450	AD	C228/9	B37F	2/13	Hampshire Bus (HA) 36839	10/14
36840	GX 62 BNZ	AD	E20D	SFD7H9BR6CGY13462	AD	C228/10	B37F	2/13	Hampshire Bus (HA) 36840	10/14
36909	GX 13 APF	AD	E20D	SFD7H7AR6DGY13796	AD	D207/1	B37F	8/13	new	8/13
36910	GX 13 APK	AD	E20D	SFD7H7AR6DGY13797	AD	D207/2	B37F	8/13	new	8/13
36911	GX 13 APO	AD	E20D	SFD7H7AR6DGY13798	AD	D207/3	B37F	8/13	new	8/13
36912	GX 13 APU	AD	E20D	SFD7H7AR6DGY13799	AD	D207/4	B37F	8/13	new	8/13
36913	GX 13 APV	AD	E20D	SFD7H7AR6DGY13800	AD	D207/5	B37F	8/13	new	8/13
36914	YX 63 GYN	AD	E20D	SFD7H7AR6DGY13801	AD	D207/6	B37F	9/13	new	9/13
36915	YX 63 KFD	AD	E20D	SFD7H7AR6DGY13805	AD	D207/7	B37F	9/13	new	9/13
36916	YX 63 KFE	AD	E20D	SFD7H7AR6DGY13806	AD	D207/8	B37F	9/13	new	9/13
36917	YX 63 KFF	AD	E20D	SFD7H7AR6DGY13807	AD	D207/9	B37F	9/13	Hampshire Bus (HA) 36917	10/14
36918	YX 63 GYA	AD	E20D	SFD7H7AR6DGY13808	AD	D208/1	B37F	9/13	Hampshire Bus (HA) 36918	10/14
36919	YX 63 GYB	AD	E20D	SFD7H7AR6DGY13809	AD	D208/2	B37F	9/13	Hampshire Bus (HA) 36919	10/14
36920	YX 63 GYC	AD	E20D	SFD7H7AR6DGY13810	AD	D208/3	B37F	9/13	Hampshire Bus (HA) 36920	10/14
36921	YX 63 GYD	AD	E20D	SFD7H7AR6DGY13811	AD	D209/1	B37F	9/13	Hampshire Bus (HA) 36921	10/14
36922	YX 63 GYE	AD	E20D	SFD7H7AR6DGY13812	AD	D209/2	B37F	9/13	Hampshire Bus (HA) 36922	10/14
36923	YX 63 GYF	AD	E20D	SFD7H7AR6DGY13816	AD	D209/3	B37F	9/13	Hampshire Bus (HA) 36923	10/14
36924	YX 63 GYH	AD	E20D	SFD7H7AR6DGY13817	AD	D209/4	B37F	9/13	Hampshire Bus (HA) 36924	10/14
36925	YX 63 GYJ	AD	E20D	SFD7H7AR6DGY13818	AD	D209/5	B37F	9/13	Southdown (WS) 36925	10/14
37261	SL 64 HWU	AD	E20D	SFD7H9ER6EGY14646	AD	E225/1	B37F	12/14	new	12/14
37262	SL 64 HWV	AD	E20D	SFD7H9ER6EGY14647	AD	E225/2	B37F	12/14	new	12/14
37263	SL 64 HWX	AD	E20D	SFD7H9ER6EGY14587	AD	E225/3	B37F	12/14	new	12/14
37264	SL 64 HWY	AD	E20D	SFD7H9ER6EGY14588	AD	E225/4	B37F	12/14	new	12/14
37265	SL 64 HWZ	AD	E20D	SFD7H9ER6EGY14591	AD	E225/5	B37F	12/14	new	12/14
37266	SL 64 HXA	AD	E20D	SFD7H9ER6EGY14592	AD	E225/6	B37F	12/14	new	12/14
37267	SL 64 HXB	AD	E20D	SFD7H9ER6EGY14675	AD	E225/7	B37F	12/14	new	12/14
37268	SL 64 HXC	AD	E20D	SFD7H9ER6EGY14674	AD	E225/8	B37F	12/14	new	12/14
37269	SL 64 HXD	AD	E20D	SFD7H9ER6EGY14593	AD	E226/1	B37F	12/14	new	12/14
37270	SL 64 HXE	AD	E20D	SFD7H9ER6EGY14596	AD	E226/2	B37F	12/14	new	12/14
37271	SL 64 HXF	AD	E20D	SFD7H9ER6EGY14598	AD	E226/3	B37F	12/14	new	12/14
37272	SL 64 HXG	AD	E20D	SFD7H9ER6EGY14595	AD	E226/4	B37F	12/14	new	12/14
37273	SL 64 HXH	AD	E20D	SFD7H9ER6EGY14597	AD	E226/5	B37F	12/14	new	12/14
37274	SL 64 HXJ	AD	E20D	SFD7H9ER6EGY14594	AD	E226/6	B37F	12/14	new	12/14
37275	SL 64 HXK	AD	E20D	SFD7H9ER6EGY14602	AD	E226/7	B37F	1/15	new	1/15
37276	SL 64 HXM	AD	E20D	SFD7H9ER6EGY14603	AD	E226/8	B37F	1/15	new	1/15
			(named *Peter Chilvers*)							
37277	SL 64 HXN	AD	E20D	SFD7H9ER6EGY14601	AD	E226/9	B37F	1/15	new	1/15
			(named *The Hayling Billy*)							
37278	SL 64 HXO	AD	E20D	SFD7H9ER6EGY14600	AD	E226/10	B37F	1/15	new	1/15
			(named *The Coppist*)							

STAGECOACH (SOUTH) (HA) (continued)

37279	SL 64 HXP	AD	E20D	SFD7H9ER6EGY14599	AD	E226/11	B37F	1/15 new	1/15
			(named *The Olive Leaf*)						
37291	YY 14 WGD	AD	E20D	SFD7LAER7EGY14315	AD	D274/1	B37F	7/14 Hampshire Bus (HA) 37291	10/14
37292	YY 14 WGE	AD	E20D	SFD7LAER7EGY14316	AD	D274/2	B37F	7/14 Hampshire Bus (HA) 37292	10/14
39651	GX 08 HBN	MAN	14.240	WMAA66ZZ38C011028	AD	7234/1	B43F	5/08 new	5/08
39652	GX 08 HBO	MAN	14.240	WMAA66ZZ08C011035	AD	7234/2	B43F	5/08 new	5/08
39653	GX 08 HBP	MAN	14.240	WMAA66ZZ08C011049	AD	7234/3	B43F	5/08 new	5/08
39654	GX 08 HBU	MAN	14.240	WMAA66ZZX8C011060	AD	7234/4	B43F	5/08 new	5/08
39655	GX 08 HBY	MAN	14.240	WMAA66ZZ68C011055	AD	7234/5	B43F	5/08 new	5/08
39656	GX 08 HBZ	MAN	14.240	WMAA66ZZ78C011059	AD	7234/6	B43F	5/08 new	5/08
47048	YK 04 KVV	Oe	M780	SAB19000000001546	Oe		B19F	7/04 Hampshire Bus (HA) 47048	10/14
47049	YK 04 KVW	Oe	M780	SAB19000000001547	Oe		B19F	7/04 Hampshire Bus (HA) 47049	10/14
47307	GX 06 DYH	Oe	M850SL	SABENFAF06L192306	Oe		B28F	6/06 new	6/06
47308	GX 06 DYJ	Oe	M850SL	SABENFAF06L192307	Oe		B28F	6/06 new	6/06
47309	GX 06 DYM	Oe	M850SL	SABENFAF06L192308	Oe		B28F	6/06 new	6/06
47310	GX 06 DYN	Oe	M850SL	SABENFAF06L192309	Oe		B28F	6/06 new	6/06
47311	GX 06 DYO	Oe	M850SL	SABENFAF06L192310	Oe		B28F	6/06 new	6/06
47312	GX 06 DYP	Oe	M850SL	SABENFAF06L192311	Oe		B28F	6/06 new	6/06
47536	GX 57 DKA	Oe	M880SL	SABENMAF07L192785	Oe	192785	B28F	12/07 Southdown (WS) 47536	6/14
47537	GX 57 DKD	Oe	M880SL	SABENMAF07L192786	Oe	192786	B28F	12/07 Southdown (WS) 47537	6/14
47538	GX 57 DKE	Oe	M880SL	SABENMAF07L192787	Oe	192787	B28F	12/07 Southdown (WS) 47538	6/14
47539	GX 57 DKF	Oe	M880SL	SABENMAF07L192788	Oe	192788	B28F	11/07 Fleet Buzz (HA) 47539	10/14
47540	GX 57 DKJ	Oe	M880SL	SABENMAF07L192789	Oe	192789	B28F	12/07 Fleet Buzz (HA) 47540	10/14
47541	GX 57 DKK	Oe	M880SL	SABENMAF07L192790	Oe	192790	B28F	12/07 Fleet Buzz (HA) 47541	10/14
47542	GX 57 DJJ	Oe	M880SL	SABENMAF07L192791	Oe	192791	B28F	12/07 Southdown (WS) 47542	10/14
47543	GX 57 DJK	Oe	M880SL	SABENMAF07L192792	Oe	192792	B28F	1/08 Southdown (WS) 47543	10/14
47544	GX 57 DJO	Oe	M880SL	SABENMAF07L192793	Oe		B28F	1/08 Hampshire Bus (HA) 47544	10/14
47545	GX 57 DJU	Oe	M880SL	SABENMAF07L192814	Oe	192814	B28F	1/08 Fleet Buzz (HA) 47545	10/14
47546	GX 57 DJV	Oe	M880SL	SABENMAF07L192815	Oe		B28F	1/08 Hampshire Bus (HA) 47546	10/14
47547	GX 57 DJY	Oe	M880SL	SABENMAF07L192816	Oe		B28F	1/08 Hampshire Bus (HA) 47547	10/14
47554	GX 57 DJZ	Oe	M880SL	SABENMAF07L192817	Oe		B28F	1/08 Hampshire Bus (HA) 47554	10/14
47625	GX 08 HBJ	Oe	M880SL	SABENFAF08L193187	Oe		B28F	8/08 new	8/08
47626	GX 08 HBK	Oe	M880SL	SABENFAF08L193188	Oe		B28F	8/08 new	8/08
47644	GX 58 GJO	Oe	M880SL	SABENMAF08L193206	Oe	193206	B28F	10/08 Southdown (WS) 47644	6/14
47645	GX 58 GJU	Oe	M880SL	SABENMAF08L193207	Oe	193207	B28F	10/08 Southdown (WS) 47645	6/14
47646	GX 58 GJV	Oe	M880SL	SABENMAF08L193208	Oe	193208	B28F	10/08 Southdown (WS) 47646	6/14
47647	GX 58 GJY	Oe	M880SL	SABENMAF08L193209	Oe		B28F	11/08 Southdown (WS) 47647	10/09
47648	GX 58 GJZ	Oe	M880SL	SABENMAF08L193210	Oe	193210	B28F	11/08 Southdown (WS) 47648	6/14
47737	YJ 57 YDA	Oe	M880SL	SABENMAF7R192971	Oe		B27F	12/07 Fleet Buzz (HA) 47737	10/14
47738	MX 08 UZM	Oe	M880SL	SABENMAF8R193071	Oe		B28F	8/08 Fleet Buzz (HA) 47738	10/14
47739	MX 08 UZL	Oe	M880SL	SABENMAF08R193070	Oe		B28F	8/08 Fleet Buzz (HA) 47739	10/14
47740	MX 09 MJJ	Oe	M880	SABEWMAF08R193094	Oe		B29F	8/09 Fleet Buzz (HA) 47740	10/14
47864	GX 13 ANF	Oe	M925SL	SABSNLVF0DS290650	Oe		B28F	7/13 new	7/13
47865	GX 13 ANP	Oe	M925SL	SABSNLVF0DS290651	Oe		B28F	7/13 new	7/13
47866	GX 13 ANR	Oe	M925SL	SABSNLVF0DS290652	Oe		B28F	7/13 new	7/13
47924	YJ 14 BVS	Oe	M920SR	SABSNLVF0ES290912	Oe		B28F	7/14 Hampshire Bus (HA) 47924	10/14
47925	YJ 14 BVT	Oe	M920SR	SABSNLVF0ES290913	Oe		B28F	7/14 Hampshire Bus (HA) 47925	10/14
47926	YJ 14 BVU	Oe	M920SR	SABSNLVF0ES290914	Oe		B28F	7/14 Hampshire Bus (HA) 47926	10/14
47927	YJ 14 BVV	Oe	M920SR	SABSNLVF0ES290915	Oe		B28F	7/14 Hampshire Bus (HA) 47927	10/14
47928	YJ 14 BVW	Oe	M920SR	SABSNLVF0ES290916	Oe		B28F	7/14 new	7/14
47929	YJ 14 BVX	Oe	M920SR	SABSNLVF0ES290917	Oe		B28F	7/14 new	7/14
47930	YJ 14 BVZ	Oe	M920SR	SABSNLVF0ES290918	Oe		B28F	7/14 new	7/14
47931	YJ 14 BVG	Oe	M920SR	SABSNLVF0ES290919	Oe		B28F	7/14 new	7/14
47932	YJ 14 BVH	Oe	M920SR	SABSNLVF0ES290920	Oe		B28F	7/14 new	6/14
47933	YJ 14 BVK	Oe	M920SR	SABSNLVF0ES290921	Oe		B28F	7/14 new	7/14
52617	NFX 667	Vo	B10M-62	YV31MA61XWC060892	Je	24821	C49FT	10/98 Hampshire Bus (HA) 52617	11/14
			(ex S457 BCE 1/10)						
52618	411 DCD	Vo	B10M-62	YV31MA611WC060893	Je	24822	C49FT	10/98 Hampshire Bus (HA) 52618	11/14
			(ex S458 BCE 1/10)						
52619	413 DCD	Vo	B10M-62	YV31MA613WC060894	Je	24823	C49FT	10/98 Hampshire Bus (HA) 52619	11/14
			(ex S459 BCE 1/10)						
52623	456 CLT	Vo	B10M-62	YV31MA61XWC060908	Je	24827	C49FT	10/98 Hampshire Bus (HA) 52623	11/14
			(ex S903 CCD 12/09)						
52655	WLT 526	Vo	B10M-62	YV31MA618XC061296	Je	25262	C49FT	10/99 Hampshire Bus (HA) 52655	11/14
			(ex V905 DPN 3/13, NSU 133 12/12, V905 DPN 8/07)						
52657	PSU 787	Vo	B10M-62	YV31MA611XC061298	Je	25264	C49FT	10/99 Hampshire Bus (HA) 52657	11/14
			(ex V907 DDY 3/13)						
52658	XYK 976	Vo	B10M-62	YV31MA613XC061299	Je	25265	C49FT	10/99 Hampshire Bus (HA) 52658	11/14
			(ex V908 DDY 3/13)						

(handwritten) Now G628

29101-9; 34628 83; 37406-23; 47312(+50313), 47974;52231; 8Ko7D4A(DEMO);

STAGECOACH (SOUTH) (HA) - Fleet Allocation / Checklist 19159-63 93; 26041-9; 26146-65; 26294-300 2-1416-25; 2777465
16698-700; 10101-719-78; 08891902/4; 16941-70; 11273; 16931 3/4; 18004; 18073 54; 18375 1254; 18437 48; 19039 98; 19063 404Dc

(left margin handwritten) 1907 / 8376 / 18386 / 18439 / 16527 / 18084 / 45374

10001 CR	16755 AT	22746 AT	27675 WG	34517 CR	36021 WI	37266 AT 32
10008 CR	16767 WI	22747 AT	27676 WG	34518 GD	36022 WI	37267 AT 33
10009 CR	16769 WI	22748 AT	27677 WG	34519 GD	36023 WI	37268 AT 33
15585 WG	16787 WI	22749 AT	27678 WG	34520 GD	36024 WI	37269 CR 33
15586 WI	16797 WI	22750 AT	27679 WG	34521 GD	36025 WI	37270 CR 33
15588 WG	16798 WI	22751 AT	27680 WG	34522 WI	36026 WI	37271 CR 34
15589 WG	16799 WI	22752 AT	27741 CR	34523 CR	36027 WI	37272 CR 34
15590 WG	17425 PM	22753 AT	27742 CR	34524 CR	36028 BE	37273 CR
15591 WG	17672 PM	22754 AT	27755 AT	34527 WG	36029 BE	37274 CR
15592 WG	17740 PM	22755 AT	27756 AT	34528 CR	36030 BE	37275 PM 34
15593 WG	18184 BE	22756 AT	27828 BE	34529 CR	36036 BE	37276 PM 34
15594 WG	18185 AR	27511 WI	27829 BE	34531 AT	36051 BE	37277 PM 34
15595 WG	18186 BE	27512 WI	27830 BE	34629 WI n/i	36052 BE	37278 PM 34
15596 WG	18187 BE	27513 WG	27831 BE	34631 WI	36053 BE	37279 PM
15597 WG	18188 BE	27514 WG	27832 BE	34632 WI	36054 BE	37291 BE
15598 PM	18191 BE	27515 WG	27833 BE	34633 BE	36055 BE	37292 BE 37
15599 PM	18193 BE	27553 PM	27834 BE	34634 BE	36056 BE	39651 AT 37
15600 PM	18194 BE	27554 PM	27835 BE	34635 BE	36057 BE	39652 AT 37
15601 PM	18310 WI	27555 PM	27836 BE	34636 BE	36431 GD	39653 AT 37
15602 WG	18311 BE	27556 PM	27837 AT	34637 res	36432 GD	39654 AT 37
15603 PM	18502 AR	27557 PM	27838 CR	34638 WG	36433 GD	39655 AT 37
15604 PM	18503 BE	27558 PM	27839 CR	34684 AT	36434 GD	39656 AT 37
15605 WG	18504 WI	27559 PM	27840 CR	34686 AT	36435 GD	47048 AR
15804 AR	18505 WI	27560 PM	27841 CR	34689 AT	36436 BE	47049 BE
15805 AR	18510 BE	27561 PM	27842 CR	34690 CR	36437 BE	47307 AT
15806 AR	18511 BE	27562 PM	27843 CR	34852 GD	36438 BE	47308 GD 3
15982 WG	18512 WI	27563 PM	27844 CR	34853 GD	36439 BE	47309 GD 5
15983 WG	18513 AR	27564 PM	28761 PM	34854 GD	36440 BE	47310 GD
15984 WG	18514 BE	27565 PM	27862 PM	34855 WG	36441 BE	47311 GD 3
15985 WG	18515 WI	27566 PM	27863 PM	34856 GD	36442 BE	47312 WI 50
15986 WG	18516 PM	27567 PM	27864 PM	34857 GD	36443 BE	47536 AT 57
15987 PM	18517 PM	27568 PM	27865 PM	34858 GD	36823 PM	47537 AT 34
15988 PM	18518 PM	27569 PM	27866 PM	35117 WG	36824 PM	47538 AT 34
15989 WG	18519 AR	27570 PM	27867 PM	35118 WG	36825 PM	47539 AT 34
15990 WG	18520 WI	27616 WI	27868 PM	35119 WG	36826 PM	47540 u 47
15991 WG	18521 WI	27617 WI	27869 PM	35120 WG	36827 PM	47541 AT
15992 WG	18522 AR	27618 WI	27870 PM	35121 WG	36828 PM	47542 AT
15993 WG	18523 BE	27619 WI	27871 PM	35122 WG	36829 PM	47543 res
16129 AR	18524 WI	27620 WI	27872 PM	35123 WG	36830 WG	47544 AR
16261 AT	18525 AR	27621 WI	27873 PM	35124 WG	36831 PM	47545 res
16262 AT	18526 WI	27622 WI	27874 PM	35125 WG	36832 PM	47546 AR
16263 BE	18527 AR	27642 w	27875 PM	35126 WG	36833 BE	47547 AT
16268 BE	19055 WI	27643 w	27876 PM	35127 WG	36834 BE	47554 AT
16269 CR	19063 PM	27644 w	27877 PM	35151 GD	36835 BE	47625 AT
16278 CR	19069 WI	27648	27878 PM	35152 GD	36836 BE	47626 AT
16282 AT	19071 PM	27649	27918 AT	35210 BE	36837 BE	47644 CR
16291 GD	19078 PM	27650 CR	33020 w	35211 BE	36838 BE	47645 CR
16292 WI	19079 WI	27651 PM	33156 PM	35212 BE	36839 BE	47646 CR
16293 w	19081 WI	27652 CR	33189 GD	35213 BE	36840 BE	47647 AT
16295 GD	19090 PM	27653 CR	33190 PM	35214 BE	36909 AT	47648 CR
16302 AT	19096 WI	27654 CR	33191 GD	35215 WI	36910 AT	47737 AT
16303 w	19097 CH	27655 CR	33306 FMs	35216 AR	36911 AT	47738 AT
16304 WI	19099 WI	27656 WG	33381 w	35217 AR	36912 AT	47739 AT
16305 AT	19881 CR	27657 WG	34414 AT	35250 WG	36913 AT	47740 AT
16312 CR	19982 CR	27658 WG	34415 AT	35251 WG	36914 AT	47864 AT
16502 WI	19883 CR	27659 WG	34416 WG	35252 WG	36915 AT	47865 AT
16523 BE	19884 CR	27660 WG	34417 WG	35253 GD	36916 AT	47866 AT
16524 BE	19885 CR	27661 WG	34418 WG	35254 WI	36917 WI	47924 AR
16525 BE	19886 CR	27662 WG	34445 WI	35255 WI	36918 AR	47925 AR
16590 BE	19887 CR	27663 WG	34446 PM	35256 WI	36919 AR	47926 AR
16591 res	19900 CR	27664 CR	34447 PM	35257 WI	36920 AR	47927 AR
16624 AT	19909 WGp	27665 CR	34448 PM	35258 WI	36921 BE	47928 CR
16625 AT	19913 p	27666 WG	34449 PM	35259 AR	36922 BE	47929 CR
16627 AT	19945 p	27667 CR	34450 res	35260 AR	36923 BE	47930 CR
16628 AT	20228 WI	27668 WG	34451 res	36014 WI	36924 BE	47931 CR
16629 AT	20937 WI	27669 WG	34452 res	36015 WI	36925 PM	47932 CR
16631 AT	22741 AT	27670 WG	34453 res	36016 WI	37261 AT	47933 CR
16632 AT	22742 AT	27671 WG	34514 AT	36017 WI	37262 AT	52617 52666
16633 AT	22743 AT	27672 WG	34515 GD	36018 WI	37263 AT	52618 52657
16748 AT	22744 AT	27673 WG	34516 GD	36019 WI	37264 AT	52619 52658
16752 CR	22745 AT	27674 WG	34516 GD	36020 WI	37265 AT	52623 53610

(handwritten) Now G628

Bell, Eastergate (Rutherfords) Plaxton Premiere 320 bodied Scania K93CRB J287 NNC was new to Shearings. It is seen on football duties at the Community stadium in Falmer in April 2014. (Alan Snatt)

Seen outside Brighton railway station on rail replacement work in January 2015 is Bird, Beeding (Southern Transit) TA1 (V301 KGW), an Alexander bodied Dennis Trident. (Richard Covey)

Brown, Crawley (Crawley Luxury) operate a large fleet of coaches most of which have been registered with CLC plates. N 60 CLC (ex PN 02 SVK, 8468 RU, PN 02 SVK) is a Volvo B10M-62 with Caetano Enigma bodywork. It is seen leaving Eastbourne station in July 2013 (Alan Snatt)

Coach Hire, Colgate run a number of services in West and East Sussex under the Sussex Bus name. Branded for route 40X is NKK 447 (ex X232 NNO), an Alexander bodied Dennis Trident seen in Gloucester Place, Brighton in November 2013. (Alan Snatt)

Emsworth & District, Southbourne operate bus services in West Sussex and Hampshire with vehicles carrying a livery reminiscent of Southdown. KV 51 KZJ is a Plaxton Pointer 2 bodied Dennis Dart SLF seen on route 54 in Chichester in August 2013. (Cliff Baker)

Sole vehicle currently recorded with Holt Services, Henfield is AE 60 DBX, an Iveco 65C18 with Indcar Wing body. It is seen on the London Road at Patcham. (Alan Snatt)

Latest additions to the fleet of Metrobus are a batch of ten Alexander Dennis Enviro200 which carry a revised livery. 6781 (YY 15 GDA) is seen in Castle Square, Brighton in May 2015. (Alan Snatt)

The fleet of Miller, Horsham (Arun Coaches) consists of three Duple 425, with another being used for spares. ARU 500A (ex A 4 SOL, E747 YSU) is seen at the Community stadium on football work in January 2013. (Alan Snatt)

Seen at Burgess Hill leisure centre in January 2014 is Mr Clive, Beeding AE 04 FUV. It is an Ayats A14-9.6/PT Platinum, one of only three in the country. (Alan Snatt)

Southdown PSV, Copthorne operate a small network of bus services in Sussex, Surrey and Kent. East Lancs Myllenium bodied Alexander Dennis Dart 114 (LK 55 AEA) is seen on layover at Crawley bus station in September 2014. (Cliff Baker)

Stagecoach has a number of routes which have names rather than the traditional numbers or letters. Branded for the Bognor Star route is Optare Solo SR 47933 (YJ 14 BVK). It is seen in Flansham Park, Bognor Regis in October 2014. (Cliff Baker)

Seen at its base in the old Beeding cement works in November 2014 is Walker, Beeding (Brightonian) NIW 6518, a Volvo B10M-61 with Van Hool body new to Shearings as C532 DND. (Richard Covey)

Woodcock, Beeding ASV 440 (ex P566 MLE) is a Volvo B10M-62 with Plaxton Premiere 320 bodywork. It is seen at Beeding cement works in November 2014. (Richard Covey)

Worthing Coaches, Worthing is owned by Luckett, Fareham and shares the livery style and fleet numbering of that operator, but retains its own separate identity. 5369 (YN 13 XYT) is an Irizar i6 bodied Scania K360IB4 seen in Arundel in June 2014. (Cliff Baker)

Adur Community Transport, Shoreham has small fleet of accessible minibuses which are used principally in the Worthing area. BU 54 GZT is a Fiat Ducato with a Swain body. (Paul Green)

Bluebird Community Partnership, Haywards Heath operates in both East and West Sussex, with the main area of operation being in Haywards Heath. DK 06 EHN, a Mercedes Benz 411CDI converted by Stanford Conversions is seen in Commercial Square, Haywards Heath. (Paul Green)

PK1111109/N: STARLINE (Sussex) Limited, 9 Market Road, CHICHESTER, PO19 1JW.
FN: Starline Taxis.   OC: Unit 3, Plot 12, Terminus Road, Chichester, PO19 8TX.   VA: 7.

	K 33 SKY	Io	45C11	ZCFC457100D201695	Eurm -?-	M15L	3/03 Essex County Council (XEX)	8/13
			(ex EU 03 RNX 12/13)					
	S800 STA	MB	413CDI	WDB9046632R739658	Cpt	M16	12/05 Chapman,	
							New Stevenston (SW)	10/12
			(ex MX 05 WZK 11/12)					
	AO 51 HZG	Io	45C11	ZCFC457100D163868	Eurm -?-	M15L	9/01 Keech, Todmorden (WY)	8/13
			(ex N 3 DKT 9/13, AO 51 HZG 3/13)					
x	KR 02 JHE	Fd	Tt	WF0VXXBDFV2J37839	Fd	M8	8/02 Starline, Chichester (YWS)	8/09
x	BU 53 TNO	Rt	Mtr	VF1FDBNH529147589	?	M8L	1/04 -?-, -?-	8/11
	LM 05 BUS	VW	Crf	WV1ZZZ2EZ96005414	Tawe	C15F	9/09 new	9/09
			(ex CU 59 FYR 11/09)					
x	KX 55 OJF	Fd	Tt	WF0VXXBDFV5B46836	Fd	M8	11/05 new	11/05
x	SH 55 WUK	Vx	Mov	VN1F9BVH534809994	?	M8	1/06 -?-, -?-	7/11
			(carries Chichester District Council private hire plate 1124)					
x	GR 07 OLO	Fd	Tt	WF0BXXBDFB7E08242	Fd	M8	6/07 Starline, Chichester (YWS)	8/09
x	KX 07 FFA	Fd	Tt	WF0BXXBDFB7C79849	Fd	M8	4/07 Starline, Chichester (YWS)	8/09
x	RX 57 BXZ	Rt	Mtr	VF1FDB2E637955360	?	M6	9/07 -?-, -?-	8/13
			(carries Chichester District Council private hire plate 1301)					
x	KY 58 FVP	Fd	Tt	WF0BXXBDFB8G83937	Fd	M8	9/08 Starline, Chichester (YWS)	8/09
x	LX 58 DJE	Rt	Mtr	VF1FDB2E639458777	?	M6	10/08 -?-, -?-	8/13
			(carries Chichester District Council private hire plate 1302)					
x	NL 58 TZX	Fd	Tt	WF0BXXBDFB8L23555	Fd	M8	9/08 Starline, Chichester (YWS)	8/09
x	ND 61 HFK	Fd	Tt	WF0BXXBDFBBU22146	Fd	M8	1/12 new	1/12
x	NJ 61 GHH	Fd	Tt	WF0SXXBDFSBS14039	Fd	M8	9/11 new	9/11
			(operating on Chichester PH plate 1145)					
x	NL 62 BUP	Fd	Tt	WF0BXXBDFBCY50561	Fd	M8	1/13 new	1/13
x	NL 13 XNZ	Fd	Tt	WF0SXXBDFSDJ56750	Fd	M8	5/13 new	5/13
	HX 63 EZU	Fd	Tt	WF0DXXTTFDDR07127	Fd	M16	9/13 new	9/13
	HX 63 EZV	Fd	Tt	WF0DXXTTFDDR07090	Fd	M16	9/13 new	9/13
	NL 14 UZO	Fd	Tt	WF0DXXTTFDDD09437	Fd	M16	4/14 new	4/14

NOTE: prior to 10/12, vehicles were licenced to PK1100694/N Starline (Chichester) Limited, Chichester.

PK1012507/I: STORBROOK Limited, 46 Newmarket Road, CRAWLEY, RH10 6NA.
FNs: Premier Transport; South East Provincial.   OC: Dunns Yard, Copthorne Road, Crawley, RH10 3ED.   VA: 13.

w	PN 04 VHF	LDV	Cy	SEYZMVSZGDN104159	LDV	M16	5/04 private owner	9/06
	WA 07 BGV	Vo	B12B(T)	YV3R8L2287A117346	VH 33978	CH59/20CT	4/07 Galleon 2009, Roydon (EX)	12/14
			(ex 924 CRT 6/14, WA 07 BGV 4/14)					
	YJ 08 EEY	Tmsa	Opalin	NLTHGJ45L01000028	Tmsa -?-	C35F	7/08 Galloway, Mendlesham (SK)	1/13
	YJ 11 GJV	VH	T916	YE2916SS351D54088	VH 54088	C44FT	6/11 Barnard, Kirton in Lindsey (LI)	4/13
	YT 11 LPO	Sca	K360EB4	YS2K4X20001868785	Lah -?-	C51FT	4/11 New City Coaches,	
							Luton Airport (BD)	10/12
	YJ 12 CJX	VH	T916	YE2916SS351D54092	VH 54092	C57FT	7/12 Grace, Crawley (WS)	2/13
	YJ 13 GVP	Tmsa Safari		NLTRJTA7R01010030	Tmsa OA07274	C53FT	6/13 new	6/13
	YJ 13 GXS	Tmsa Safari		NLTRJTA7R01010025	Tmsa -?-	C53FT	3/13 new	3/13
	YJ 13 GXT	Tmsa Safari		NLTRJTA7R01010019	Tmsa -?-	C53FT	5/13 new	5/13
	WN 63 BKL	MB	516CDI	WDB9066572S796336	Swansea Coachworks	C19F	2/14 new	2/14
	YJ 14 CAO	VH	TX16	YE2X16SS351D54007	VH 54097	C??FT	5/14 new	5/14
	YJ 14 CAX	VH	TDX20	YE2X20SU351D53280	VH 53280	CH??/??FT	5/14 new	5/14
	YJ 14 CDY	VH	TX16	YE2X16SH249D55135	VH 55135	C57FT	7/14 new	7/14

PK1001042/I: SUSSEX COMMERCIAL SERVICES Limited, Beedingwood Farm, Forest Road, COLGATE, Horsham,
RH12 4TB.   OC: Mackley Industrial Estate, Henfield Road, Small Dole, Henfield, BN5 9XQ.   VA: 7.

See joint entry under Coach Hire, Colgate

PK1135514/R: SUSSEX TRAVEL SERVICES Limited, 34 West Way, LANCING, BN15 8LX.
OC: as address.   VA: 2.

New application currently pending

PK1130993/R: Pamela Jean SWEETMAN, 21 Bramble Close, COPTHORNE, Crawley, RH10 3QB.
FN: Hello Travel.　**OC:** Moorhouse Farm, Ditchling Road, Haywards Heath, RH17 7RE.　**VA:** 2.

No vehicles yet recorded

PK1099918/I: TAKE-A-BREAK Care & Travel Limited, 17 Fleet Close, LITTLEHAMPTON, BN17 6SD.
OC: as address.　**VA:** 2.

T 10 ACL	MB	O814D	WDB6703742N074204	Pn	998.5MZE9609	C29F	3/99 Avon Mini Buses.	
							Longwell Green (GL)	3/11

PK1039457/R: Roy THOMAS, 14 Carylls Cottages, Faygate Lane, FAYGATE, Horsham, RH12 4SQ.
FN: Park Limos.　**OC:** Millfield Farm, Horsham Road, Rusper, Horsham, RH12 4PR.　**VA:** 2.

No vehicles currently recorded

PK1125007/I: TRAVELSTAR Gatwick Limited, Travelstar Garages, Lakeland Business Centre, Parish Lane, Pease Pottage, CRAWLEY, RH10 5NY.　**OC:** as address.　**VA:** 10.

YT 59 NZO	Sca	K340EB4	YS2K4X20001864063	Lah YK900L3409R008597	C55F	9/09 Heffernan, Perivale (LN)	12/11
PO 11 LNC	MB	O816D	WDB6703742N141011	UNVI -?-	C29F	7/11 new	7/11
PO 61 LUT	MB	O816D	WDB6703742N142377	UNVI -?-	C27F	1/12 new	1/12
YT 62 JAO	Sca	K400EB4	YS2K4X20001878683	Lah YK900L360CR008506	C53FT	9/12 new	9/12
YT 13 AMX	Sca	K360EB4	YS2K4X20001884530	Ir 133352	C49FT	8/13 new	8/13
YT 13 AOG	Sca	K400EB4	YS2K4X20001884182	Lah YK900L360DR008793	C53FT	3/13 new	3/13
PE 63 PZZ	MB	1524L	WDB9702782L780662	UNVI 2155	C37F	1/14 new	1/14
YN 14 PLF	Sca	K360EB4	YS2K4X20001887208	Ir 141425	C53FT	3/14 new	3/14

NOTE: prior to 1/14, vehicles were licenced to PK1053854/I Anthony George Grace, Crawley.

PK0002283/I: TURBOSTYLE Coaches Limited, 82 Southgate Drive, Southgate, CRAWLEY, RH10 6EY.
OC: The Old Goods Yard, Wallage Lane, Rowfant, Crawley, RH10 4NF.　**VA:** 16.

W344 MKY	Sca	K124IB4	1836903	Ir 93316	C49FT	5/00 Romsey Coaches, Romsey (HA)	9/04
YN 03 NHT	Ds	Jv	SFD741BR52GJ22424	Pn 0212GRX4792	C55F	3/03 new	3/03
YN 05 VST	MB	O814D	WDB6703742N115341	Pn -?-	C33F	4/05 new	4/05
YN 56 NSE	Sca	K94IB4	1853992	Ir 151620	C70FL	11/06 APT Coaches, Rayleigh (EX)	4/10
WA 07 KXT	MB	O815DT	WDB6703742N123099	Sitcar 2229	C29F	6/07 new	6/07
SN 08 CNJ	Sca	K310IB4	YS2K4X20001859908	Ir 152073	C70F	4/08 Doigs, Glasgow (SW)	10/12
SN 08 CNK	Sca	K310IB4	YS2K4X20001859912	Ir -?-	C70F	4/08 Doigs, Glasgow (SW)	6/13
YN 08 MMX	Sca	K310IB4	YS2K4X20001858207	Ir 152035	C70F	4/08 new	4/08
FN 09 AOO	Vo	B7R	YV3R6K6278A128687	Ssd B-4866	C57F	5/09 new	5/09
FJ 59 CCO	Vo	B7R	YV3R6K6229A130428	Ssd B-4954	C57F	9/09 new	9/09
YN 60 FMJ	MB	O816D	WDB6703742N139271	Pn 108.5MBJ8609	C33F	10/10 new	10/10
BX 11 GWK	Vo	B7R	YV3R6R623AA141080	Ssd B-5342	C57F	6/11 new	6/11
SN 11 CTO	MB	O816D	WDB6703742N141010	UNVI 1217	C33F	4/11 MCH, Uxbridge (LN)	8/13
		(ex 87 MCH 3/14, SN 11 CTO 5/13)					
SN 61 CXJ	MB	O816D	WDB6703742N142443	UNVI 1420	C33F	1/12 MCH, Uxbridge (LN)	1/14
		(ex MCH 999 2/14, SN 61 CXJ 5/13)					
YN 63 BYX	Sca	K360IB4	YS2K4X20001884576	Ir 141006	C53FT	9/13 new	9/13

PK1012657/I: W & H MOTORS Limited, Unit 7-9, Kelvin Business Centre, Kelvin Way, CRAWLEY, RH10 2SE.
OCs: as address; Bonehurst Road, Salfords, Surrey, RH1 2SE.　**VA:** 14.

W587 DGU	Ta	BB50R	TW043BB5000001571	Co 951211	C18F	6/00 Carter, North Acton (LN)	1/06
		(ex W 11 RAN 12/04)					
W547 RNB	As	A3E/BR1	VS946VB33YA031304	As 10086	CH57/16DT	5/00 Waterhouse, Polegate (ES)	4/01
WH 02 WOW	As	A3E/BR1	VS946VB33YA031312	As 10094	CH57/18DT	8/02 new	8/02
YN 03 AWM	MAN	18.360	WMAA51ZZZ3S001176	Noge N-5068	C51FT	5/03 new	5/03
YN 03 AWP	MAN	18.360	WMAA51ZZZ3S001178	Noge N-5080	C51FT	5/03 new	5/03
FN 05 DGE	Vo	B12B	YV3R8G1295A104921	Ssd B-3151	C49FT	7/05 new	7/05
FJ 06 ZLU	Vo	B12B	YV3R8G1245A103076	Ssd B-3083	C49FT	4/06 new	4/06
SF 07 XNV	Vo	B12M	YV3R9L2237A118384	Je 27979	C53F	3/07 Park, Hamilton (SW)	2/10
		(ex LSK 500 12/08)					

W & H MOTORS, CRAWLEY (continued)

SF 07 XOK	Vo	B12M	YV3R9L2247A118524	Je	27983	C53F	3/07 Park, Hamilton (SW)	2/10
		(ex LSK 504 1/09)						
MV 08 HUK	Vo	B12M	YV3R9L2288A125171	Je	28577	C53F	3/08 Park, Hamilton (SW)	2/11
		(ex LSK 496 11/10, LSK 555 3/10)						
WH 08 AGH	Vo	B12B	YV3R8L2297A118697	Ssd	B-4061	C53F	3/08 new	3/08
CN 09 JYD	Vo	B12M	YV3R9L2239A131641	Je	29008	C53F	3/09 Park, Hamilton (SW)	4/12
		(ex LSK 499 12/11)						
WH 09 SUN	Vo	B12B	YV3R8L2277A119671	Ssd	B-4072	C53F	5/09 new	5/09
BX 13 BYF	Vo	B11R	YV3T2S921DA159098	Ssd	-?-	C53FT	4/13 new	4/13
BX 13 BYG	Vo	B11R	YV3T2S920DA159108	Ssd	B-5845	C53FT	4/13 new	4/13

NOTE: prior to 11/02, vehicles were licensed to PK0002675/I A G & G M Heron, Crawley.

PK0001237/I: Laurence Reginald WALKER, 3 The Avenue, Brighton, BN2 4GF.
FN: Brightonian. OC: Old Cement Workshops, BEEDING, West Sussex, BN44 3TX. VA: 3.

NIW 6518	Vo	B10M-61	YV31MED13GA0011461	VH	12029	C57F	3/86 Cheney, Banbury (OX) 110	5/08
		(ex C532 DND 5/93)						
182 KWC	Vo	B10M-62	YV31M2B18SA042702	Bf	2787	C55F	5/95 APT Coaches, Rayleigh (EX)	7/11
		(ex M786 NBA 5/12, APT 42S 7/11, M786 NBA 5/11)						

NOTE: prior to 1/09 (nominal date) vehicles were recorded in the East Sussex section of News Sheet 2.

PK1036192/N: Stephen WALLIS, 27 Newport Road, BURGESS HILL, RH15 8QG.
FN: Wallis Logistics. OC: Silverwood, Snow Hill, Copthorne, RH10.3EN. VA: 1.

No vehicles currently recorded

PK1103403/I: WESTRINGS Travel Limited, 46 Graydon Avenue, CHICHESTER, PO19 8RG.
OC: Nunnington Farm, Rookwood Road, West Wittering, Chichester, PO20 8LZ. VA: 2.

WEZ 2563	Sca	K340EB4	YS2K4X20001860591	Ir	-?-	C49FT	8/08 Wilfreda-Beehive,	
		(ex YN 08 MPZ 8/13)					Adwick-le-Street (SY)	8/13

PH1091274/N: WHEEL DRIVE Limited, Unit 8, Liss Business Centre, Station Road, LISS, GU33 7AW.
OC: The Workshop, Ironhill, HOLLYCOMBE, Liphook, GU30 7LP. VA: 5.

x	M 10 HNH	Fd	Tt	WF0RXXRDFB9K54812	Fd		M7	6/10 -?-, -?-	6/11
			(operates on East Hampshire Private Hire plate 318)					
x	W212 RKK	Vx	Mov	VN1F9CEL521877666	Ts		M8L	4/00 Studio Landia, Mendham(XSK) 12/08
x	RA 02 CMK	Rt	Mtr	VF1FDCNL526503882	?		M8L	4/02 -?-, -?-	9/08
			(operates on East Hampshire Private Hire plate 328)					
x	EU 03 ONF	Rt	Mtr	VF1FDCML527891093	Csd		M8L	3/03 Watford & District Old People's	
								Welfare (XHT)	6/10
x	VU 03 HCD	Vx	Mov	VN1F9CML527862319	O&H		M8L	4/03 Leeds City Council	
								(XWY) 80450	8/08
x	VU 03 HKG	Vx	Mov	VN1F9CML527862319	O&H		M8L	4/03 Leeds City Council	
								(XWY) 80454	5/08
x	WA 03 OLC	Rt	Mtr	VF1FDBNH528076383	?		M8L	4/03 Somerset County Council,	
								Taunton (SO) 735-62	9/11
	WX 03 LEU	Io	50C13	ZCFC5090005364276	Eurm	-?-	M16L	3/03 Blaenau Gwent Council	
								(XCS) 442	11/09
x	RX 53 AXR	Rt	Mtr	VF1FDBNH528691648	?		M8L	9/03 -?-, -?-	8/10
x	BV 04 VPG	Fd	Tt	WF0LXXGBFL3S30076	?		M8L	6/04 -?-, -?-	9/10
			(operates on East Hampshire Private Hire plate 399)					
x	RL 04 KTX	Rt	Mtr	VF1FDBVH531211252	Atl		M8L	7/04 Barchester Healthcare,	
								Rochester (XKT)	6/11
x	NK 54 RLO	Rt	Mtr	VF1PDMUL632605280	O&H		M8L	1/05 Gateshead Council	
								(XTW) 3018	by2/12
x	YJ 05 UJN	Rt	Mtr	VF1FDBVE533874128	O&H		M8L	7/05 -?-, -?-	8/09
			(operates on East Hampshire Private Hire plate 361)					
x	RE 06 VFT	Rt	Mtr	VF1FDBVH535809968	?		M8	6/06 -?-, -?-	9/12
x	EU 56 JZK	Rt	Mtr	VF1FDCWL636173571	O&H		M8L	9/06 -?-, -?-	11/10
x	LX 56 OTH	Vx	Mov	VN1F9BMH636264328	?		M8L	12/06 -?-, -?-	9/11

WHEEL DRIVE, LISS (continued)

PN 07 RVJ	Rt	Mtr	VF1NDD2L637682264	Rt		M15	6/07 Club La Costa,			
								Auchterarder (XSE)	9/11	
x YJ 07 UHR	lo	50C15	ZCFC50A2005633937	Me	4483	M8L	4/07 Calderdale Council,			
								Halifax (WY) 3123	c6/13	
CN 08 CWA	Rt	Mtr	VF1FDC1M638390826	Tawe		M16	3/08 HK Chauffeurs,			
		(ex OO 08 HKS 10/08, CN 08 CWA 5/08)						Sutton Courtenay (OX)	5/10	
EY 58 RZR	MB	311CDI	WDB9066352S348081	?		M16	10/08 -?-, -?-		6/13	
x LR 10 NRL	Fd	Tt	WF0SXXBDFSAS67013	Fd		M8	6/10 -?-, -?-		6/11	
		(operates on East Hampshire Private Hire plate 340)								

PK0003175/N: WHITE HORSE Caravan Co Limited, Paddock Lane, SELSEY, Chichester, PO20 9EJ.
FN: Bunn Leisure.   OC: Main Stores, Warner Lane, Selsey.   VA: 2.

BX 07 AOS	Etpr	Plasma	TS9EB01GS6P130054	Pn	077.9BAR6980	B28F	4/07 Flights Hallmark,		
								Hounslow (LN) 7020	5/11

PK1109916/R: WICKEDLY WONDERFUL Limited, 40 Marine Drive West, WEST WITTERING, Chichester, PO20 8HH.
OC: Wickedly Wonderful Camp, Birdham Road, Chichester, PO20 7EJ.   VA: 2.

No vehicles yet recorded

PK1059568/R: WILLIAM REED Publishing Limited, Broadfield Park, Brighton Road, PEASE POTTAGE, Crawley,
RH11 9RT.   OC: as address.   VA: 1.

CV 05 CZF	Fd	Tt	WF0EXXTTFE4S79613	Fd		M14	3/05 -?-, -?-	4/08
CV 11 JXD	Fd	Tt	WF0DXXTTFDAA82888	Fd		M16	3/11 -?-, -?-	10/14

PK1095087/N: Brian WILLIAMS & Clare JOHNSON, 32 Hartington Road, Brighton, East Sussex, BN2 3LS.
FN: Brighton Travel.   OC: Old Cement Works, BEEDING, BN44 3TX.   VA: 6.

See joint entry with Ace Travel, Beeding

PK0001690/N: Peter J & C M F WOODCOCK, 19 Stonery Close, Portslade, Brighton, BN41 2TD.
FN: Ocean Coaches.   OC: Cement Workshops, Shoreham Road, BEEDING, West Sussex, BN44 3TX. VA: 2.

ASV 440	Vo	B10M-62	YV31MA61XVA047019	Pn	9612VUM6437	C57F	4/97 Brown, Crawley (WS)	8/13
		(ex P566 MLE 3/10)						

PK0001633/I: WOODS Travel Limited, Park Road, BOGNOR REGIS, PO21 2PX.
FN: Woods Holidays.   OCs: Unit R, Rudford Industrial Estate, Rodney Grescent Ford, Arundel, BN18 ODB; WSCC
Drayton Depot, Drayton Lane, Drayton, Chichester, PO20 2BW   VA: 15.

FYL 122	MB	O815D	WDB6703742N117500	Sitcar	2115	C25F	6/05 London Mini, Isleworth (LN)	4/09
		(ex WA 05 JWL 5/09)						
112 FYA	Ba	FLC12-280	XL9AA12NGW7003130	Ba		C53F	1/98 Thurlby, Aldershot (HA)	11/02
		(ex R 57 EDW 3/03)						
198 FYB	Ba	MHD131.460	XL9259EK511320543	Ba		C49FT	3/10 Whytes, Newmachar (SN)	3/13
		(ex SN 10 ANR 3/15)						
503 FYC	Ba	FHD13-340	XL9AA38P632003811	Ba		C53FT	12/06 new	12/06
		(ex WA 56 ENP 11/08)						
666 FYD	Ba	MHD131.460	XL9259EK511320460	Ba		C49FT	6/09 D Coaches, Morriston (CW)	8/11
		(ex WA 09 HTL 9/13)						
587 FYF	Ba	MHD131.460	XL9259EK511320417	Ba		C53F	3/09 Whytes, Newmachar (SN)	5/14
		(ex SN 09 AKV 7/14)						
307 FYG	Ba	FLC12-280	XL9AA12NGW7003149	Ba		C53F	1/98 Thurlby, Aldershot (HA)	11/02
		(ex R 61 EDW 3/04)						
436 FYM	Ba	MHD131.460	XL9259EK511320461	Ba		C49FT	6/09 D Coaches, Morriston (CW)	9/11
		(ex WA 09 HTN 9/13)						
498 FYN	Ba	FHD127.365	XL9AA38R834003256	Ba		C55FT	3/10 Austin, Earlston (SS)	10/12
		(ex SK 10 CVW 3/15, ESU 974 6/12)						

WOODS, BOGNOR REGIS (continued)

274 FYP	Ba	FHD12-340 XL9AA18P632003479	Ba		C49FT	3/06 Anderson, Bermondsey		
		(ex YJ 06 GKZ 9/10)				(LN) B119	8/10	
253 FYW	Ba	FHD13-340 XL9AA38R833003434	Ba		C53FT	2/08 new	2/08	
348 FYY	Ba	FHD12-340 XL9AA18P431003252	Ba		C49FT	3/04 new	3/04	
		(ex WA 04 EWK 2/05)						
J 40 YRS	Ba	XHD122-340XL9158AK310320682	Ba		C49FT	3/06 Stacey's, Carlisle (CA)	9/10	
		(ex YJ 06 GOE 9/10, M 2 DNT 4/10, YJ 06 GOE 8/09)						
S 55 FYE	Ba	XHD122.410 XL9158EF511320098	Ba		C53FT	1/08 DAC Coaches, St Ann's Chapel		
		(ex WA 57 CYZ 4/11)				(CO)	12/09	
S 55 FYX	VW	Crf WV1ZZZ2EZ96020295 Excel -?-			M16	8/10 Milburn, Birtley (TW)	1/14	
		(ex HM 06 GJM 2/14, YN 10 GYU 1/11)						
X 70 BUS	Ba	FHD12-340 XL9AA18P230003259	Ba		C70F	3/02 Grimmett, Minehead (SO)	2/05	
		(ex 498 FYN 9/14, WJ 02 KDK 3/05)						
WA 64 CVV	VDL	FHD2-129 XNL501E100D003025	VDL		C57FT	11/14 Moseley, Wellington (Qd)	2/15	

PK1030840/R: Richard WOOLLEY, 17 Highclere Way, WORTHING, BN13 3RF.
FNs: Richards Minibuses; Brighton Minibus. OC: as address. VA: 2.

See joint entry under Brighton Minibus, Worthing

PK1004668/R: WORKMATES PREMIER Limited, 24 Station Road, BOGNOR REGIS, PO21 1QE.
OC: Hobbs New Barn, Gravetts Lane, Climping, Littlehampton, BN17 5RE. VA: 2.

NA 08 YEV	Fd	Tt	WF0DXXTTFD8B69437	Fd	M16	4/08 -?-, -?-	3/11

PK0000115/I: WORTHING COACHES Limited, 117 King George V Road, WORTHING, BN11 5SA. *also refer Luckett group.*
OCs: Spencer Road, Lancing, BN15 8TX; c/o Eastbourne Buses, Birch Road, Eastbourne, East Sussex, BN23 6PD.
VA: 16. FJ61EWA; YN13X95; YR13RJX; YN64AGZ; YR17RJV; BU18OSL; OSM; OSN; OSO; OSP; YR17RJX; BFS1WJE; YR17RJX;

4202 YR 02 ZZC	Sca	K114IB4		1842029	Ir	95092	C53F	4/02 Luckett, Fareham (HA) 4202	8/06
X4808 FN 62 CAO	Vo	B9R	YV3S5P725CA156691	Co	F123043065	C48FT	2/13 new	2/13
X4809 FN 62 CBV	Vo	B9R	YV3S5P727CA156692	Co	F123043066	C48FT	2/13 new	2/13
X4810 FN 62 CDX	Vo	B9R	YV3S5P729CA156693	Co	F123043067	C48FT	2/13 new	2/13
X4811 FN 62 CEY	Vo	B9R	YV3S5P722CA156700	Co	F123043068	C48FT	2/13 new	2/13
X4812 FN 62 CFG	Vo	B9R	YV3S5P724CA156701	Co	F123043069	C48FT	2/13 new	2/13
X4813 FN 62 CFX	Vo	B9R	YV3S5P726CA156702	Co	F123043070	C48FT	2/13 new	2/13
X4814 FN 62 CGE	Vo	B9R	YV3S5P728CA156703	Co	F123043071	C48FT	2/13 new	2/13
4928 YN 04 GOJ	Sca	K114EB4		1847504	Ir	96303	C49FT	4/04 Luckett, Fareham (HA) 4928	3/08
4929 YN 04 GOC	Sca	K114EB4		1847508	Ir	96193	C49FT	4/04 Luckett, Fareham (HA) 4929	12/05
4943 YN 56 FGM	Sca	K114EB4		1853753	Ir	13215	C49FT	9/06 new	9/06
4947 YN 08 DFD	Sca	K340FR4	YS2K4X20001859622	Ir	131704	C49FT	3/08 new	3/08
4948 YN 08 DFE	Sca	K340EB4		1859620	Ir	131705	C49FT	3/08 new	3/08
4949 DL 03 GRZ	Sca	K114IB4	YS2K4X20001844582	Ir	95614	C49FT	5/03 Luckett, Fareham (HA) 4949	5/14
		(ex 8830 RU 2/08)						
4974 YR 62 EAF	Sca	K340	YS2K4X20001878351	Ir	-?-	C49FT	1/13 new	1/13
5343 YR 02 ZZB	Sca	K114IB4		1841758	Ir	95035	C53F	3/02 Luckett, Fareham (HA) 5343	2/08
5369 YN 13 XYT	Sca	K360IB4	YS2K4X20001883800	Ir	140908	C53F	3/13 new	3/13

3 YN13 XY6 Sca K360EB4 Ir C53Ft 2013

WEST SUSSEX NON-PSV OPERATORS (XWS)

1st CASTLE LGV TRAINING, Springfield Park, CHICHESTER, PO20 1EJ.

NG 04 RVN	Fd	Tt	WF0EXXGBFE3P67386	Fd	M16	6/04 Amalga, Heathrow (YLN)	7/07

1st FELPHAM SEA SCOUTS, c/o 11 The Grove, Felpham, PO22 7EY.

NG 06 LXD	Fd	Tt	WF0EXXTTFE5K10244	Fd	M14	5/06 Transmore Vehicle Hire,	
						Stockton (YCD)	5/11

1ST ROFFEY SCOUT GROUP, Roffey.
No vehicles currently recorded

1st RUSTINGTON Explorer SCOUTS, RUSTINGTON.
CA 05 OZR   Fd   Tt   WF0EXXTTFE5U45569   Fd   M16   8/05 -?-, -?-   4/06

1st SHIPLEY SCOUTS, The Scout Hut, Dragons Green, SHIPLEY, Horsham, RH13 8GE.
No vehicles currently recorded

2nd WORTHING SCOUTS, Bruce Avenue, Worthing, BN11 5LN.
No vehicles currently recorded

2351 BOGNOR REGIS SQUADRON ATC, Bognor Regis.
R319 NRR   LDV Cy   SEYZMYSJEDN030936   LDV   M16   5/98 Ash Lea School,
                                                          Cotgrave (XNG)   3/11

2464 SQUADRON ATC, Washington Road, STORRINGTON, RH20 4RE.
No vehicles currently recorded

ABBEY DEAN CARE HOME, 102 Barnham Road, BARNHAM, PO22 0EW.
No vehicles currently recorded

ACTION FOR BLIND PEOPLE, Norworth, Kings Parade, BOGNOR REGIS, PO21 2QR.
HG 03 JPF   Pt   Bxr   VF3ZCPMNC17200812   RKC   M16   5/03 new   5/03

ADUR COMMUNITY TRANSPORT, Room 5, Shoreham Centre, Pond Road, SHOREHAM, BN43 5WU.
Y336 TKJ   VW   LT46   WV1ZZZ2DZ1H031307   Wre   B8FL   5/01 new   5/01
YK 03 EZV   VW   LT46   WV1ZZZ2DZ2H030916   UVM 9725   M16   5/03 new   5/03
BU 54 GZT   Ft   Do (3 axle)   ZFA24400007410675   Swain   B16FL   10/04 new   10/04

ADUR OUTDOOR ACTIVITIES CENTRE, Brighton Road, SHOREHAM-BY-SEA, BN43 5LT.
HJ 06 VTZ   Pt   Bxr   VF3ZCPMNC17703973   RKC   M16   3/06 new   3/06

AGE CONCERN, The Laburnum Centre, Lyon Street, BOGNOR REGIS, PO21 1UX.
GV 53 WZO   VW   LT35   WV1ZZZ2DZ4H013793   ?   M?L   11/03 -?-, -?-   9/09

AGE CONCERN (Burgess Hill), Fairfield Road, BURGESS HILL, RH15 8QB.
EO 07 DVM   MB   311CDI   WDB9066332S167844   ?   M10L   5/07 new   5/07

AGE CONCERN, Shackleton Road, Tilgate, CRAWLEY, RH10 5DE.
GX 55 GOP   Rt   Mtr   VF1PDMUL633467293   ?   M16L   9/05 -?-, -?-   4/08

AGE CONCERN, 105 Queens Road, EAST GRINSTEAD, RH19 1BE.
No vehicles currently recorded

AGE CONCERN (Haywards Heath), Perrymount Road, HAYWARDS HEATH, RH16 3DN.
EK 09 OES   Fd   Tt   WF0XXXTTFX8C29337   Eurm -?-   M11L   3/09 -?-, -?-   7/09

AGE CONCERN, New Road, SOUTHBOURNE, Emsworth, PO10 8JX.

J875 ODV	MB	308D	WDB6023672P210997	DC	244M	M12L	5/92 new	5/92

AGE UK HORSHAM District, Lavinia House, Dukes Square, Horsham, RH12 1GZ.

BV 53 AVK	Rt	Mtr	VF1FDCUL529156283	?		M??L	12/03 new	12/03
EU 56 EKW	Rt	Mtr	VF1FDCWLH36280365	?		M??	9/06 new	9/06
EU 09 ERX	Rt	Mtr	VF1FDC2L641358248	Stan		M12L	6/09 new	6/09

AGE UK WEST SUSSEX, Suite 2, First Floor, Anchor Springs, LITTLEHAMPTON, BN17 6BP.

R486 TTP	Pt	Bxr	VF3233J5215280708	?		M16	8/97 -?-, -?-	6/10
S634 CBD	Rt	Mtr	VF1FDCEL519342603	?		M16	2/99 -?-, -?-	10/11

The ALDINGBOURNE TRUST, Blackmill Lane, NORTON, Chichester, PO18 0JP.

BJ 07 XHH	Fd	Tt	WF0DXXTTFD7D07593	Fd		M14	6/07 1car1.com (Y)	11/09
NA 07 ASX	Fd	Tt	WF0DXXTTFD6P42031	Fd		M14	3/07 Northgate (Y)	11/09

ALL ABOUT KIDS, Stafford House, 91 Keymer Road, HASSOCKS, BN6 8QJ.

LV 02 XHN	MB	311CDI	WDB9036632R387761	?		M?	7/02 new	7/02
GN 10 KAU	Io	40C12	ZCFC4082005801867	?		M16L	5/10 new	5/10
		(VCGB donation)						
YT 11 YZN	Fd	Tt	WF0DXXTTFDAA85852	Fd		M16	4/11 -?-, -?-	1/13

The ANGMERING SCHOOL, Station Road, ANGMERING, BN16 4HH.

BW 51 OHN	Ctn	Rly	VF7233JL216196474	Km		M16	2/02 pre-registered by dealer	3/02
GX 07 FHS	Fd	Tt	WF0XXXTTFX7C62672	Stan -?-		M16L	4/07 new	4/07
		(Taverners donation, number 02/2007-824)						
HY 60 XNH	Fd	Tt	WF0DXXTTFDAU54588	Fd		M14	9/10 pre-registered by dealer	10/10

ANGMERING YOUTH FORUM, Angmering.

OJD 817Y	MCW	DR101/16	MB7065	MCW		H43/28D	3/83 Archer, Poulton-le-Fylde (LA)	5/08
		(mobile coffee bar / drop-in centre)						

ARDINGLY COLLEGE, ARDINGLY, Haywards Heath, RH17 6SQ.

YC 10 HCN	Fd	Tt	WF0DXXTTFD9E34266	Fd		M14	4/10 new	4/10
YP 60 ABN	Fd	It	WF0DXXTTFDAB17307	Fu		M16	11/10 new	11/10
YP 60 HCU	Fd	Tt	WF0DXXTTFDAR48335	Fd		M14	12/10 new	12/10
YP 60 KJJ	Fd	Tt	WF0DXXTTFDAR48366	Fd		M14	12/10 new	12/10
YR 60 WHC	Fd	Tt	WF0DXXTTFDAB17287	Fd		M16	11/10 new	11/10

ARDINGLY RIDING CLUB, South of England Showground, Ardingly, RH17 6TL.

MRJ 52W	MCW	DR102/21	MB6100	MCW		H--/--F	3/81 Cancer Research Campaign, Hull (XEY)	6/05

ARUN Co-ordinated COMMUNITY TRANSPORT, Unit S3, The Rudford Industrial Estate, Ford Road, ARUNDEL, BN18 0BD.

Arun1	RX 04 UFW	MB	411CDI	WDB9046632R624838	Eurm	M15L	5/04 new	5/04
Arun3	WU 04 FHA	Rt	Mtr	VF1FDCUL631598079	?	M12L	7/04 Bradbury Hotel, East Preston (XWS)	10/14
Arun4	KC 03 LHM	MB	413CDI	WDB9046122R539377	UVM -?-	B16FL	7/03 West Sussex County Council, Chichester (XWS)	by2/15
Arun5	CK 02 VMO	MB	413CDI	WDB9046122R370611	UVG -?-	M16	7/02 West Sussex County Council, Chichester (XWS)	4/09
Arun10	MX 10 EMF	Io	45C15	ZCFC45A2005766361	Cpt	M15L	3/10 new	3/10
		(named *Mary*)						

ARUN TRANSPORT FOR VISUALLY IMPAIRED.
GN 07 TBY   lo   50C15   ZCFC50A2005669089   ?   M16L   7/07 new   7/07

ARUNCARE, 88 Sea Road, East Preston, LITTLEHAMPTON, BN16 1NP.
No vehicles currently recorded

ASDA DAIRY BUS c/o The Staging House Limited, The Studio, Worthing Road, Dial Post, HORSHAM, RH13 8NH.
A629 BCN   MCW   DR102/43   MB7715   MCW   H46/31F   5/84 Chariots, Stanford-le-Hope (EX) 1/09

ASHTON PARK SCHOOL, Brinsbury Campus East, Stane St, North Heath, PULBOROUGH, RH20 1DJ.
OU 12 DJF	MB	313CDI	WDB9066332S682301	O&H -?-	M12	7/12 new	7/12
OU 12 DMO	MB	313CDI	WDB9066332S710593	O&H -?-	M12	8/12 new	8/12
OU 12 DNO	MB	313CDI	WDB9066332S682616	O&H -?-	M12	7/12 new	7/12
OU 12 DNX	MB	313CDI	WDB9066332S683296	O&H -?-	M12	7/12 new	7/12
OU 12 DVT	MB	313CDI	WDB9066332S697744	O&H -?-	M12	8/12 new	8/12
OU 12 DVW	MB	313CDI	WDB9066332S697746	O&H -?-	M12	7/12 new	7/12

AUTOMANIA Garage Services, Units 1 & 2, Forge Wood Industrial Estate, Gatwick Road, CRAWLEY, RH10 9PG.
No vehicles currently recorded

BARCHESTER HEALTHCARE, Westergate House Care Home, FONTWELL, BN18 0SU.
HN 61 CHD   Rt   Mtr   VF1MLJ2DF45828426   ?   M8L   12/11 new   12/11

BARCHESTER HEALTHCARE, Kingsland Close, off Middle Road, SHOREHAM-BY-SEA, BN43 6LT.
RY 54 ERK   Rt   Mtr   VF1FDBVH532493405   Atl   M8L   2/05 new   2/05
HN 61 CJO   Rt   Mtr   VF1MLJ2DF45828439   ?   M8L   12/11 new   12/11

BAY TREE HOUSE Care Home, 28 Chesswood Road, WORTHING, BN11 2AD.
P303 RCW   lo   49.10   ZCFC4970105115686   ?   M?L   9/96 -?-, -?-   4/03

BISHOP LUFFA SCHOOL, Bishop Luffa Close, CHICHESTER, PO19 3LT.
No vehicles currently recorded

BLUEBIRD COMMUNITY PARTNERSHIP, Wivelsden Farm, North Common Road, North Chailey, East Sussex BN8 4EH.
but provides community transport services in the HAYWARDS HEATH/Burgess Hill area of West Sussex.
BU 02 FNF	VW	LT35	WV1ZZZ2DZ2H022164	MCC	M11L	3/02 WMSNT, Birmingham (WMx) 0203	8/10
CK 02 VMR	MB	413CDI	WDB9046122R379696	UVG -?-	B16FL	7/02 West Sussex County Council, Chichester (XWS)	4/09
HV 02 RKA	MB	411CDI	WDB9046632R348343	?	M15L	3/02 EGBus Community Transport, East Grinstead (XWS)	10/10
KC 03 LHK	MB	413CDI	WDB9046122R536546	UVM 9758	B16FL	7/03 West Sussex County Council, Chichester (XWS)	by1/15
KC 03 LHL	MB	413CDI	WDB9046122R539376	UVM -?-	B16FL	7/03 West Sussex County Council, Chichester (XWS)	by8/14
DK 06 EHN	MB	411CDI	WDB9046632R914765	Stan	M16L	3/06 new	3/06
RX 07 PNY	MB	511CDI	WDB9066552S179285	Eurm-?-	M15	6/07 Henfield Community Transport (XWS)	7/10
LK 57 HBP	MB	311CDI	WDB9066332S252154	?	M13L	1/08 -?-, -?-	11/09
LK 08 NDJ	MB	511CDI	WDB9066552S285637	Stan	M16L	5/08 new	5/08

BOURNE COMMUNITY COLLEGE, Park Road, SOUTHBOURNE, PO10 8PJ.
GX 63 YKD   Fd   Tt   WF0DXXTTFDDA09307   Fd   M16   10/13 new   10/13

BRAMBLETYE SCHOOL, EAST GRINSTEAD, RH19 3PD.

LJ 04 JJL	LDV	Cy	SEYZMVSZGDN102220	LDV	M16	3/04	new	3/04
GU 58 CUX	Fd	Tt	WF0DXXTTFD8A53142	Fd	M16	9/08	new	9/08
RX 60 HPF	Pt	Bxr	VF3YCBMFC11831133	?	M16	12/10	new	12/10

BURGESS HILL BOYS' BRIGADE company, Burgess Hill.

N557 LAM	Fd	Tt	SFALXXBDVLSU42262	?	M14	11/95	Expect the Best,	
							Reading (BE) 009	2/99

BURGESS HILL SCHOOL FOR GIRLS, Keymer Road, Burgess Hill, RH15 0EG.

RX 54 CMZ	LDV	Cy	SEYZMVXZGDN107007	LDV	M16	9/04	new	9/04
RX 58 AOS	LDV	Max	SEYL6RXE21N231487	LDV	M16	11/08	new	11/08
HG 09 UCV	Fd	Tt	WF0DXXTTFD9B04830	Fd	M16	6/09	Welwyn & Hatfield 14-19 Consortium,	
							Welwyn Garden City (XHT)	8/12
EU 59 CAE	Fd	Tt	WF0DXXTTFD9D17363	Fd	M16	5/10	-?-, -?-	6/12
HJ 10 VMT	Fd	Tt	WF0DXXTTFD9C71792	Fd	M16	3/10	-?-, -?-	4/13
PY 10 DXJ	Fd	Tt	WF0DXXTTFD9E32474	Fd	M16	6/10	Thrifty (Y)	8/11
GV 60 GEU	Fd	Tt	WF0DXXTTFDAA75490	Fd	M16	1/11	new	1/11
GY 60 XCK	Fd	Tt	WF0DXXTTFDAA75494	Fd	M16	12/10	new	12/10

CAFE ZONE HOLIDAY CLUB, c/o Reflections Nursery, Westerfields House, 54 Richmond Road, WORTHING, West Sussex, BN11 1PS.

N100 BUS	LDV	Max	SEYL6P6A20N211175	LDV	M14	10/06	Easyfleet Vehicle Hire,	
		(ex AE 56 OEW 12/08)					Peterborough (YCM)	10/08

CENTRAL SUSSEX COLLEGE, College Road, CRAWLEY, RH10 1NR.

LF 52 ZFU	LDV	Cy	SEYZMVSYGDN089111	LDV	M16	9/02	new	9/02
BD 07 EDR	Fd	Tt	WF0DXXTTFD7E42516	Fd	M16	7/07	-?-, -?-	10/08
BD 07 EEG	Fd	Tt	WF0DXXTTFD7E42523	Fd	M16	7/07	-?-, -?-	10/08
CN 57 HVV	LDV	Max	SEYL6RXE20N221330	LDV	M16	11/07	Thrifty (Y)	2/11
YM 08 CUO	Fd	Tt	WF0DXXTTFD8K35384	Fd	M16	8/08	Sixt Kenning (Y)	9/10

CHATSMORE Catholic High SCHOOL, Goring Street, WORTHING, BN12 5AF.

No vehicles currently recorded

CHICHESTER & WITTERINGS PHAB CLUB, c/o United Reformed Church, 2 Oakfield Avenue, EAST WITTERING, PO20 8BU.

No vehicles currently recorded

CHICHESTER COLLEGE, Westgate Fields, CHICHESTER, PO19 1SB.

HJ 53 RVM	Pt	Bxr	VF3ZCPMNC17266519	RKC	M16	9/03	new	9/03
PE 04 UBV	Fd	Tt	WF0EXXGBFE3P67620	Fd	M16	3/04	-?-, -?-	2/12
PO 54 AUH	Fd	Tt	WF0EXXTTFE4D00078	Fd	M16	11/04	-?-, -?-	5/12
LX 58 ZXK	Rt	Tc	VF1JLAMA69V332288	Rt	M8	9/08	new	9/08
LX 58 ZXN	Rt	Tc	VF1JLAMA69V332287	Rt	M8	9/08	new	9/08
HN 09 WKE	Fd	Tt	WF0BXXBDFB9M43489	Fd	M8	7/09	-?-, -?-	4/10
HN 09 WKF	Fd	Tt	WF0BXXBDFB9M43679	Fd	M8	7/09	-?-, -?-	4/10
LX 59 EFS	Rt	Mtr	VF1NDD1L642554759	Rt	M15	2/10	new	2/10
HY 60 XRN	Fd	Tt	WF0DXXTTFDAU67711	Fd	M16	9/10	pre-registered by dealer	10/10
LV 11 ORX	Rt	Tc	VF1JLAHASBY386647	Rt	M8	6/11	new	6/11
HK 13 KNM	Fd	Tt	WF0DXXTTFDDR07081	Fd	M13	8/13	new	8/13
HK 13 KNO	Fd	Tt	WF0DXXTTFDDR07101	Fd	M13	8/13	new	8/13

CHICHESTER HIGH SCHOOL for Girls, Kingsham Road, Chichester, PO19 8EB.

S435 KFX	LDV	Cy	SEYZMYSJEDN035249	LDV	M16	8/98	new	8/98
HV 12 XRG	Fd	Tt	WF0DXXTTFDCA89231	Fd	M16	5/12	new	5/12

CHICHESTER LIONS CLUB, c/o Chichester Park Hotel, Madgwick Lane, Chichester, PO19 7QL.

BP 11 JVF	Vx	Viv	W0LF7BHA6BV650917	?	M?	8/11 -?-, -?-	6/12

CHICHESTER NURSERY SCHOOL AND CHILDREN'S CENTRE, St James Road, Chichester, PO19 7AB.

LB 54 LNW	Fd	Tt	WF0EXXTTFE4S73830	Fd	M16	1/05 -?-, -?-	11/08

CHRIST'S HOSPITAL SCHOOL, The Avenue, HORSHAM, RH13 0YP.

Y875 KDY	VW	Ce	WV2ZZZ70Z1H136552	VW	M8	4/01 new	4/01
GU 59 XVP	Fd	Tt	WF0DXXTTFD9G65447	Fd	M16	10/09 new	10/09
GV 59 ONP	Fd	Tt	WF0DXXTTFD9G65473	Fd	M16	1/10 new	1/10
HJ 60 KXE	Fd	Tt	WF0DXXTTFDAT18414	Fd	M16	9/10 new	9/10
HJ 60 KXF	Fd	Tt	WF0DXXTTFDAT18365	Fd	M16	9/10 new	9/10

CONIFERS SCHOOL, Egmont Road, Easebourne, MIDHURST, GU29 9BG.

DN 53 GGK	Fd	Tt	WF0PXXBDFP3J17784	Fd	M11	11/03 -?-, -?-	2/09

CONTACT 88 (Chichester Voluntary Transport for Disabled and Elderly), Tozer Way, CHICHESTER, PO19 7LT.

6 HX 56 BNU	Rt	Mtr	VF1FDCUM632228291	Atl	M8L	12/06 pre-registered by dealer	3/07
7 HY 07 EXF	Rt	Mtr	VF1FDCML636587984	Atl	M14L	4/07 new	4/07
LC 14 WPZ	Ctn	Rly	VF7YCTMFC12633471	?	M8L	6/14 new	6/14

COPTHORNE HOTEL London Gatwick, Copthorne Way, Copthorne, RH10 3PG.

192 COP	Fd	Tt	SFACXXBDVCFK12078	Agh 001188	C7F	12/87 KF Cars, Gatwick (WS)	c4/91

COPTHORNE PREPARATORY SCHOOL, Effingham Lane, COPTHORNE, RH10 3HR.

YJ 02 LKV	Fd	Tt	WF0EXXGBFE1D11792	Fd	M14	3/02 -?-, -?-	8/04
AY 06 XAU	Fd	Tt	WF0EXXTTFE5G69903	Fd	M16	3/06 -?-, -?-	8/08
GX 06 TZZ	Fd	Tt	WF0TXXBDFT6L00375	Fd	M8	3/06 MoD (X)	11/10
			(ex #394923 *(MoD)* 10/10)				
6 YK 59 WVP	Fd	Tt	WF0DXXTTFD9R36346	Fd	M16	9/09 -?-, -?-	1/13
7 MW 10 DWG	Fd	Tt	WF0DXXTTFDAJ42307	Fd	M16	7/10 -?-, -?-	2/14

COUNTRY LODGE NURSING HOME, Cote Street, High Salvington, WORTHING, BN13 3EX.

GU 52 HDD	Rt	Mtr	VF1FDCNL526921681	O&H	M9	11/02 South East Coast Ambulance, Lewes (XES) 321	9/13

CRAWLEY COMMUNITY TRANSPORT Limited, Gleneagles Court, Brighton Road, CRAWLEY.

OU 05 BWF	VW	LT46	WV1ZZZ2DZ4H007093	?	M14L	4/05 West Sussex County Council (XWS)	5/10
BX 60 EJC	Rt	Mtr	VF1MAF4BR43684486	?	M12L	2/11 new	2/11
BX 11 KXV	Rt	Mtr	VF1MAF4BR44828745	MinO	M12L	4/11 new	4/11
BX 11 KYR	Rt	Mtr	VF1MAF4BR44828841	MinO	M12L	4/11 new	4/11
BX 11 KYS	Rt	Mtr	VF1MAF4BE43684537	MinO	M12L	4/11 new	4/11
FJ 11 DBY	Ft	Do	ZFA25000001715063	?	M16L	3/11 new	3/11

CRAWLEY DIAL-a-RIDE, The Trees, 103 High Street, CRAWLEY, RH10 1DD.

GU 52 ZYW	MB	411CDI	WDB9046632R461974	?	M??L	2/03 new	2/03
GN 55 PZV	MB	411CDI	WDB9046632R895739	Eurm -?-	M7L	2/06 -?-, -?-	6/09

CRAWLEY OPEN HOUSE, Riverside House, Stephenson Way, Three Bridges, CRAWLEY, RH10 1TN.

No vehicles currently recorded

CRAWLEY YOUTH CENTRE, Longmore Road, CRAWLEY, RH10 8ND.
No vehicles currently recorded

CUMNOR HOUSE SCHOOL, London Road, Danehill, HAYWARDS HEATH, RH17 7HT.

T544 FJT	Fd	Tt	WF0LXXBDVLWU51439	RKC	M16	5/99 -?-, -?-	11/05
Y841 VGN	Ctn	Rly	VF7233J5216094997	AVB	M16	6/01 new	6/01
HN 57 VFD	Ctn	Rly	VF7YCDMFC11298356	RKC	M16	1/08 Exsportise, Brighton (XES)	8/13
HG 60 CJU	Fd	Tt	WF0DXXTTFDAJ37429	Fd	M14	10/10 new	10/10
HG 60 CJV	Fd	Tt	WF0DXXTTFDAJ37368	Fd	M14	10/10 new	10/10
WA 62 FHV	Pt	Bxr	VF3YCTMFC12212534	GM	M16	11/12 new	11/12
WA 62 FJY	Pt	Bxr	VF3YCTMFC12221368	GM	M16	11/12 new	11/12

DAVISON Church of England HIGH SCHOOL FOR GIRLS, Selborne Road, WORTHING, BN11 2JX.

GU 09 YBC	Fd	Tt	WF0DXXTTFD9M80180	Fd	M14	5/09 new	5/09

DIAL-A-RIDE MOBILITY, WORTHING.

OKZ 8958	MB	311CDI	WDB9036622R832427	?	M??L	9/05 -?-, -?- (NI)	8/10
YX 08 KNN	Rt	Mtr	VF1FDC2L639460934	O&H -?-	M13L	6/08 Cirencester Dial-a-Ride (XGL)	8/12

DIGNITY COMMUNITY MINIBUS, WEST SUSSEX.

VK 13 BJE	Fd	Tt	WF0DXXTTFDDJ44438	Fd	M16	4/13 new	4/13

DORSET HOUSE SCHOOL, The Manor, Church Lane, BURY, Pulborough, RH20 1PB.

GU 11 YPW	Fd	Tt	WF0DXXTTFDAB37767	Fd	M16	3/11 new	3/11
GU 11 YRW	Fd	Tt	WF0DXXTTFDAB37658	Fd	M16	3/11 new	3/11
YS 64 UJP	Fd	Tt	WF0HXXTTGHEA25023	Fd	M11	1/15 new	1/15

DOWNLANDS COMMUNITY SCHOOL, Dale Avenue, HASSOCKS, BN6 8LP.

YJ 55 JWF	LDV	Cy	SEYZMVSZGDN111764	LDV	M16	9/05 new	9/05
YR 13 OEB	Fd	Tt	WF0DXXTTFDDM12264	Fd	M13	5/13 new	5/13

DOWNSBROOK MIDDLE SCHOOL, Dominion Road, WORTHING, BN14 8GD.

HK 60 NVT	Fd	Tt	WF0DXXTTFDAA82701	Fd	M16	2/11 new	2/11

DUDLEY HOUSE TRUST, Dudley House, High Street, HANDCROSS, RH17 6BL.
No vehicles currently recorded

DURRINGTON HIGH SCHOOL, The Boulevard, WORTHING, BN13 1JX.

HT 06 KDZ	Fd	Tt	WF0DXXTTFD6U02060	Fd	M14	8/06 -?-, -?-	12/12
AE 56 GZG	LDV	Max	SEYL6P6B20N209527	LDV	M14	9/06 Global Self Drive, Cambridge (YCM)	2/10
SL 07 KXT	Fd	Tt	WF0DXXTTFD7D16281	Fd	M14	6/07 -?-, -?-	12/12

EARNLEY CONCOURSE, Earnley, CHICHESTER, PO20 7JN.

GN 06 PUK	Io	40C12	ZCFC4081005568645	?	M16L	7/06 new	7/06

EAST GRINSTEAD FOOTBALL ACADEMY, East Court, College Lane, East Grinstead, RH19 3LS.

BX 58 OKN	LDV	Max	SEYL6RXH21N230252	LDV	M16	10/08 Europcar (Y)	9/13

EASTBROOK PRIMARY SCHOOL, Manor Hall Road, SOUTHWICK, Brighton, BN42 4NF.

RJ 06 VHE	Pt	Bxr	VF3ZCPMNC17821566	?	M16	7/06 Portsmouth Grammar School	
			(ex S111 PGS 9/09, RJ 06 VHE by8/09)			(XHA)	11/10

ELAN NURSERY, Chanctonfold, Horsham Road, STEYNING, BN44 3AA.

DS 03 VCA	Fd	Tt	WF0EXXGBFE3Y11536	Fd	M16	7/03 -?-, -?-	10/07

ENGLISH LANGUAGE HOMESTAYS, Global-ATS Building, 25 Cecil Pashley Way, SHOREHAM-BY-SEA, BN43 5FF.
No vehicles currently recorded

ERSKINE DAY NURSERY, Brighton Road, HURSTPIERPOINT, BN6 9EF.
No vehicles currently recorded

FARLINGTON SCHOOL, Strood Park, HORSHAM, RH12 3PN.

PK 54 ZJU	Pt	Bxr	VF3ZCPMNC17404052	Km	M16	11/04 -?-, -?-	12/09
MX 59 PFZ	Pt	Bxr	VF3YCBMFC11700550	?	M16	2/10 new	2/10
YR 10 ZDC	Fd	Tt	WF0DXXTTFDAS89718	Fd	M16	4/10 new	4/10

FARNEY CLOSE SCHOOL, Bolney Court, BOLNEY, Haywards Heath, RH17 5RD.

GN 03 ENR	Io	35S11	ZCFC357100D201972	Eurm -?-	M16L	4/03 new	4/03
		(VCGB donation)					

FELPHAM COMMUNITY COLLEGE, Felpham Way, FELPHAM, Bognor Regis, West Sussex, PO22 8EL.

GY 62 LGL	Fd	Tt	WF0DXXTTFDCY65910	Fd	M14	11/12 new	11/12
GY 13 VEM	Fd	Tt	WF0DXXTTFDCT14362	Fd	M13	6/13 new	6/13

FIRST STEPS DAY NURSERY, Chichester College, Westgate Fields, CHICHESTER, PO19 1SB.

V 34 FEL	Fd	Tt	WF0LXXBDVLWA81564	May	M16	10/99 new	10/99
HJ 53 UAT	Pt	Bxr	VF3ZCPMNC17302704	RKC	M16	10/03 Chichester College (XWS)	by6/13

FORDWATER SCHOOL, Summersdale Road, CHICHESTER, PO19 6PP.

GN 08 VTD	Io	45C15	ZCFC45A200D390991	Eurm -?-	M16L	7/08 new	7/08
		(VCGB donation)					

The FOREST SCHOOL, Comptons Lane, HORSHAM, RH13 5NW.

HJ 03 XML	Pt	Bxr	VF3ZCPMNC17159755	?	M16	4/03 -?-, -?-	1/04
HG 57 EVF	Fd	Tt	WF0DXXTTFD7S36348	Fd	M14	10/07 Ryedale School, Nawton (XNY)	9/12

FREDDYSMILE Childrens Cancer Charity, 40 Leconfield Road, LANCING, BN15 9JB.

NJ 55 YPH	Fd	Tt	WF0EXXTTFE5A48798	Fd	M14	11/05 Northgate (Y)	3/13

GREAT WALSTEAD SCHOOL, East Mascalls Lane, LINDFIELD, RH16 2QL.

GX 63 HJZ	Fd	Tt	WF0DXXTTFDDR72199	Fd	M16	9/13 new	9/13

GUILD CARE, Methold House, North Street, WORTHING, BN11 1DU.

T369 RPG	Rt	Tc	VF1F8ALA520651766	?	M8L	8/99 -?-, -?-	8/00
KE 53 EKR	MB	411CDI	WDB9046632R552425	Eurm -?-	M??L	9/03 new	9/03
RX 54 XJG	MB	411CDI	WDB9046632R733824	Eurm -?-	M12L	2/05 new	2/05
GN 57 ASO	MB	511CDI	WDB9066552S201410	?	M12	9/07 new	9/07
RA 08 YSD	MB	111CDI	WDF63960323424233	Eurm -?-	M??	8/08 new	8/08
RE 11 YZK	MB	513CDI	WDB9066552S551548	Eurm -?-	M12L	6/11 new	6/11
RX 13 FSD	MB	513CDI	WDB9066552S784825	?	M13L	6/13 new	6/13

HANDCROSS District COMMUNITY BUS, Dumbledore, High Street, Handcross, RH17 6BN.

SN 58 BZC	VW	Crf	WV1ZZZ2EZ96006881	Ks	M16	10/08 new	10/08

NOTE: prior to 10/13, vehicles were recorded in the PSV section under licence PKC0002805/CB.

HANDCROSS PARK SCHOOL, HANDCROSS, Haywards Heath, RH17 6HF.

GU 59 FXR	Fd	Tt	WF0DXXTTFD9P87070	Fd	M16	9/09 new	9/09
GU 59 GHA	Fd	Tt	WF0DXXTTFD9P86421	Fd	M16	9/09 new	9/09

HARTING PARISH COUNCIL, North Lane, SOUTH HARTING, GU31 5NN.
FN: Harting Minibus.

YD 09 AUE	MB	311CDI	WDB9066352S361178	?	M16	3/09 converted from van	6/14

HENFIELD & DISTRICT SELF HELP CLUB, Henfield.

GV 56 KWD	Vx	Mov	VN1N9DUL635804254	Vx	M15	10/06 -?-, -?-	8/09

HERONS DALE Primary SCHOOL, Hawkins Crescent, SHOREHAM-BY-SEA, BN 43 6TN.

GN 03 FUJ	VW	LT46	WV1ZZZ2DZ3H023017	Stan 3/554.2	M16L	7/03 London Hire, Rotherhithe (XLN)	11/07
GK 63 LXU	Ft	Do	ZFA25000002470479	?	M16	12/13 new	12/13

HOLLYWYND CARE HOME, 5-9 St Botolphs Road, WORTHING BN11 4JN.
No vehicles currently recorded

The HOLY TRINITY Church of England Secondary SCHOOL, Buckswood Drive, Gossops Green, CRAWLEY, RH11 8JE.

CN 55 EXS	Rt	Mtr	VF1PDMUL633467249	?	M16	1/06 pre-registered by dealer	2/06
BN 15 LGX	Fd	Tt	WF0HXXTTGHEJ19536	Fd	M16	4/15 new	4/15

HOMELINK, The Ark, 1 New Road, LITTLEHAMPTON, BN17 5AX.
No vehicles currently recorded

HORSHAM District COMMUNITY TRANSPORT, Lavinia House, Dukes Square, HORSHAM, RH12 1GZ.

7 BX 11 KXT	Rt	Mtr	VF1MAF4BC44828710	?	M8L	4/11 Crawley Community Transport, Crawley (XWS)	by8/14

HORSHAM LEISURE LINK, Horsham District Council, 1st Floor, North Point, North Street, HORSHAM, RH12 1RL.

AD 53 EEY	Fd	Tt	WF0LXXGBFL3S39020	Stan -?-	M16L	11/03 -?-, -?-	7/06

HORSHAM SEA CADETS (TS GLORY), HORSHAM.

AF 52 OPW	LDV	Cy	SEYZMVSYGDN088705	LDV	M16	10/02 Arriva (Y)	11/06

HORSHAM YOUTH, Hurst Road, HORSHAM, RH12 2DN.

GY 56 BZR	VW	LT35	WV1ZZZ2DZ6H028998	?	M14	9/06 Euro Self Drive, Westham (YES)	4/09

HURST & HASSOCKS COMMUNITY BUS Association, McKenzie House, 2 Station Approach, East Hassocks, BN6 8HN.

BU 06 CUG	MB	413CDI	WDB9046632R607758	Koch	M16L	6/06 Evobus, Coventry (Qd)	4/08

NOTE: prior to 10/13, vehicles were recorded in the PSV section under licence PKC0002674/CB.

HURSTPIERPOINT COLLEGE (Hurst), College Road, Hurstpierpoint, BN6 9JS.

GY 51 PVT	Fd	Tt	WF0EXXGBFE1C06972	Fd	M14	10/01 new	10/01
EU 05 EMF	LDV	Cy	SEYZLWSYGDN111520	LDV	M12	7/05 Servecorp, Burgess Hill (YWS)	10/08
LC 59 WEX	Fd	Tt	WF0DXXTTFD9K09356	Fd	M16	11/09 new	11/09
LC 59 WFE	Fd	Tt	WF0DXXTTFD9K07404	Fd	M14	11/09 new	11/09
LC 59 WFG	Fd	Tt	WF0DXXTTFD9K05900	Fd	M14	11/09 new	11/09
LC 59 WFO	Fd	Tt	WF0BXXBDFB9D56186	Fd	M8	11/09 new	11/09
LC 59 WFX	Fd	Tt	WF0DXXTTFD9K09879	Fd	M16	11/09 new	11/09
LC 59 WGE	Fd	Tt	WF0DXXTTFD9K09866	Fd	M16	11/09 new	11/09
VN 12 GNP	Vx	Mov	W0LMVN4JECB025442	Vx	M16	4/12 -?-, -?-	8/13

IFIELD COMMUNITY COLLEGE, Crawley Avenue, CRAWLEY, RH11 0DB.

RX 57 JDO	LDV	Max	SEYL6RXE20N223211	LDV	M16	2/08 new	2/08
WA 12 HUV	Pt	Bxr	VF3YCTMFC12123615	GM	M16	5/12 new	5/12

IMBERHORNE SCHOOL, Imberhorne Lane, EAST GRINSTEAD, RH19 1QY.

GV 62 KCG	Fd	Tt	WF0DXXTTFDCS00299	Fd	M16	1/13 new	1/13
GX 14 LTK	Fd	Tt	WF0DXXTTFDDC65717	Fd	M16	3/14 new	3/14

The JAIL HOUSE CAFE, 1 Little Park Enterprises, Charlwood Road, IFIELD, Crawley, RH11 0JZ.

TUA 161W	Bd	YMT	KW452429	Pn	8011TC221/S	C53F	3/81 café, Henstridge (XSO)	7/13

Gordon Skeggs t/a JUST UNIQUE Hospitality Vehicles, 5 Lamberhurst, Furnace Green, CRAWLEY, RH10 6SN.

4730 EL	DAF	MB200DKTL600	207800 VH 10466		C49FT	3/82 Marksman, Gatwick (WS)	5/94

(ex RHE 610X 5/88, PWM 123 by2/87, YUG 788X 10/84)

KANGAROOS, Syresham Gardens, HAYWARDS HEATH, RH16 3LB.

X514 OGP	Fd	Tt	WF0LXXGBFLYC34047	Eurm -?-	M12L	12/00 London Borough of Sutton (XLN) S25	5/10
GX 61 AZF	Fd	Tt	WF0XXXTTFXBE21337	Stan -?-	M16L	9/11 new	9/11

(Taverners donation, number 19/2011-984)

KIDZONE, Worthing College, Bolsover Road, WORTHING, BN13 1NS.

No vehicles currently recorded

KINGDOM FAITH CHURCH, Foundry Lane, HORSHAM, RH13 5PX.

No vehicles currently recorded

KNOWLES TOOTH CENTRE, Langton Lane, HURSTPIERPOINT, BN6 9EZ.

RK 02 EKZ	MB	311CDI	WDB9036622R320018	?	M?	4/02 -?-, -?-	2/05

L V S HASSOCKS, London Road, SAYERS COMMON, BN6 9HT.

LR 61 NKJ	Fd	Tt	WF0DXXTTFDBP24391	Fd	M13	1/12 new	1/12
LR 61 NKL	Fd	Tt	WF0DXXTTFDBP24491	Fd	M14	1/12 new	1/12

LADYBIRDS NURSERY SCHOOL, 4th Littlehampton Scout HQ, Linden Park, East Ham Road, LITTLEHAMPTON, BN17 7BH.

RY 02 PKU	Fd	Tt	WF0EXXGBFE2J83952	Fd	M14	6/02 -?-, -?-	7/08

LANCING COLLEGE, Coombes Road, Lancing, BN15 0RW.

HF 54 GKU	Fd	Tt	WF0EXXTTFE4D06622	Fd	M16	9/04 -?-, -?-	10/06
HJ 54 KYO	Pt	Bxr	VF3ZCPMNC17409860	RKC	M16	9/04 -?-, -?-	5/09
HG 55 VSD	Pt	Bxr	VF3ZCPMNC17669638	RKC	M16	1/06 -?-, -?-	10/06
HJ 55 KLP	Pt	Bxr	VF3ZCPMNC17638359	RKC	M16	1/06 -?-, -?-	10/06
HJ 57 RWU	Fd	Tt	WF0DXXTTFD7D11317	Fd	M16	9/07 -?-, -?-	1/11
YP 08 WFF	Fd	Tt	WF0BXXBDFB8G83950	Fd	M8	5/08 -?-, -?-	6/10
HY 12 KCO	Fd	Tt	WF0DXXTTFDCB52735	Fd	M16	3/12 new	3/12
GX 13 UWH	Fd	Tt	WF0DXXTTFDCT15011	Fd	M16	3/13 new	3/13

LANCING YOUTH CENTRE, Penhill Road, LANCING, BN15 8HA.

GN 06 LFM	Fd	Tt	WF0EXXTTFE5C87497	Fd	M16	4/06 new	4/06

LAVANT HOUSE SCHOOL, WEST LAVANT, Chichester, PO18 9AB.

RV 60 DKO	MB	313CDI	WDB9066352S492607	MB	M16	9/10 new	9/10
RV 60 DMU	MB	313CDI	WDB9066352S507211	MB	M16	11/10 new	11/10
RV 60 DMX	MB	313CDI	WDB9066352S505451	MB	M16	11/10 new	11/10
RV 60 DMY	MB	313CDI	WDB9066352S508083	MB	M16	11/10 new	11/10

LAVENDER LODGE CARE HOME, 32 Mill Road, WORTHING BN11 5DR.

ML 05 UAR	Rt	Mtr	VF1FDBVH533862973	?	M??	6/05 -?-, -?-	5/11

The LITTLEHAMPTON ACADEMY, Hill Road, LITTLEHAMPTON, West Sussex, BN17 6DQ.

LB 05 HHS	Fd	Tt	WF0EXXTTFE5P86059	Fd	M14	6/05 Nehemiah Project, Streatham (XLN)	9/10
AK 10 CCU	Fd	Tt	WF0DXXTTFDAY68710	Fd	M16	3/10 -?-, -?-	9/10

LITTLEHAMPTON TOWN FOOTBALL CLUB, Littlehampton.

V260 FRV	LDV	Cy	SEYZKSFXCDN053265	?	M16	10/99 -?-, -?-	12/03

LITTLEHAMPTON & RUSTINGTON HOUSING SOCIETY, Rustington Hall, Station Road, Rustington, BN16 3AY.

X307 FGC	Ctn	Rly	VF7233J4215930417	?	M?	9/00 new	9/00
LJ 62 GKY	Ctn	Rly	VF7YDTMFC12288888	?	M8L	11/12 new	11/12

LODGE HILL CENTRE, Watersfield, PULBOROUGH, RH20 1LZ.

X931 HBP	Fd	Tt	WF0EXXBDVEXJ53735	Fd	M14	11/00 -?-, -?-	6/08

MANOR GREEN COLLEGE, Lady Margaret Road, Ifield, CRAWLEY, RH11 0DX.

GX 04 GMG	Fd	Tt	WF0EXXGBFE3M48001	Fd	M16	5/04 new	5/04
GN 54 BVL	Io	45C13	ZCFC459000D232908	Eurm -?-	M16L	9/04 new	9/04
GX 06 EWA	Fd	Tt	WF0EXXTTFE5M51669	Fd	M16	4/06 new	4/06
			(Taverners donation number 2/2006-778)				
GN 11 KKA	Ft	Do	ZFA25000001916415	Eurm -?-	M12L	6/11 new	6/11
			(VCGB donation, number 5119)				

MIDHURST COMMUNITY BUS Association, The Grange Centre, Bepton Road, Midhurst, GU29 9HD.

MX 56 HWA	MB	811D	WDB6683222N124493	Me -?-	B16FL	9/06 new	9/06

NOTE: prior to 10/13, vehicles were recorded in the PSV section under licence PKC0002796/CB.

MIDHURST ROTHER COLLEGE, North Street, MIDHURST, GU29 9DT.

HT 57 BUW	Fd	Tt	WF0DXXTTFD7S20922	Fd	M16	1/08 Midhurst Grammar School (XWS)	1/09
GU 13 FPG	Fd	Tt	WF0DXXTTFDCY56970	Fd	M16	4/13 new	4/13

MILLAIS SCHOOL, Depot Road, HORSHAM, RH13 5HR.

HG 53 NSY	Pt	Bxr	VF3ZCPMNC17302743	RKC	M16	1/04 new	1/04
YP 13 KLC	Fd	Tt	WF0DXXTTFDDM07914	Fd	M16	5/13 new	5/13

NEW LIFE CHURCH, 10 Greenland Road, DURRINGTON, Worthing, BN13 2RR.
No vehicles currently recorded

NORTHBROOK COLLEGE, Broadwater Road, WORTHING, BN14 8HJ.

HY 59 GXS	Fd	Tt	WF0DXXTTFD9R25974	Fd	M16	9/09 -?-, -?-	8/10

OAK GROVE COLLEGE, The Boulevard, WORTHING, BN13 1JX.

HY 57 UMT	Pt	Bxr	VF3YCDMFC11127514	RKC	M16	9/07 new	9/07
HY 57 UMU	Pt	Bxr	VF3YCDMFC11131276	RKC	M16	9/07 new	9/07

OAKMEEDS COMMUNITY COLLEGE, Station Road, BURGESS HILL, RH15 9EA.

FX 08 YLA	Fd	Tt	WF0DXXTTFD8B88731	Fd	M16	3/08 new	3/08
LJ 62 JFO	Ft	Do	ZFA25000002092782	?	M13L	10/12 pre-registered by dealer	12/12

OATHALL COMMUNITY COLLEGE, Appledore Gardens, HAYWARDS HEATH, RH16 2AQ.

KV 05 UGY	Fd	Tt	WF0EXXTTFE5M66197	Fd	M16	3/05 new	3/05
YH 58 EZN	Fd	Tt	WF0DXXTTFD8B89809	Fd	M14	9/08 new	9/08

OFFINGTON PARK METHODIST CHURCH, South Park Road, WORTHING, BN14 7TN.

WX 04 FWB	Rt	Mtr	VF1PDMVL531625532	?	M16	7/04 -?-, -?-	8/07

ORCHARDS Community Middle SCHOOL, Nelson Road, Goring-by-Sea, WORTHING, BN12 6EN.

HX 61 HCA	Pt	Bxr	VF3YEHMFC12058126	RKC	M16	1/12 new	1/12

ORIEL HIGH SCHOOL, Maidenbower Lane, Maidenbower, CRAWLEY, RH10 7XW.

PE 56 KMZ	Pt	Bxr	VF3ZCPMNC17790310	Km	M16	11/06 new	11/06

OUR LADY OF SION SCHOOL, Gratwicke Road, WORTHING, BN11 4BL.

YK 53 HAA	LDV	Cy	SEYZMVSYGDN093795	LDV	M16	12/03 pre-registered by dealer	2/04
RV 58 ORO	Pt	Bxr	VF3YCBMFC11500721	?	M16	9/08 new	9/08
GU 59 FYJ	Fd	Tt	WF0DXXTTFD9P86503	Fd	M16	9/09 Shoreham College, Shoreham (XWS) 1	6/14
GU 59 MYX	Fd	Tt	WF0DXXTTFD9B10876	Fd	M16	9/09 new	9/09
GU 12 ZHG	Fd	Tt	WF0DXXTTFDBM06205	Fd	M16	3/12 new	3/12

PC POWER DOWN Limited, The Priory, Syresham Gardens, BURGESS HILL, RH16 3LB.

K777 DAO	Vo	B10M-55	YV31MGB19PA031597	Ar	27PS/3492/6	DP48F	5/93 Big Lemon, Brighton (ES)	6/11

PAGHAM & District RESIDENTS ASSOCIATION, Pagham.

HK 55 BYO	Rt	Mtr	VF1FDCVL534863747	?	M15	2/06 new	2/06

PALATINE SCHOOL, Palatine Road, WORTHING, BN12 6JP.

GN 12 GYS	Ft	Do	ZFA25000002072914	?	M16L	5/12 new	5/12

(VCGB donation, number 5183)

PENNTHORPE SCHOOL, Church Street, RUDGWICK, RH12 3HJ.

Y773 XCW	Pt	Bxr	VF3233JL216050455	Km	M16	3/01 new		3/01
HJ 54 XFN	Pt	Bxr	VF3ZCPMNC17487556	RKC	M16	9/04 pre-registered by dealer		11/04
LX 61 BFE	Rt	Mtr	VF1MEN4JE45894562	Rt	M16	10/11 new		10/11
LX 12 BGV	Rt	Mtr	VF1MEN4JE46765130	?	M16	3/12 new		3/12

PIONEER CHILDCARE, 30 Marchants Road, HURSTPIERPOINT, BN6 9UU.

BV 58 GNJ	Fd	Tt	WF0DXXTTFD8K40154	Fd	M16	9/08 Midhire, Birmingham (XWM)	7/13
YS 12 ELO	Fd	Tt	WF0DXXTTFDBP26749	Fd	M16	7/12 new	7/12
YT 14 UUD	Fd	Tt	WF0DXXTTFDDK73522	Fd	M16	4/14 new	4/14
YT 14 UVH	Fd	Tt	WF0DXXTTFDDK73538	Fd	M16	3/14 new	3/14

The QUEEN ALEXANDRA HOME for Disabled ex-Servicemen, Boundary Road, WORTHING, BN11 4LJ.

Y663 NAY	Ds	Jv	SFD731BR4YGJ52307	Mpo -?-	C14FTL	3/01 new	3/01

QUEEN ELIZABETH II SILVER JUBILEE SCHOOL, Comptons Lane, HORSHAM, RH13 5NW.

X 83 MKM	Fd	Tt	WF0LXXBDVLYC08471	Eurm -?-	M13L	10/00 new	10/00
GN 06 OXK	Io	45C14	ZCFC45A100D299668	Eurm -?-	M16L	5/06 new	5/06

RAF Benevolent Fund, Princess Marina House, Seafield Road, RUSTINGTON BN16 2JG.

FJ 09 DXH	Ta	XZB50R	TW1FC518306000259	Co -?-	C16FL	4/09 new	4/09
EX 10 RAF	MB	513CDI	WDB9066572S440656	Stan -?-	M14L	4/10 new	4/10

RAFA (Royal Air Force Association) BRANCH 761, The Harbour Club, Harbour Way, SHOREHAM-BY-SEA, BN43 5HG.

J111 RAF	Ctn	Rly	VF7YCBMFC11129547	AVB	M16	6/07 -?-, -?-	4/11
		(ex FN 07 DZR 5/11)					

RSPCA, Wilberforce Way, HORSHAM, RH13 9RS.

No vehicles currently recorded

RED OAKS CARE HOME, The Hooks, HENFIELD, BN5 9UY.

HY 08 WLN	Rt	Mtr	VF1FDB2H639031240	?	M8L	3/08 new	3/08

REGIS SCHOOL, Westloats Lane, Bognor Regis, PO21 5LH.

HN 58 LLE	Fd	Tt	WF0DXXTTFD8Y27995	Fd	M16	11/08 -?-, -?-	8/09
HV 11 TLY	Fd	Tt	WF0DXXTTFDBC42835	Fd	M14	4/11 new	4/11

RICHARD COLLYER COLLEGE, Hurst Road, HORSHAM, RH12 2EJ.

YG 56 FHV	Fd	Tt	WF0DXXTTFD6P51679	Fd	M14	11/06 -?-, -?-	5/07

ROCKING HORSE, Chalkhill Unit, Princess Royal Hospital, Lewes Road, HAYWARDS HEATH, RH16 4EX.

BX 59 LZD	Rt	Mtr	VF1FDC2L641124750	?	M12L	11/09 new	11/09

ROUNDABOUT HOUSE KIDZ CLUB, Albemarle Centre, Oathall Community College, Appledore Gardens, HAYWARDS HEATH,West Sussex RH16 2AQ.

YG 58 SVZ	Fd	Tt	WF0DXXTTFD8K38058	Fd	M16	9/08 new	9/08

RYDON COMMUNITY COLLEGE, Rock Road, STORRINGTON, Pulborough, RH20 3AA.

HJ 03 JFF	Pt	Bxr	VF3ZCPMNC17160063	RKC	M16	3/03 new	3/03

ST ANDREWS C of E High SCHOOL for Boys, Sackville Road, WORTHING, BN14 8BG.

GY 58 UOG	Fd	Tt	WF0DXXTTFD8Y40998	Fd	M16	12/08 new	12/08

ST ANTHONY'S SCHOOL, Woodlands Lane, CHICHESTER, PO19 5PA.

W926 PAP	Fd	Tt	WF0EXXBDVEXP65834	Fd	M14	7/00 new	7/00
			(Taverners' donation)				
LD 57 DKU	Ctn	Rly	VF7YCBMFC11200247	?	M8L	9/07 new	9/07

ST BARNABAS HOUSE, Titnore Lane, WORTHING, BN12 6NZ.

LJ 55 JVV	VW	LT46	WV1ZZZ2DZ6H016575	Stan -?-	M16L	2/06 new	2/06

ST BRIDGET'S CHESHIRE HOME, Ilex Close, RUSTINGTON, BN16 2RX.

W754 TJH	Rt	Mtr	VF1FDCEH521988572	?	M8L	5/00 new	5/00

ST CATHERINE'S HOSPICE, Malthouse Road, CRAWLEY, RH10 6BH.

Y425 GCD	Fd	Tt	WF0LXXGBFLYS69589	?	M??L	5/01 new	5/01

ST JOHN'S CHURCH, Main Road, SOUTHBOURNE, PO10 8PD.

TND 409X	DAF	MB200DKTL600	222158	Pn	8212DKS5C017	C51DL	5/82 Emsworth & District,	
		(mobile outreach unit)					Southbourne (WS)	10/13

ST PAUL'S CATHOLIC COLLEGE, Jane Murray Way, BURGESS HILL RH15 8GA.

GU 07 NCJ	Fd	Tt	WF0DXXTTFD6G31909	Fd	M16	3/07 new	3/07
YL 07 FMJ	Fd	Tt	WF0DXXTTFD7E49274	Fd	M16	7/07 new	7/07
YH 58 FKD	Fd	Tt	WF0DXXTTFD8A53166	Fd	M14	11/08 new	11/08
LJ 62 JGV	Ft	Do	ZFA25000002095364	?	M13	10/12 pre-registered by dealer	12/12

ST PETER'S CHURCH, SELSEY, PO20 0NA.

No vehicles currently recorded

ST PHILIP HOWARD Catholic HIGH SCHOOL, Elm Grove South, BARNHAM, PO22 0EN.

HN 09 JYX	Fd	Tt	WF0DXXTTFD9B13118	Fd	M16	7/09 -?-, -?-	4/10
YR 62 CNV	Fd	Tt	WF0DXXTTFDCD18397	Fd	M16	9/12 new	9/12

SACKVILLE SCHOOL, Lewes Road, EAST GRINSTEAD, RH19 3TY.

LJ 55 AWH	LDV	Cy	SEYZMVSZGDN111730	LDV	M16	12/05 Sixt Kenning (Y)	7/08
LJ 55 AWO	LDV	Cy	SEYZMVSZGDN111715	LDV	M16	12/05 Sixt Kenning (Y)	7/08
YT 08 URO	Fd	Tt	WF0DXXTTFD8B88074	Fd	M16	3/08 Sixt Kenning (Y)	11/10
WF 63 JYX	Pt	Bxr	VF3YCTMFC12463070	GM	M16	9/13 new	9/13

SALVINGTON LODGE, Salvington Hill, WORTHING, BN13 3BW.

No vehicles currently recorded

SAMMY COMMUNITY TRANSPORT Limited, 285 Chichester Road, Bognor Regis, PO21 5AH.

HN 02 BFY	Rt	Mtr	VF1FDCNL526406029	?	M16L	4/02 new	4/02
HY 06 FTX	Rt	Mtr	VF1FDCVL535756494	Atl	M13L	7/06 new	7/06
HY 06 FTZ	Rt	Mtr	VF1FDCVL535756485	Atl	M13L	7/06 new	7/06
		(named *Sammy 3*)					
HY 06 FUA	Rt	Mtr	VF1FDCVL535756464	Atl	M13L	7/06 new	7/06
GK 63 OTB	Ft	Do	ZFA25000002496463	?	M11L	1/14 new	1/14
GN 14 DVW	Ft	Do	ZFA25000002512743	?	M16L	4/14 new	4/14

SEAFORD COLLEGE, Lavington Park, PETWORTH, GU28 0NB.

	HJ 56 VPF	Fd	Tt	WF0DXXTTFD6M31929	Fd	M16	9/06 Ousedale School,	
							Newport Pagnell (XBK)	10/11
	HJ 57 RWV	Fd	Tt	WF0DXXTTFD7D11320	Fd	M16	9/07 -?-, -?-	9/12
SEA007	HJ 60 KXU	Fd	Tt	WF0DXXTTFD9K12058	Fd	M16	9/10 -?-, -?-	9/13
SEA008	LN 62 TXU	Fd	Tt	WF0DXXTTFDCK81144	Fd	M16	9/12 -?-, -?-	9/14

SEAHORSES SWIMMING CLUB, Dolphin Leisure Centre, Pasture Hill Road, HAYWARDS HEATH, RH16 1LY.

R795 GNJ	LDV	400	SEYZNHPFEDN022016	Cu	6400	B??FL	11/97 new	11/97

SEAL Primary ACADEMY, East Street, SELSEY, PO20 0BN.

YS 63 NMX	Fd	Tt	WF0DXXTTFDDA28474	Fd	M16	3/14 new	3/14

SELSEY COMMUNITY BUS Association, Selsey.

MX 10 DVH	Io	45C15	ZCFC45A2005760544	?	M15L	3/10 new	3/10

SELSEY VENTURE CLUB, Clifford Rhodes House, Elm Grove, SELSEY, Chichester, PO20 0RP.

HN 52 KMO	MB	411CDI	WDB9046632R447022	?	M16L	12/02 new	12/02
HX 54 EGC	MB	411CDI	WDB9046632R686810	?	M14	11/04 new	11/04
HX 09 CVN	MB	411CDI	WDB9066552S393081	?	M14	7/09 new	7/09

SHAW HEALTHCARE (FM Services) Limited, 1 Links Court, Links Business Park, St Mellons, Cardiff.
OCs: various locations within West Sussex and the nominal location used will be CRAWLEY.

BX 11 KYN	Rt	Mtr	VF1MAF4BE44663453	MinO	M13L	6/11 new	6/11
FJ 11 DFF	Ft	Do	ZFA25000001885342	MinO	M13L	4/11 new	4/11
FJ 61 BVS	Ft	Do	ZFA25000002080659	MinO	M13L	12/11 new	12/11
FJ 61 BVT	Ft	Do	ZFA25000002067552	MinO	M13L	12/11 new	12/11

SHOREHAM ACADEMY, Kingston Lane, SHOREHAM-BY-SEA, BN43 6YT.

BL 57 XHG	Fd	Tt	WF0DXXTTFD7M13440	Fd	M14	12/07 -?-, -?-	11/10
BK 58 ACV	Fd	Tt	WF0DXXTTFD7P53660	Fd	M14	3/08 -?-, -?-	9/10

SHOREHAM COLLEGE, St Julians Lane, Shoreham-by-Sea, BN43 6YW.

1	GX 14 LHZ	Fd	Tt	WF0DXXTTFDDC57160	Fd	M16	4/14 new	4/14
2	GX 14 LJZ	Fd	Tt	WF0DXXTTFDDC54136	Fd	M16	4/14 new	4/14
3	GX 14 LNO	Fd	Tt	WF0DXXTTFDDC57225	Fd	M16	4/14 new	4/14
4	GX 14 LOA	Fd	Tt	WF0DXXTTFDDC57134	Fd	M16	4/14 new	4/14
5	GX 14 LSV	Fd	Tt	WF0DXXTTFDDC62720	Fd	M16	4/14 new	4/14
6	GX 14 LSY	Fd	Tt	WF0DXXTTFDDB65172	Fd	M16	4/14 new	4/14
7	GX 14 LTN	Fd	Tt	WF0DXXTTFDDC57204	Fd	M16	4/14 new	4/14

SIR ROBERT WOODARD ACADEMY, Upper Boundstone Lane, LANCING, BN15 9QZ.

HX 60 EFH	Pt	Bxr	VF3YCBMFC11669400	RKC	M16	9/10 new	9/10

SLINDON COLLEGE, Top Road, Slindon, Arundel, BN18 0RH.

GP 10 ABU	Fd	Tt	WF0DXXTTFDAU55427	Fd	M14	7/08 new	7/08
GU 62 EXK	Fd	Tt	WF0DXXTTFDCB44704	Fd	M16	9/12 new	9/12

SLINFOLD MINIBUS CLUB, Slinfold.

NL 02 FKJ	Fd	Tt	WF0EXXGBFE2Y86517	Fd	M14	5/02 Groundstar,	
							Newcastle Airport (YTW)	10/05

SOMPTING ABBOTTS SCHOOL, Church Lane, SOMPTING, Lancing, BN15 0AZ.

AO 52 VAK	Fd	Tt	WF0TXXGBFT2R88064	Fd	M8	12/02 -?-, -?-	8/05
GY 09 NUV	Fd	Tt	WF0BXXBDFB9P44842	Fd	M8	6/09 pre-registered by dealer	9/09

SOUTHWATER GUIDES, Shipley Road, Southwater, HORSHAM, RH13 9BG.

GV 05 YLT	Fd	Tt	WF0EXXTTFE5B15915	Fd	M16	6/05 new	6/05

The SPRINGBOARD PROJECT, 52 Hurst Road, HORSHAM, RH12 2EP.

GR 04 ECN	Fd	Tt	WF0EXXGBFE3P61134	Fd	M14	7/04 -?-, -?-	7/06
WA 08 ULB	Fd	Tt	WF0XXXTTFX8R15122	GM	M16L	7/08 -?-, -?-	11/11
GN 10 FXC	Io	50C15	ZCFC50A2005686415	Eurm -?-	M16L	4/10 new	4/10
GN 10 FXD	Io	45C15	ZCFC45A2005755417	?	M16L	4/10 new	4/10

STEYNING GRAMMAR SCHOOL, Shooting Field, STEYNING, BN44 3RX.

RX 57 BSU	LDV	Max	SEYL6RXE20N217664	LDV	M16	9/07 new	9/07
RX 57 BSV	LDV	Max	SEYL6RXE20N216576	LDV	M16	9/07 new	9/07
GY 11 EFK	Fd	Tt	WF0DXXTTFDBC36533	Fd	M14	3/11 new	3/11
GU 13 KAA	Fd	Tt	WF0DXXTTFDDU73299	Fd	M13	3/13 new	3/13

STORM MINISTRIES, 19 Ardsheal Road, WORTHING, BN14 7RN.

P144 NBP	LDV	Cy	SEYZMYSFEDN016302	LDV	M16	4/97 new	4/97

The SUSSEX COLLEGE OF GOLF, East Mascalls Lane, LINDFIELD, Haywards Heath, RH16 2QN.

GY 05 VSX	Fd	Tt	WF0EXXTTFE5M67421	Fd	M16	5/05 -?-, -?-	9/07

SUSSEX HEALTH CARE, Tylden House, Dorking Road, WARNHAM, RH12 3RZ.

X239 KVN	Rt	Mtr	VF3PDMEL523149052	Me 11111	M16	2/01 Enterprise Rent-a-car (Y)	9/04
LY 52 ZFV	Rt	Mtr	VF1PDMML527948863	Me 11715	M16	2/03 -?-, -?-	5/06
GN 03 WBK	MB	411CDI	WDB9046632R484111	?	M??L	4/03 new	4/03
PJ 53 UPY	Rt	Mtr	VF1PDMVL529945719	Me 11911	M16	2/04 Read, Beeston Regis (NK)	2/08
EU 04 KZW	Rt	Mtr	VF1FDCVL529796807	?	M13L	3/04 new	3/04
HX 04 NRE	Rt	Mtr	VF1PDMVL529945738	Me 11932	M14	3/04 -?-, -?-	2/06
EU 54 SZC	Rt	Mtr	VF1FDCVL532498569	Stan -?-	M8L	11/04 new	11/04
EU 54 SZT	Rt	Mtr	VF1FDCVL532902392	Stan -?-	M8L	1/05 new	1/05
VX 54 LSZ	Rt	Mtr	VF1PDMUL632141237	Me 12097	M16	11/04 -?-, -?-	4/06
EU 55 KUH	Rt	Mtr	VF1FDCVL534824056	?	M8L	11/05 new	11/05
EU 55 KWF	Rt	Mtr	VF1FDCVL535054426	Stan -?-	M8L	1/06 new	1/06
EU 06 EWP	Rt	Mtr	VF1FDCVL535732278	?	M13L	7/06 new	7/06
EY 57 ACU	Rt	Mtr	VF1FDC2L638188559	?	M13L	10/07 new	10/07
RX 57 MTU	Rt	Mtr	VF1NDD2L638618849	Rt	M15	11/07 University of Surrey, Guildford (XSR)	9/10
YA 57 XCG	Rt	Mtr	VF1FDC2L638956997	?	M8L	1/08 -?-, -?-	9/09
EU 08 KAX	Rt	Mtr	VF1FDC2L639822272	Stan -?-	M13L	6/08 new	6/08
LT 08 TCK	Rt	Mtr	VF1PDM2L638608890	?	M16	3/08 -?-, -?-	2/10
EU 58 EBM	Rt	Mtr	VF1FDC2L640034432	?	M12	10/08 new	10/08
EU 10 EBV	Rt	Mtr	VF1FDC2L642303934	?	M12L	7/10 new	7/10
BJ 12 YBM	Fd	Tt	WF0DXXTTFDCC47756	Fd	M16	7/12 Hertz (Y)	9/13

SUSSEX WASTE RECYCLING Ltd., Unit 2, Chartwell Road, LANCING, BN15 8TU.

SWB 287L	Ld	AN68/1R	7204459	Ar AL13/2170/3	O43/31F	3/73 Guide Friday (WK)	7/04

TANBRIDGE HOUSE SCHOOL, Farthings Hill, Guildford Road, HORSHAM, RH12 1SR.

GY 56 SYX	Vx	Mov	VN1P9MUL636069243	?	M16	9/06 pre-registered by dealer	10/06
LK 56 GVM	Rt	Mtr	VF1NDDML636443279	Rt	M15	11/06 KICC, Hackney (XLN)	1/10

TANDEM, The Grange, MIDHURST, GU29 9HD.

HV 52 NDN	Ctn	Rly	VF7ZBRMNB17096432	Atl	M8L	9/02 new		9/02
HY 06 BUV	Rt	Mtr	VF1FDBUH635446498	?	M8L	6/06 new		6/06
GN 57 FBU	Io	50C15	ZCFC50A2005689186	?	M14L	9/07 new		9/07

TANYA'S TINKERS, 39 Kipling Avenue, GORING-BY-SEA, BN12 6LQ.

SM 04 HYX	Fd	Tt	WF0EXXGBFE3P71613	Fd	M14	4/04 -?-, -?-	5/10

TAVISTOCK & SUMMERHILL SCHOOL, Summerhill Lane, HAYWARDS HEATH, RH16 1RP.

YK 56 MKZ	Fd	Tt	WF0DXXTTFD6U12873	Fd	M16	9/06 new	9/06
YK 58 JRV	Fd	Tt	WF0DXXTTFD8D76516	Fd	M16	9/08 new	9/08

THE ACADEMY, School Lane, SELSEY, Chichester, PO20 9EH.

HN 58 ZDJ	Pt	Bxr	VF3YCBMFC11565853	RKC	M16	2/09 new	2/09

THE POINT (SCOPE WEST SUSSEX), Sunray Building, Little Breach, CHICHESTER, PO19 5UA.

LA 05 FGP	Ctn	Rly	VF7ZCPMNC17611101	?	M6L	8/05 new	8/05
LJ 09 MJF	Ctn	Rly	VF7YCDMFC11628124	?	M8L	3/09 new	3/09
LJ 61 BZL	Ctn	Rly	VF7YCBMFC12097190	?	M8L	12/11 new	12/11

THE PREBENDAL SCHOOL, 54 West Street, CHICHESTER, PO19 1RT.

HK 07 MJF	Pt	Bxr	VF3CPMNC17826609	RKC	M16	7/07 new	7/07

THE REDEEMED CHRISTIAN CHURCH OF GOD, Albemarle Centre, HAYWARDS HEATH, RH15 0RB.

BU 54 DDZ	LDV	Cy	SEYZLWSYGDN101753	LDV	M12	11/04 Practical (Y)	8/11

THE REDEEMED CHRISTIAN CHURCH OF GOD, East Worthing Community Centre, Pages Lane, WORTHING, BN11 2NQ.

No vehicles currently recorded

THE WEALD SCHOOL, Station Road, BILLINGSHURST, RH14 9RY.

GU 07 FMV	Fd	Tt	WF0DXXTTFD07K76718	Fd	M16	3/07 new	3/07
GU 07 FSV	Fd	Tt	WF0DXXTTFD7K76721	Fd	M16	4/07 new	4/07

THOMAS A BECKET Middle SCHOOL, Glebeside Avenue, WORTHING, BN14 7PR.

R248 FMJ	Fd	Tt	WF0FXXBDVFWY22904	Fd	M8	5/98 new	5/98
HN 10 ZYZ	Fd	Tt	WF0DXXTTFDAJ43471	Fd	M13	6/10 pre-registered by dealer	8/10

THOMAS BENNETT Community COLLEGE, Ashdown Drive, Tilgate, CRAWLEY, RH10 5AD.

X761 WFX	Ft	Do	ZFA23000005945693	RKC	M16	9/00 new	9/00
X762 WFX	Ft	Do	ZFA23000005929112	RKC	M16	9/00 new	9/00
CN 09 AOE	Ft	Do	ZFA25000001413913	?	M16	3/09 -?-, -?-	10/09

TIC TOC PLAY CLUBS Limited, 40 Busticle Lane, SOMPTING, Lancing, BN15 0DJ.

GU 08 ACZ	Fd	Tt	WF0DXXTTFD8B74702	Fd	M16	3/08 Gapton Vehicle Hire, Great Yarmouth (YNK)	11/11

The TOWERS CONVENT SCHOOL, Henfield Road, UPPER BEEDING, BN44 3TF.

1	GU 58 CZB	Fd	Tt	WF0DXXTTFD8D66462	Fd	M16	9/08 -?-, -?-	9/11
2	GY 62 XPS	Fd	Tt	WF0DXXTTFDCY69241	Fd	M16	12/12 new	12/12
3	GY 61 VYX	Fd	Tt	WF0DXXTTFDBM82703	Fd	M16	1/12 new	1/12
4	GY 12 OCS	Fd	Tt	WF0DXXTTFDCB50426	Fd	M16	4/12 new	4/12
5	GV 10 ZWR	Fd	Tt	WF0DXXTTFDAJ32104	Fd	M16	7/10 new	7/10
6	SJ 09 VXD	Fd	Tt	WF0DXXTTFD8Y38067	Fd	M16	3/09 Homefield Preparatory School, Sutton (XLN)	4/15

TS IMPLACABLE (NAUTICAL TRAINING CORPS), 50th Division, 72 Wick Farm Road, Wick, LITTLEHAMPTON, West Sussex, BN17 7HG.

No vehicles currently recorded

T S INTREPID N T C [Training Ship Intrepid Nautical Training Corps], Lancing APC College, Grinstead Lane, LANCING, BN15 9DP.

EF 05 YDR	Fd	Tt	WF0EXXTTFE5B06155	Fd	M16	6/05 Bedford High School, Bedford (XBD)	12/12

TULLETT Plant and COMMERCIAL Services Limited, Pond Lane, Durrington, WORTHING, BN13 2RH.

B803 AOP	MCW	DR102/27 (immobile office)	MB7877	MCW	H--/--F	10/84 Archer, Poulton (LA)	4/13

UNIVERSITY OF CHICHESTER, College Lane, CHICHESTER, PO19 6PE.

GU 62 PJX	Fd	Tt	WF0DXXTTFDBP40240	Fd	M16	9/12 new	9/12
GX 63 DFE	Fd	Tt	WF0DXXTTFDDR02780	Fd	M16	9/13 new	9/13

UNSOLVED? YOUTH GROUP, The Weald Community Church, The Smithy, Bolney Road, COWFOLD, RH13 8AA.

RX 53 NXM	LDV	Cy	SEYZMVXZGDN098068	LDV	M16	9/03 Burgess Hill School For Girls (XWS)	9/12

VILLAGE BUS Committee of Amberley & Slindon, Pump Cottage, Church Hill, SLINDON, Arundel.

SN 09 EMV	VW	Crf	WV1ZZZ2EZ76036084	VDL Kusters	M16L	4/09 new	4/09

NOTE: prior to 10/13, vehicles were recorded in the PSV section under licence PKC0001405/CB.

Kew Botanical Gardens {WAKEHURST PLACE}, Wakehurst Place, ARDINGLY, Haywards Heath, RH17 6TN.

LN 02 HXR	MB	313CDI	WDB9036622R361178	?	M?	5/02 new	5/02

WARDEN PARK SCHOOL, Broad Street, CUCKFIELD, Haywards Heath, RH17 5DP.

PN 52 NBY	Fd	Tt	WF0EXXGBFF2S26999	Fd	M14	9/02 -?-, -?-	9/06
BV 53 CEN	LDV	Cy	SEYZMVSYGDN099890	LDV	M16	12/03 -?-, -?-	4/06

WEST SUSSEX COUNTY COUNCIL, County Hall, West Street, CHICHESTER, PO19 1RQ.

ANA 565Y	Ld	AN68D/1R (tree lopper)	8200807	NC 2298	O--/--F	10/82 Ryan, Langridge (SO)	8/07
KC 03 LHH	MB	413CDI	WDB9046122R539017	UVM -?-	B16FL	7/03 Medway Council, Rochester (XKT)	by10/10
KC 03 LHJ	MB	413CDI	WDB9046122R536545	UVM 9757	B16FL	7/03 Medway Council, Rochester (XKT)	by10/10
RY 05 AXD	MB	109CDI	WDF63970523155366	Traveliner	M8	7/05 Accord Operations, Chichester (WS)	7/06
RX 55 BZL	MB	411CDI	WDB9046632R833159	Eurm-?-	M12L	10/05 Accord Operations, Chichester (WS)	7/06
RX 55 BZN	MB	411CDI	WDB9046632R834335	Eurm-?-	M12L	10/05 Accord Operations, Chichester (WS)	7/06

WEST SUSSEX COUNTY COUNCIL, CHICHESTER (continued)

Reg			Chassis	Body				
RX 55 CCN	MB	411CDI	WDB9046632R849021	Eurm-?-	M12L	10/05	Accord Operations, Chichester (WS)	7/06
RX 55 CDK	MB	411CDI	WDB9046632R848692	Eurm-?-	M12L	10/05	Accord Operations, Chichester (WS)	7/06
RX 55 CEK	MB	411CDI	WDB9046632R863034	Eurm-?-	M12L	11/05	Accord Operations, Chichester (WS)	7/06
RX 55 CEN	MB	411CDI	WDB9046632R848691	Eurm-?-	M12L	11/05	Accord Operations, Chichester (WS)	7/06
RX 55 UKB	MB	411CDI	WDB9046632R863033	Eurm-?-	M12L	11/05	Accord Operations, Chichester (WS)	7/06
RX 55 UKC	MB	411CDI	WDB9046632R862749	Eurm-?-	M12L	11/05	Accord Operations, Chichester (WS)	7/06
HX 06 BLJ	LDV	Cy	SEYZMVSZGDN112129	LDV	M16	3/06	new	3/06
WX 56 WWC	MB	515CDI	WDB9061532N318292	UVM -?-	B16FL	2/07	new	2/07
WX 56 WWD	MB	515CDI	WDB9061532N318293	UVM -?-	B16FL	2/07	new	2/07
WX 56 WWK	MB	515CDI	WDB9061532N308060	UVM -?-	B16FL	2/07	new	2/07
WX 56 WWL	MB	515CDI	WDB9061532N308061	UVM -?-	B16FL	2/07	new	2/07
WX 56 WWM	MB	515CDI	WDB9061532N308062	UVM -?-	B16FL	2/07	new	2/07
WX 56 WWN	MB	515CDI	WDB9061532N308063	UVM -?-	B16FL	2/07	new	2/07
WX 56 WWO	MB	515CDI	WDB9061532N308064	UVM -?-	B16FL	2/07	new	2/07
WX 56 WWP	MB	515CDI	WDB9061532N308272	UVM -?-	B16FL	2/07	new	2/07
WX 56 WWR	MB	515CDI	WDB9061532N308273	UVM -?-	B16FL	2/07	new	2/07
WX 56 WWS	MB	515CDI	WDB9061532N308166	UVM -?-	B16FL	2/07	new	2/07
WX 07 DDV	MB	515CDI	WDB9061532N320021	UVM -?-	B16FL	3/07	new	3/07
WX 07 DDY	MB	515CDI	WDB9061532N320391	UVM -?-	B16FL	3/07	new	3/07
WX 07 DDZ	MB	515CDI	WDB9061532N320392	UVM -?-	B16FL	3/07	new	3/07
WX 07 DEU	MB	515CDI	WDB9061532N318294	UVM -?-	B16FL	3/07	new	3/07
WX 07 DFA	MB	515CDI	WDB9061532N317537	UVM -?-	B16FL	3/07	new	3/07
WX 07 DFC	MB	515CDI	WDB9061532N317538	UVM -?-	B16FL	3/07	new	3/07
WX 07 DFD	MB	515CDI	WDB9061532N317912	UVM -?-	B16FL	3/07	new	3/07
WX 07 DFE	MB	515CDI	WDB9061532N317302	UVM 11388	B16FL	3/07	new	3/07
WX 07 DFF	MB	515CDI	WDB9061532N317303	UVM -?-	B16FL	3/07	new	3/07
GR 57 GWG	Fd	Tt	WF0DXXTTFD7M13442	Fd	M16	2/08	new	2/08
RX 57 JHV	MB	515CDI	WDB9066552S223205	Eurm -?-	B16FL	3/07	new	3/07
RX 57 JHY	MB	515CDI	WDB9066552S223200	Eurm -?-	B16FL	3/07	new	3/07
RX 57 JHZ	MB	515CDI	WDB9066552S223201	Eurm -?-	B16FL	3/07	new	3/07
RX 57 JJE	MB	515CDI	WDB9066552S223203	Eurm -?-	B16FL	3/07	new	3/07
RX 57 JJK	MB	515CDI	WDB9066552S223202	Eurm -?-	B16FL	3/07	new	3/07
RX 57 JJL	MB	515CDI	WDB9066552S223204	Eurm -?-	B16FL	3/07	new	3/07
RX 57 JJO	MB	515CDI	WDB9066552S231026	Eurm -?-	B16FL	3/07	new	3/07
WX 08 BCK	MB	515CDI	WDB9061532N363926	UVM -?-	B16FL	4/08	new	4/08
WX 08 BCO	MB	515CDI	WDB9061532N365698	UVM -?-	B16FL	4/08	new	4/08
WX 08 BCU	MB	515CDI	WDB9061532N365944	UVM -?-	B16FL	4/08	new	4/08
WX 08 BDE	MB	515CDI	WDB9061532N365699	UVM -?-	B16FL	4/08	new	4/08
WX 08 BDO	MB	515CDI	WDB9061532N365321	UVM -?-	B16FL	4/08	new	4/08
WX 08 BDV	MB	515CDI	WDB9061532N365778	UVM -?-	B16FL	4/08	new	4/08
WX 08 BDY	MB	515CDI	WDB9061532N366158	UVM -?-	B16FL	4/08	new	4/08
GV 58 EFU	Fd	It	WF0DXXTTFD0Y38866	Fd	M16	12/08	new	12/08
GV 58 EFX	Fd	Tt	WF0DXXTTFD8Y40312	Fd	M16	12/08	new	12/00
GV 58 EHO	Fd	Tt	WF0DXXTTFD8Y40320	Fd	M16	1/09	new	1/09
GV 58 EKK	Fd	Tt	WF0DXXTTFD7M19060	Fd	M16	12/08	new	12/08
GV 58 EKP	Fd	Tt	WF0DXXTTFD8S43545	Fd	M16	1/09	new	1/09
GV 58 ENU	Fd	Tt	WF0DXXTTFD8Y37941	Fd	M16	12/08	new	12/08
GV 58 EOM	Fd	Tt	WF0DXXTTFD8Y40316	Fd	M16	12/08	new	12/08
GV 58 EOO	Fd	Tt	WF0DXXTTFD8S43547	Fd	M16	1/09	new	1/09
GV 58 EOX	Fd	Tt	WF0DXXTTFD8Y40319	Fd	M16	1/09	new	1/09
GV 58 VLH	Fd	Tt	WF0DXXTTFD8Y40313	Fd	M16	1/09	new	1/09
WR 58 ZWL	MB	515CDI	WDB9061532N385695	UVM -?-	B16FL	1/09	new	1/09
WR 58 ZWM	MB	515CDI	WDB9061532N385696	UVM -?-	B16FL	1/09	new	1/09
WR 58 ZWN	MB	515CDI	WDB9061532N386715	UVM -?-	B16FL	1/09	new	1/09
WR 58 ZWU	MB	515CDI	WDB9061532N400006	UVM -?-	B16FL	1/09	new	1/09
WR 58 ZWW	MB	515CDI	WDB9061532N399801	UVM -?-	B16FL	1/09	new	1/09
WR 58 ZXL	MB	515CDI	WDB9061532N400442	UVM -?-	B16FL	1/09	new	1/09
WR 58 ZXM	MB	515CDI	WDB9061532N400008	UVM -?-	B16FL	1/09	new	1/09
DY 59 NBM	Fd	Tt	WF0SXXBDFS9C53497	Fd	M8	12/09	-?-, -?-	9/10
AE 10 GGV	lo	50C15	ZCFC50A2005781962	?	M16	6/10	-?-, -?-	by5/14
YM 62 CZC	Fd	Tt	WF0DXXTTFDCT20212	Fd	M16	2/13	new	2/13
YS 62 CPV	Fd	Tt	WF0DXXTTFDCT20089	Fd	M16	2/13	new	2/13
YS 62 CVR	Fd	Tt	WF0DXXTTFDCT19307	Fd	M16	2/13	new	2/13
YS 62 HWZ	Fd	Tt	WF0DXXTTFDCT19873	Fd	M16	2/13	new	2/13
YS 62 LNC	Fd	Tt	WF0DXXTTFDCT18744	Fd	M16	2/13	new	2/13
YS 62 RVJ	Fd	Tt	WF0DXXTTFDCT19405	Fd	M16	2/13	new	2/13
YS 62 WGZ	Fd	Tt	WF0DXXTTFDCT19991	Fd	M16	2/13	new	2/13
YT 13 HXA	Fd	Tt	WF0DXXTTFDCT18772	Fd	M16	3/13	new	3/13

WEST SUSSEX COUNTY COUNCIL, CHICHESTER (continued)

YT 13 KHF	Fd	Tt	WF0DXXTTFDCT20019	Fd		M16	3/13 new	3/13
YT 13 KKL	Fd	Tt	WF0DXXTTFDCT19238	Fd		M16	3/13 new	3/13
YT 13 KKU	Fd	Tt	WF0DXXTTFDCT19444	Fd		M16	3/13 new	3/13
YT 13 KWD	Fd	Tt	WF0DXXTTFDCT20029	Fd		M16	3/13 new	3/13
YT 13 KWG	Fd	Tt	WF0DXXTTFDCT19184	Fd		M16	3/13 new	3/13
YT 13 KWK	Fd	Tt	WF0DXXTTFDCT18708	Fd		M16	3/13 new	3/13
YT 13 KWO	Fd	Tt	WF0DXXTTFDCT20190	Fd		M16	3/13 new	3/13
YT 13 LOJ	Fd	Tt	WF0DXXTTFDCT20052	Fd		M16	3/13 new	3/13
YT 13 MFA	Fd	Tt	WF0DXXTTFDCT19794	Fd		M16	3/13 new	3/13
YT 13 NYO	Fd	Tt	WF0DXXTTFDCT20157	Fd		M16	3/13 new	3/13
YT 13 OFY	Fd	Tt	WF0DXXTTFDCT19457	Fd		M16	3/13 new	3/13
YT 13 POU	Fd	Tt	WF0DXXTTFDCT19275	Fd		M16	3/13 new	3/13
LJ 14 BGO	MB	513CDI	WDB9066572S901256	Treka	-?-	M16L	4/14 new	4/14
LJ 14 BGV	MB	513CDI	WDB9066572S916763	Treka	-?-	M16L	6/14 new	6/14
LJ 14 BHA	MB	513CDI	WDB9066572S915546	Treka	-?-	M16L	7/14 new	7/14
LJ 14 BHD	MB	513CDI	WDB9066572S917976	Treka	-?-	M16L	6/14 new	6/14
LJ 14 BKV	MB	513CDI	WDB9066572S913042	Treka	-?-	M16L	6/14 new	6/14
LJ 14 BKX	MB	513CDI	WDB9066572S913397	Treka	-?-	M16L	6/14 new	6/14
LJ 14 BKY	MB	513CDI	WDB9066572S916762	Treka	-?-	M16L	7/14 new	7/14
LJ 14 BLV	MB	513CDI	WDB9066572S915544	Treka	-?-	M16L	8/14 new	8/14
LJ 14 BPE	MB	513CDI	WDB9066572S901257	Treka	-?-	M16L	5/14 new	5/14
LJ 14 BPF	MB	513CDI	WDB9066572S903961	Treka	-?-	M16L	5/14 new	5/14
LJ 14 BPU	MB	513CDI	WDB9066572S901796	Treka	-?-	M16L	5/14 new	5/14
LJ 14 BPY	MB	513CDI	WDB9066572S902892	Treka	-?-	M16L	5/14 new	5/14
LJ 14 BTF	MB	513CDI	WDB9066572S905624	Treka	-?-	M16L	6/14 new	6/14
LJ 14 BTU	MB	513CDI	WDB9066572S905622	Treka	-?-	M16L	6/14 new	6/14
LJ 14 BUA	MB	513CDI	WDB9066572S903963	Treka	-?-	M16L	6/14 new	6/14
LJ 14 BUE	MB	513CDI	WDB9066572S903962	Treka	-?-	M16L	5/14 new	5/14
LJ 14 BXC	MB	513CDI	WDB9066572S915545	Treka	-?-	M16L	8/14 new	8/14
LJ 14 BXH	MB	513CDI	WDB9066572S917381	Treka	-?-	M16L	8/14 new	8/14
LJ 64 BHZ	MB	513CDI	WDB9066572S915543	Treka	-?-	M16L	9/14 new	9/14
LJ 64 BJF	MB	513CDI	WDB9066572S910759	Treka	-?-	M16L	10/14 new	10/14
LJ 64 BJO	MB	513CDI	WDB9066572S913398	Treka	-?-	M16L	10/14 new	10/14
LJ 64 BJU	MB	513CDI	WDB9066572S912716	Treka	-?-	M16L	9/14 new	9/14
LJ 64 BJX	MB	513CDI	WDB9066572S917385	Treka	-?-	M16L	10/14 new	10/14
LJ 64 BKK	MB	513CDI	WDB9066572S917978	Treka	-?-	M16L	9/14 new	9/14
LJ 64 BKL	MB	513CDI	WDB9066572S917384	Treka	-?-	M16L	10/14 new	10/14
LJ 64 BKO	MB	513CDI	WDB9066572S915547	Treka	-?-	M16L	9/14 new	9/14
LJ 64 BKV	MB	513CDI	WDB90665725917383	Treka	-?-	M16L	10/14 new	10/14

WEST SUSSEX FIRE BRIGADE, Fire Brigade Headquarters, Northgate, CHICHESTER PO19 1BD.

u	E890 KYW	Ld	LX1126LXCTZR1		LX1073	Ld	B47F	10/87 Arriva Kent & Sussex (KT) 2044	4/06
A00151	P831 JPO	Ds	Dt	9SDL3056/2399	LCB	-?-	B--F	2/97 new	2/97
			(command unit)						

WEST SUSSEX FIRE and Rescue SERVICE, Northgate, CHICHESTER, PO19 1BD.
No vehicles currently recorded

WEST SUSSEX MINIBUS, STORRINGTON.
OCs: Ashington, Billingshurst, Five Villages, Petworth, Pulborough, Steyning, Storrington, and Wisborough Green.

CU 03 LXN	Fd	Tt	WF0EXXGBFE3D30906	Fd	M14	6/03 pre-registered by dealer	7/03
CU 03 LXP	Fd	Tt	WF0EXXGBFE3D30907	Fd	M14	6/03 pre-registered by dealer	7/03
CK 56 TKE	Fd	Tt	WF0DXXTTFD6P52495	Fd	M14	11/06 -?-, -?-	5/13
GU 56 HYC	Fd	Tt	WF0DXXTTFD6M35172	Fd	M14	9/06 new	9/06
BF 57 LGY	VW	Tr	WV2ZZZ7HZ8H032118	VW	M8	9/07 new	9/07
RX 57 JYO	LDV	Max	SEYL6P6A20N210241	LDV	M14	11/07 -?-, -?-	7/08
GU 08 BTO	Fd	Tt	WF0DXXTTFD7P63890	Fd	M14	3/08 pre-registered by dealer	4/08
GV 08 VDD	Fd	Tt	WF0DXXTTFD8R05929	Fd	M14	5/08 new	5/08
GV 08 VEF	Fd	Tt	WF0DXXTTFD8R05927	Fd	M14	5/08 new	5/08
BN 58 POU	VW	Tr	WV2ZZZ7HZ9H035900	VW	M8	9/08 new	9/08
RX 58 AOK	LDV	Max	SEYL6P6E21N230838	LDV	M11L	11/08 new	11/08

NOTE: Vehicles were observed with the following lettering at the dates shown. Ashington Village Minibus - RX 57 JYO (5/12).
Billingshurst Village Minibus - GU 08 BTO (7/11). Five Villages Minibus - RX 58 AOK (4/12). Petworth Area Minibus – GV 08 VEF (2/15).
Pulborough Area Minibus - CU 03 LXN (7/12); CK 56 TKE (12/14). Steyning Area Minibus - GU 56 HYC. Storrington Area Minibus –
HJ 03 JFU, BF 57 LGY, CU 03 LXP (12/10), RX 57 JYO (11/10), GV 08 VDD (7/10, 12/10). Wisborough Green Minibus - BN 58 POU
(6/11).

WESTBOURNE HOUSE SCHOOL, Coach Road, Shopwyke, CHICHESTER, West Sussex, PO20 2BH.

R736 YCK	Pt	Bxr	F3233J5215509581	Km	M16	4/98	new	4/98
V299 LRN	Pt	Bxr	VF3233J5215783690	Km	M16	1/00	new	1/00
HY 58 PFG	Pt	Bxr	VF3YCBMFC11312626	RKC	M16	9/08	new	9/08

WESTERGATE Community SCHOOL, Lime Avenue, WESTERGATE, Chichester, PO20 3UE.

Y339 JFB	Ft	Do	ZFA23000006056297	?	M16	3/01 -?-, -?-		10/04
			(lettered for Gators Sports Club)					

WESTLAKE HOUSE Care Home, Pondtail Road, HORSHAM, RH12 5HT

HY 11 PXF	Rt	Mtr	VF1MAF2BN44188040	?	M?L	3/11	pre-registered by dealer	5/11

WINDLESHAM HOUSE SCHOOL, WASHINGTON, Pulborough, West Sussex, RH20 4AY.

AS 07 WHS	Fd	Tt	WF0DXXTTFDBM06002	Fd	M16	1/12	new	1/12
			(ex GY 61 VLJ 3/12)					
BS 07 WHS	Fd	Tt	WF0DXXTTFDBM05103	Fd	M16	1/12	new	1/12
			(ex GY 61 VKD 3/12)					
CS 07 WHS	Fd	Tt	WF0DXXTTFDBM05270	Fd	M16	1/12	new	1/12
			(ex GV 61 HPC 3/12)					
DS 07 WHS	Fd	Tt	WF0DXXTTFDBM05301	Fd	M16	1/12	new	1/12
			(ex GV 61 HJG 9/13)					
ES 07 WHS	Pt	Bxr	VF3YCBMFC11679166	?	M14	9/10	new	9/10
FS 07 WHS	Pt	Bxr	VF3YCBMFC11681955	?	M14	9/10	new	9/10

WOODLANDS MEED (School), Chanctonbury Road, BURGESS HILL, RH15 9EY.

W487 YKM	Fd	Tt	WF0LXXBDVLYB71968	Eurm -?-	M13L	5/00	Newick House School, Burgess Hill (XWS)	9/12
GN 04 RJU	Io	35S12	ZCFC358100D229130	Eurm -?-	M8L	4/04	Court Meadow School, Cuckfield (XWS)	9/12
AE 54 PTZ	LDV	Cy	SEYZMVSZGDN108759	LDV	M16	12/04	Newick House School, Burgess Hill (XWS)	9/12
GN 55 CHC	Io	40C12	ZCFC408100D280010	Eurm -?-	M8L	9/05	Court Meadow School, Cuckfield (XWS)	9/12
GN 09 PVJ	Io	35S12	ZCFC3583005784656	Eurm -?-	M13L	7/09	Court Meadow School, Cuckfield (XWS)	9/12
CN 11 GFK	Ft	Do	ZFA25000001876970	Eurm -?-	M13L	5/11	new	5/11
			(VCGB donation number 5095)					
GN 13 AKP	Ft	Do	ZFA25000002246376	Eurm -?-	M13L	4/13	new	4/13
			(VCGB donation number 5230)					

NOTE: prior to 9/12, vehicles were licenced either to Court Meadow School, Cuckfield or Newick House School, Burgess Hill. It is not known which GN 11 GFK operated for.

WORTH ABBEY COMMUNITY SERVICE, Paddockhurst Road, TURNERS HILL, RH10 4SD

KE 53 EHU	MB	411CDI	WDB9046632R560793	?	M?L	11/03	new	11/03

WORTH SCHOOL, Paddockhurst Road, TURNERS HILL, RH10 4SD.

YP 58 AOG	Fd	Tt	WF0DXXTTFD8L22325	Fd	M16	10/08	new	10/08
YT 59 FDN	Fd	Tt	WF0DXXTTFD9A40707	Fd	M16	9/09	new	9/09
YT 59 GDO	Fd	Tt	WF0DXXTTFD9A40691	Fd	M16	9/09	new	9/09
YT 59 JWA	Fd	Tt	WF0DXXTTFD9A40676	Fd	M16	9/09	new	9/09
YT 60 RHY	Fd	Tt	WF0DXXTTFDAM80979	Fd	M16	11/10	new	11/10
YT 60 RRX	Fd	Tt	WF0DXXTTFDAM82492	Fd	M16	11/10	new	11/10
YS 61 RXW	Fd	Tt	WF0DXXTTFDBP27107	Fd	M16	2/12	new	2/12
YS 61 UYL	Fd	Tt	WF0DXXTTFDBP26907	Fd	M16	2/12	new	2/12
YT 63 PMU	Fd	Tt	WF0DXXTTFDDC53824	Fd	M16	12/13	new	12/13
YT 63 RKE	Fd	Tt	WF0DXXTTFDDC53865	Fd	M16	11/13	new	11/13

WORTHING COLLEGE, Bolsover Road, Worthing BN13 1NS.

HY 61 NXM	Fd	Tt	WF0DXXTTFDBK44660	Fd		M16	9/11 new	9/11
HY 61 NXO	Fd	Tt	WF0DXXTTFDAR41960	Fd		M16	9/11 new	9/11
YD 61 GWM	Fd	Tt	WF0DXXTTFDAR60390	Fd		M16	9/11 new	9/11

WORTHING DIAL-A-RIDE, c/o Worthing Council for Voluntary Service, Colonnade House, Warwick Street, Worthing, West Sussex, BN11 3DH.

No vehicles currently recorded

WORTHING HIGH SCHOOL, South Farm Road, WORTHING, BN14 7AR.

| PO 51 RLX | LDV | Cy | SEYZMVSHEDN076707 | LDV | | M16 | 9/01 new | 9/01 |

WORTHING MENCAP, 121 South Farm Road, WORTHING, BN 14 7AX.

| RJ 05 YYZ | Fd | Tt | WF0EXXTTFE5M65829 | Fd | | M14 | 6/05 National Car Rental (Y) | 12/07 |

WORTHING SEA CADETS (TS VANGUARD), 9A Broadwater, WORTHING, BN14 8AD.

| HN 04 FND | Fd | Tt | WF0EXXGBFE3S25750 | Fd | | M14 | 3/04 -?-, -?- | 10/09 |

WORTHING SOCIETY FOR THE BLIND, 48 Rowlands Road, WORTHING, BN11 3JT.

| LJ 07 WWW | VW | Crf | WV1ZZZ2EZ76036148 | ? | | M16L | 8/07 new | 8/07 |

WEST SUSSEX – REGISTRATION / PAGE NUMBER INDEX

Reg	Page	Reg	Page	Reg	Page	Reg	Page	Reg	Page
"BU 6043"	6	MIL 1850	23	XSU 612	28	401 DCD	24	SMK 660F	8	A889 FPM	15
"BU 6046"	6	MIL 1851	23	XSU 682	28	402 DCD	31	SMK 742F	8	A829 SUL	15
"BU 6047"	6	MIL 1852	23	XYK 976	33	403 DCD	29	SMK 755F	8	A883 SUL	15
"BU 6048"	6	MIL 8322	23	YFV 722	11	404 DCD	26	AML 30H	15	A101 SYE	8
"BU 6049"	6	MIL 9337	23	YIL 4058	13	406 DCD	25	WHE 349J	8	A103 SYE	8
"BU 6050"	6	MSV 617	11	YLJ 332	27	407 DCD	31	MLK 708L	15	A715 THV	7
CD 7045	28	NCZ 8070	18	YSL 847	11	408 DCD	31	SWB 287L	54	A113 TRP	18
CL 5561	8	NDZ 3017	28	YYL 370	11	409 DCD	28	NPX 998M	18	A 12 YOU	15
KV 4644	11	NDZ 3018	28			411 DCD	33	HPB 664N	18		
SV 9314	11	NDZ 3019	28	2722 CD	25	412 DCD	25	JGV 332N	15	B803 AOP	56
UF 4813	28	NDZ 3020	27	2719 DT	12	413 DCD	33	KJD 434P	8	B 29 BMC	15
		NFX667	33	4730 EL	48	414 DCD	31	KJD 530P	23	B194 BLG	8
AEZ 1361	4	NIL 2458	11	3544 FH	12	416 DCD	25	KMW 175P	25	B999 CUS	15
AIG 7944	11	NIL 9248	7	8957 FN	12	417 DCD	31	OJD 93R	8		
ASV 440	38	NIW 6518	37	8357 KV	12	418 DCD	31	OUC 45R	15	C 8LEA	15
BJZ 2804	11	NKK 447	11	9022 KV	12	420 DCD	31	VNK 595S	15		
BNZ 3466	11	NLE 701	17	1725 LJ	9	421 DCD	31	CLC 553T	9	D 32 CLC	9
CCZ 6148	7	NUI 5155	4	1455 MV	12	112 FYA	38	CLC 983T	9	D150 FYM	7
CLC 145	9	NXP 796	8	7572 MW	12	198 FYB	38	CTM 407T	18	D862 GCD	8
CSU 978	27	OBY 443	11	2851 NX	12	503 FYC	38	TTP 592T	18	D113 GHY	7
DEZ 8491	4	OKF 580	11	1194 PO	12	666 FYD	38	BYW 382V	23	D602 RGJ	15
DJI 654	9	OKZ 8958	45	7855 PU	12	587 FYF	38	CDL 677V	18		
ESV 183	11	PSU 787	33	9041 PU	12	307 FYG	38	HDL 232V	18	E890 KYW	58
FIL 7617	11	PSV 339	11	6170 PX	12	436 FYM	38	LUA 255V	15	E749 VWT	18
FYL 122	38	PUI 6623	7	6300 RU	12	498 FYN	38	LVS 441V	18		
HIL 7746	9	RHZ 4536	7	8665 UB	12	274 FYP	39	HJB 635W	9	F 1 LGW	25
HIL 8961	18	RIL 9469	8	4885 UR	12	253 FYW	39	MRJ 52W	41	F 2 LGW	25
HJI 8686	11	RYY 544	9	2941 VU	12	348 FYY	39	OPE 613W	15	F 3 LGW	25
HSV 989	11	SCZ 1562	17	48 WT	24	644 HKX	18	TUA 161W	48	F464 NRT	18
HXN 190	11	SJI 8128	11	1521 YG	12	331 HWD	12	UNO 100W	18		
IIL 4820	18	SNZ 7259	11			182 KWC	37	CBM 12X	7	G 67 RGG	18
JBZ 5056	11	TFK 696	11	227 BWD	12	869 UYB	12	CPU 125X	8	G 2 TSW	10
JEZ 8957	4	TUI 6946	7	264 CHX	12	978 VYD	9	RDL 686X	15	G516 VYE	15
JFZ 9942	7	UHE 604	11	52 CLC	9	930 YUE	12	TND 409X	52		
JIG 9768	7	UIL 4207	17	171 CLC	9	120 YUR	12	ANA 565Y	15	H536 CTR	15
KIG 3429	7	UOI 2679	15	685 CLC	9			NYH 161Y	15	H201 DVM	15
KIG 3430	7	VIL 6773	7	687 CLC	9	ACY 178A	23	OJD 817Y	41	H204 DVM	15
LIW 9272	9	WEZ 2563	37	784 CLC	9	ARU 99A	23	YPD 101Y	8	H552 GKX	4
LUI 9692	7	WLT 526	33	789 CLC	9	ARU 100A	23			H421 GPM	18
LUO 391	9	WLZ 3488	24	456 CLT	33	ARU 500A	23	A629 BCN	41	H 6 WTR	4
LXI 4409	18	WTE 506	11	192 COP	44	ERV 254D	8	A129 EPA	7	H532 XGK	15
MIB 927	7	WVT 618	27	964 CUF	25	HCD 350E	25	A144 EPA	7		

WEST SUSSEX – REGISTRATION / PAGE NUMBER INDEX (continued)

Reg	Pg	Reg	Pg	Reg	Pg	Reg	Pg	Reg	Pg	Reg	Pg
J617 CEV	23	P 15 CLC	9	S 55 FYE	39	X613 JCS	30	CK 02 VMO	41	LK 03 CEV	13
J501 GCD	30	P268 FPK	12	S 55 FYX	39	X614 JCS	30	CK 02 VMR	42	LX 03 OJN	20
J502 GCD	15	P727 GND	27	S399 HVV	16	X616 JCS	30	FK 02 CLC	10	LX 03 OJP	20
J504 GCD	15	P728 GND	27	S435 KFX	43	X617 JCS	30	FN 02 VCC	4	PM 03 EHV	25
J511 GCD	15	P729 GND	27	S 10 KTC	19	X239 KVN	54	HN 02 BFY	52	PM 03 EHW	26
J524 GCD	15	P831 JPO	58	S769 RVU	27	X 83 MKM	51	HV 02 RKA	42	SN 03 WKU	20
J548 GCD	15	P144 NBP	54	S800 STA	35	X831 NWX	5	KR 02 JHE	35	SN 03 WKY	20
J552 GCD	15	P303 RCW	41			X832 NWX	5	KW 02 DRO	12	SN 03 WLA	20
J812 GGW	4	P817 REX	16	T 10 ACL	36	X833 NWX	5	LN 02 HXR	56	SN 03 WLE	20
J137 HMT	7	P686 RWU	12	T222 ADY	9	X835 NWX	5	LV 02 XHN	41	SN 03 WLF	20
J208 KTT	13	P514 UUG	24	T527 AOB	16	X837 NWX	5	NC 02 VSD	17	SN 03 WLH	20
J231 NNC	19	P224 VCK	27	T132 AUA	25	X839 NWX	5	NL 02 FKJ	53	SN 03 WLL	20
J287 NNC	7	P225 VCK	27	T139 AUA	26	X840 NWX	5	PJ 02 AAA	12	SN 03 WLP	22
J127 OBU	18	P227 VCK	27	T593 CGT	30	X841 NWX	5	PK 02 PUJ	24	SN 03 WLU	22
J875 ODV	41	P228 VCK	27	T 16 CLC	9	X842 NWX	5	RA 02 CMK	37	SN 03 WMT	20
J111 RAF	51	P229 VCK	27	T 17 CLC	9	X514 OGP	48	RK 02 EKZ	48	SN 03 WMV	20
J 46 SNY	7	P231 VCK	27	T 19 CLC	9	X104 UAO	24	RY 02 PKU	48	SN 03 YCL	20
J 28 UNT	7	P232 VCK	27	T183 CLO	13	X531 UAT	16	SW 02 VTT	15	SN 03 YCM	20
J240 VVN	12	P233 VCK	27	T184 CLO	13	X761 WFX	55	WC 02 CLC	10	SN 03 YCT	20
J 40 YRS	39	P268 VPN	27	T544 FJT	45	X762 WFX	55	WH 02 WOW	36	VU 03 HCD	37
		P269 VPN	27	T 4 HMC	12	X224 WNO	12	YJ 02 LKV	44	VU 03 HKG	37
K 2 CLC	9	P278 VPN	27	T373 JWA	7	X227 WNO	12	YR 02 OAX	18	WA 03 HRF	15
K 3 CLC	9	P282 VPN	27	T991 NOK	9	X236 WNO	12	YR 02 ZZB	39	WA 03 OLC	37
K 5 CLC	9	P261 WPN	27	T927 PNV	30	X344 YGU	20	YR 02 ZZC	39	WL 03 KSE	4
K128 DAO	7	P262 WPN	27	T369 RPG	46	X575 YUG	7			WX 03 LEU	37
K777 DAO	50	P263 WPN	27	T999 RRS	17	X576 YUG	7	AF 52 OPW	47	YJ 03 PSY	16
K556 NHC	15							DA 52 YGR	4	YK 03 EZV	40
K655 NHC	15	R148 CHT	4	V 22 CLC	9	Y425 GCD	52	FE 52 HFW	4	YN 03 AVZ	7
K 96 SAG	15	R 20 CLC	9	V172 DFT	27	Y853 GDV	4	FY 52 GUJ	23	YN 03 AWM	36
K 33 SKY	35	R228 CRW	28	V750 DSE	4	Y815 GFM	4	GU 52 HDD	44	YN 03 AWP	36
K 60 TCC	24	R 11 CXA	8	V930 EWP	16	Y363 HMY	20	GU 52 ZYW	44	YN 03 NHT	36
		R789 DHB	24	V 34 FEL	46	Y365 HMY	20	HN 52 KMO	53	YN 03 UWU	21
L 6 CLC	9	R748 DRJ	27	V 1 FOR	16	Y372 HMY	20	HV 52 NDN	55	YN 03 UWY	21
L 9 CLC	9	R752 DRJ	27	V260 FRV	48	Y377 HMY	20	KL 52 LZX	12	YN 03 WPM	21
L250 JBV	23	R756 DRJ	27	V301 KGW	8	Y378 HMY	20	KN 52 NFM	12	YN 03 WPP	21
L999 RRS	17	R129 EVX	27	V299 LRN	59	Y379 HMY	20	KU 52 RYG	12	YN 03 WPR	21
L635 TDY	24	R248 FMJ	55	V380 SVV	26	Y297 HUA	16	LB 52 XHF	10	YN 03 WRL	8
L452 UEB	15	R795 GNJ	53			Y339 JFB	59	LF 52 UGL	14	YV 03 RBU	20
L486 XOU	7	R291 HCD	27	W463 BCW	26	Y875 KDY	44	LF 52 URM	45	YV 03 RBX	20
		R293 HCD	27	W464 BCW	26	Y858 LRX	13	LF 52 ZFU	43	YX 03 FCU	4
M 8 HAT	16	R295 HCD	27	W465 BCW	26	Y663 NAY	51	LY 52 ZFV	54		
M 10 HNH	37	R175 HHK	7	W912 BEC	13	Y386 NHK	8	LY 52 ZDX	27	AD 53 EEY	47
M 3 KFC	16	R 6 HLC	4	W195 CDN	16	Y514 NHK	8	PN 52 NHK	56	BU 53 TNO	30
M452 LLJ	16	R370 LGH	8	W 30 CLC	9	Y517 NHK	8	PN 52 XBP	24	BV 53 AVK	41
M456 LLJ	16	R475 NPR	16	W 40 CLC	10	Y157 NLK	12	SK 52 MPY	7	BV 53 CEN	56
M602 ORJ	19	R478 NPR	16	W 44 CLC	10	Y432 PBD	16	WF 52 ESY	15	DG 53 EHK	23
M589 OSO	24	R479 NPR	16	W 55 CLC	10	YR34 TGH	26	WV 52 HSX	13	DN 53 GGK	44
M803 ROP	12	R319 NRR	40	W 66 CLC	10	Y839 TGH	26	YD 52 JAU	13	DS 53 OFM	10
M 71 RJW	16	R486 TTP	4	W 77 CLC	10	Y840 TGH	26	YP 52 CTO	21	GV 53 WZO	40
M461 VCW	24	R569 UOT	16	W587 DGU	36	Y841 TGH	26			GX 53 MWE	30
		R171 VLA	16	W129 EON	7	Y336 TKJ	40	BU 03 UJN	4	GX 53 MWF	30
N100 BUS	43	R173 VLA	16	W608 FUM	10	Y841 VGN	45	CU 03 KVH	17	GX 53 MWG	30
N 7 CLC	9	R149 VPU	7	W609 FUM	10	Y773 XCW	51	CU 03 LXN	58	GX 53 MWJ	30
N 12 CLC	9	R511 WDC	12	W344 NRY	36			CU 03 LXP	58	GX 53 MWK	30
N 60 CLC	9	R423 XFC	27	W212 RKK	37	AE 51 VFV	30	DF 03 NTE	13	GX 53 MWL	30
N869 EKR	4	R424 XFC	27	W926 PAP	52	AO 51 HZG	35	DL 03 GRZ	39	GX 53 MWM	30
N431 FKK	4	R425 XFC	27	W372 RKS	13	BW 51 OHN	41	DS 03 VCA	46	GX 53 MWN	30
N 65 FWU	23	R937 XVM	28	W547 RNB	36	CN 51 BKU	18	EF 03 NWU	10	GX 53 MWO	30
N557 LAM	43	R736 YCK	59	W754 TJH	52	GU 51 PVT	48	EU 03 ONF	37	GX 53 MWP	30
N906 NAP	16	R473 YDT	4	W681 TNV	16	KM 51 BFZ	12	GN 03 ERN	46	GX 53 MWU	30
N731 RDD	16	R524 YRP	16	W341 VGX	26	KP 51 SYA	16	GN 03 FUJ	47	GX 53 MWV	30
N 92 SKG	19			W343 VGX	26	KV 51 KZJ	16	GN 03 WBK	54	GX 53 MWW	30
N982 TPG	9	S590 BCE	27	W401 WGH	7	LK 51 JYJ	22	HG 03 JPF	40	GX 53 MWY	30
N470 VPJ	6	S591 BCE	27	W431 YBN	9	LK 51 JYL	22	HJ 03 JFF	51	GX 53 MWZ	30
N472 VPJ	6	S634 CBD	41	W752 YDM	4	LK 51 JYN	22	HJ 03 XML	46	HG 53 NSY	50
N 3 YCL	9	S302 CCD	27	W487 YKM	59	LX 51 FJY	27	HN 03 ZYM	10	HJ 53 RVM	43
		S303 CCD	27			OC 51 CLC	10	KC 03 LHH	56	HJ 53 UAT	46
		S304 CCD	27	X601 AHE	12	PO 51 RLX	60	KC 03 LHJ	56	KE 53 EHU	59
P991 AFV	16	S305 CCD	27	X533 AKY	17	SJ 51 FHV	4	KC 03 LHK	42	KE 53 EKR	46
P849 BPB	6	S312 CCD	27	X 70 BUS	39	VC 51 CLC	10	KC 03 LHL	42	OU 53 VPJ	10
P 2 CAP	9	S 8 CTD	4	X 50 CLC	10			KC 03 LHM	41	PG 53 YCT	25
P 3 CAP	9	S874 DPN	15	X307 FGC	48	AO 52 VAK	54	KV 03 ZFJ	13	PJ 53 UPY	54
P 14 CLC	9	S 12 ECH	18	X931 HBP	48	BU 02 FNF	42	KV 03 ZFK	13	RX 53 AXR	37

WEST SUSSEX – REGISTRATION / PAGE NUMBER INDEX (continued)

Reg	Pg	Reg	Pg	Reg	Pg	Reg	Pg	Reg	Pg	Reg	Pg
RX 53 NXM	56	BU 54 DDZ	55	VX 05 UHS	13	GN 06 PUK	45	GV 56 KWD	47	BD 07 EEG	43
SN 53 ETK	13	BU 54 GZT	40	YJ 05 PVY	16	GX 06 AOE	25	GX 56 KVU	31	BJ 07 XHH	41
SN 53 ETL	13	EU 54 SZC	54	YJ 05 UJN	37	GX 06 DXA	31	GX 56 KVV	31	BS 07 WHS	59
SN 53 LWL	25	EU 54 SZT	54	YN 05 BUH	7	GX 06 DXB	31	GX 56 KVW	31	BU 07 NUY	18
YK 53 HAA	50	FJ 54 MMX	17	YN 05 HAA	7	GX 06 DXC	31	GX 56 KVY	31	BU 07 RZB	18
YN 53 RYA	20	GN 54 BVL	49	YN 05 HCA	21	GX 06 DXD	31	GX 56 KVZ	31	BX 07 AOS	38
YN 53 RYB	20	GX 54 DVW	30	YN 05 HCC	21	GX 06 DXE	31	GX 56 KWA	31	CS 07 WHS	59
YN 53 RYC	20	GX 54 DVZ	30	YN 05 HCD	21	GX 06 DXF	31	GX 56 KWB	31	DS 07 WHS	59
YN 53 RYD	20	GX 54 DWA	30	YN 05 HCE	21	GX 06 DXG	31	GX 56 KWC	31	EO 07 DVM	40
YN 53 RYF	20	GX 54 DWC	30	YN 05 HCF	21	GX 06 DXH	27	GX 56 KWD	31	ES 07 WHS	59
YN 53 RYH	20	GX 54 DWD	30	YN 05 HCG	21	GX 06 DXJ	28	GX 56 KWE	31	FS 07 WHS	59
YN 53 RYK	21	GX 54 DWE	30	YN 05 VST	36	GX 06 DXL	28	GX 56 KWF	31	GN 07 AVR	21
YN 53 RYT	21	GX 54 DWF	30			GX 06 DXM	28	GX 56 KWG	31	GN 07 AVT	21
YN 53 RYV	21	GX 54 DWG	30	AU 55 DYO	13	GX 06 DXO	28	GX 56 KWH	31	GN 07 AVU	21
YN 53 RYW	21	GX 54 DWJ	30	CN 55 EXS	47	GX 06 DXP	28	GX 56 KWJ	31	GN 07 AVV	21
YN 53 RYX	21	HF 54 GKU	49	EU 55 KUH	54	GX 06 DXU	28	GX 56 KWK	31	GN 07 AVW	21
YN 53 RYY	21	HJ 54 KYO	49	EU 55 KWF	54	GX 06 DXV	28	GX 56 KWL	31	GN 07 AVY	21
YN 53 RYZ	21	HJ 54 XFN	51	GN 55 CHC	59	GX 06 DXY	28	GX 56 KWM	31	GN 07 TBY	42
YN 53 RZA	21	HX 54 EGC	53	GN 55 PZV	44	GX 06 DXZ	28	GX 56 KWN	31	GR 07 OLO	39
YN 53 RZB	21	KX 54 NKE	13	GN 55 VOB	17	GX 06 DYA	28	GX 56 KWO	31	GU 07 FMV	55
YN 53 RZC	21	KX 54 TWG	27	GX 55 GOP	40	GX 06 DYB	28	GX 56 KWP	31	GU 07 FSV	55
YN 53 RZD	21	KX 54 TWJ	27	HG 55 VSD	49	GX 06 DYC	28	GX 56 OGA	31	GU 07 NCJ	52
YN 53 RZE	21	LB 54 LNW	44	HJ 55 KLP	49	GX 06 DYH	33	GX 56 OGB	31	GX 07 AVO	14
YN 53 RZF	21	MX 54 KXR	13	HK 55 BYO	50	GX 06 DYJ	33	GX 56 OGC	31	GX 07 BYO	14
YN 53 USG	20	MX 54 LPK	27	KC 55 KTC	19	GX 06 DYM	33	GX 56 OGD	31	GX 07 FHS	41
		MX 54 LPL	27	KX 55 OJF	35	GX 06 DYN	33	GX 56 OGE	31	GX 07 FXC	31
AE 04 FUV	23	MX 54 LPN	27	LJ 55 AWH	52	GX 06 DYO	33	GX 56 OGF	31	GX 07 FXD	31
BU 04 EXV	10	MX 54 LPO	27	LJ 55 AWO	52	GX 06 DYP	33	GX 56 OGG	31	GX 07 FXG	31
BV 04 VPG	37	MX 54 LPP	27	LJ 55 JVV	52	GX 06 DZF	28	GX 56 OGJ	31	GX 07 HUJ	31
EU 04 KZW	54	MX 54 LPY	27	LK 55 ACV	25	GX 06 DZG	28	GX 56 OGK	31	GX 07 HUK	31
GN 04 RJU	59	MX 54 LRA	27	LK 55 ADX	25	GX 06 DZH	28	GX 56 OGL	31	GX 07 HUO	31
GR 04 ECN	54	MX 54 LRE	27	LK 55 ADZ	25	GX 06 DZJ	28	GY 56 BZR	47	GX 07 HUP	31
GX 04 EXH	30	NK 54 RLO	37	LK 55 AEA	25	GX 06 DZK	28	GY 56 SYX	54	GX 07 HUY	31
GX 04 EXJ	30	PK 54 ZJU	46	MX 55 NWK	13	GX 06 EWA	49	HJ 56 VPF	53	GX 07 HUZ	31
GX 04 EXK	30	PO 54 AUH	43	NJ 55 YPH	46	GX 06 TZZ	44	HX 56 BNU	44	HK 07 MJF	55
GX 04 EXL	30	RX 54 CMZ	43	OE 55 SVJ	8	HJ 06 VTZ	40	LK 56 GVM	54	HY 07 EXF	44
GX 04 EXM	30	RX 54 XJG	46	RX 55 BZL	56	HT 06 KDZ	45	LX 56 OTH	37	KX 07 FFA	35
GX 04 EXN	30	RY 54 ERK	42	RX 55 BZN	56	HX 06 BLJ	57	MX 56 ABZ	14	LJ 07 WWW	60
GX 04 EXP	30	SN 54 HXG	13	RX 55 CCN	57	HX 06 FOT	4	MX 56 FSE	28	LK 07 CBO	30
GX 04 EXR	30	VX 54 LSZ	54	RX 55 CDK	57	HY 06 BUV	55	MX 56 FSP	28	LK 07 CBU	30
GX 04 EXS	30	YN 54 AJU	21	RX 55 CEK	57	HY 06 FTX	52	MX 56 FTA	28	MX 07 HLP	28
GX 04 EXT	30	YN 54 AJV	21	RX 55 CEN	57	HY 06 FTZ	52	MX 56 FTD	28	MX 07 HLR	28
GX 04 EXU	30	YN 54 AJX	21	RX 55 UKB	57	HY 06 FUA	52	MX 56 FTP	28	MX 07 HLV	28
GX 04 EXZ	30	YN 54 AJY	21	RX 55 UKC	57	KX 06 LYU	27	MX 56 FTT	28	NA 07 ASX	41
GX 04 EYA	30	YN 54 DDO	7	SH 55 WUK	35	KX 06 LYV	27	MX 56 FTU	28	PN 07 RVJ	38
GX 04 EYB	30			SK 55 POJ	4	KX 06 LYW	27	MX 56 FTY	28	RX 07 PNY	42
GX 04 EYD	30	AJ 05 NHD	17	SN 55 DUU	13	KX 06 LYY	27	MX 56 FUM	28	SF 07 XNV	36
GX 04 GMG	49	BU 05 EEG	4	SN 55 FPL	16	LK 06 BWB	30	MX 56 HWA	49	SF 07 XOK	37
GX 04 YCL	50	CA 05 OZR	40	YJ 55 BGU	13	MV 06 KUA	25	MX 56 NLN	14	SL 07 KXT	45
GY 04 ZGA	20	CV 05 CZF	38	YJ 55 BGV	13	MX 06 ACY	14	PE 56 KMZ	50	TN 07 SWT	18
HN 04 FND	60	EF 05 YDR	56	YJ 55 JWF	45	MX 06 XSY	5	SN 56 AXC	14	WA 07 BGV	35
HX 04 NRE	54	EU 05 EMF	48	YJ 55 YGZ	14	NC 06 CLC	10	WA 56 ENK	15	WA 07 KXT	36
LD 04 YVP	14	FN 05 DGE	36	YK 55 ATV	13	NG 06 LXD	39	WX 56 WWC	57	WX 07 DDV	57
LF 04 PJX	18	GJ 05 RJX	17	YM 55 SXO	21	RE 06 VFT	37	WX 56 WWD	57	WX 07 DDY	57
LJ 04 JJL	43	GV 05 YLT	54	YM 55 SXP	21	RJ 06 VHE	46	WX 56 WWK	57	WX 07 DDZ	57
MW 04 TGJ	24	GX 05 AOP	13	YM 55 SXR	21	SD 06 HSY	17	WX 56 WWL	57	WX 07 DEU	57
NG 04 RVN	39	GY 05 VSX	54	YN 55 PWJ	21	WA 06 CDX	15	WX 56 WWM	57	WX 07 DFA	57
PE 04 UBV	43	HX 05 DYH	8	YN 55 PWK	21	YC 06 GYS	19	WX 56 WWN	57	WX 07 DFC	57
PN 04 VHF	35	KV 05 UGY	50	YN 55 PWL	21	YJ 06 LEU	13	WX 56 WWO	57	WX 07 DFD	57
RL 04 KTX	37	LA 05 FGP	55	YN 55 PWO	21	YJ 06 LFA	13	WX 56 WWP	57	WX 07 DFE	57
RX 04 UFW	41	LB 05 HHS	49	YN 55 PWU	21	YJ 06 LFX	13	WX 56 WWR	57	WX 07 DFF	57
SM 04 HYX	55	LM 05 BUS	35	YN 55 PWV	21	YN 06 JXU	21	WX 56 WWS	57	YJ 07 UHR	38
WU 04 FHA	41	ML 05 UAR	49	YN 55 PWX	21	YN 06 JXV	21	YG 56 FHV	51	YL 07 FMJ	52
WX 04 FWB	50	MX 05 OTC	13			YN 06 JXW	21	YK 56 MKZ	55	YN 07 EXX	7
YJ 04 BJE	16	OU 05 BWF	44	AY 06 XAU	44	YN 06 JXX	21	YN 56 FDO	22	YN 07 LKF	21
YK 04 KVV	33	PN 05 SYF	24	BU 06 CUG	47	YN 06 JXY	21	YN 56 FDP	22	YN 07 LKG	21
YK 04 KVW	33	PX 05 EKT	31	CN 06 BXP	14	YN 06 JXZ	21	YN 56 FEM	7	YN 07 NUF	24
YN 04 GOC	39	PX 05 EKV	31	DC 06 CLC	10			YN 56 FFM	39		
YN 04 GOJ	39	PX 05 EKZ	31	DK 06 EHN	42	AE 56 GZG	45	YN 56 NSE	36	BF 57 LGY	54
YU 04 XJV	24	PX 05 ELC	31	EU 06 EWP	54	CK 56 TKE	58			BL 57 XHG	53
YX 04 FYH	16	RJ 05 YYZ	60	FJ 06 ZLU	36	EU 56 EKW	41	AS 07 WHS	59	CN 57 HVV	43
		RY 05 AXD	56	GN 06 LFM	49	EU 56 JZK	37			CU 57 FRK	8
AE 54 PTZ	59	SN 05 FHL	13	GN 06 OXK	51	GU 56 HYC	58	BD 07 EDR	43	EY 57 ACU	54

WEST SUSSEX – REGISTRATION / PAGE NUMBER INDEX (continued)

Reg	Pg	Reg	Pg	Reg	Pg	Reg	Pg	Reg	Pg	Reg	Pg
GU 57 GXT	6	LK 08 NDJ	42	GX 58 GLF	31	YH 58 FKD	52	BK 10 EHU	5	MX 10 EMF	41
GN 57 ASO	46	LT 08 TCK	54	GX 58 GLJ	31	YK 58 JRV	55	BK 10 EHV	5	PY 10 DXJ	43
GN 57 FBU	55	MV 08 HUK	37	GX 58 GLK	32	YN 58 NDG	24	BK 10 EHW	5	YC 10 HCN	41
GR 57 GWG	57	MX 08 UZL	33	GX 58 GLV	32	YP 58 AOG	59	BK 10 EHX	5	YR 10 ZDC	46
GX 57 AFV	14	MX 08 UZM	33	GX 58 GLY	32			BK 10 EHY	5		
GX 57 BHZ	31	NA 08 YEV	39	GX 58 GLZ	32	CN 09 AOE	55	BK 10 EHZ	5	AE 60 DBX	17
GX 57 BXG	25	RA 08 YSD	46	GX 58 GME	28	CN 09 JYD	37	BK 10 EJU	6	AX 60 BCY	17
GX 57 DJJ	33	SA 08 RWO	19	GX 58 GMF	28	EK 09 OES	40	BK 10 EJV	6	BX 60 EJC	44
GX 57 DJK	33	SN 08 AAF	13	GX 58 GMG	28	EU 09 ERX	41	BK 10 EJX	6	GV 60 GEU	43
GX 57 DJO	33	SN 08 CNJ	36	GX 58 GMO	28	FJ 09 DXH	51	BK 10 EJY	6	GX 60 PBY	29
GX 57 DJU	33	SN 08 CNK	36	GX 58 GMU	28	FN 09 AOO	36	BK 10 EJZ	6	GX 60 PBZ	29
GX 57 DJV	33	WA 08 ULB	54	GX 58 GMV	28	FV 09 VYS	20	EU 10 EBV	54	GX 60 PCV	29
GX 57 DJY	33	WH 08 AGH	37	GX 58 GMY	28	GN 09 PVJ	59	EX 10 RAF	51	GX 60 PCY	29
GX 57 DJZ	33	WX 08 BCK	57	GX 58 GMZ	28	GU 09 YBC	45	GN 10 FXC	54	GX 60 PCZ	29
GX 57 DKA	33	WX 08 BCO	57	GX 58 GNF	29	GX 09 AGO	14	GN 10 FXD	54	GX 60 PDK	29
GX 57 DKD	33	WX 08 BCU	57	GX 58 GNJ	28	GX 09 AGU	14	GN 10 KAU	41	GX 60 PDO	29
GX 57 DKE	33	WX 08 BDE	57	GX 58 GNK	29	GX 09 AGV	14	GP 10 ABU	53	GX 60 PDU	29
GX 57 DKF	33	WX 08 BDO	57	GX 58 GNN	29	GX 09 AGY	14	GV 10 ZWR	56	GX 60 PDV	29
GX 57 DKJ	33	WX 08 BDV	57	GX 58 GNO	29	GX 09 AGZ	14	GX 10 HAA	26	GX 60 PDY	29
GX 57 DKK	33	WX 08 BDY	57	GX 58 GNP	29	GY 09 NUV	54	GX 10 HAE	26	GX 60 PDZ	29
HG 57 EVF	46	YJ 08 EEY	35	GX 58 GNU	29	HG 09 UCV	43	GX 10 HAO	26	GY 60 XCK	45
HJ 57 RWU	49	YM 08 CUO	43	GX 58 GNV	29	HN 09 JYX	52	GX 10 HAU	26	HG 60 CJU	45
HJ 57 RWV	53	YN 08 DFD	39	GX 58 GNY	29	HN 09 WKE	43	GX 10 HBA	26	HG 60 CJV	45
HN 57 VFD	45	YN 08 DFE	39	GX 58 GNZ	29	HN 09 WKF	43	GX 10 HBB	26	HJ 60 KXE	44
HT 57 BUW	49	YN 08 DFJ	21	GX 58 MVE	28	HX 09 CVN	53	GX 10 HBC	26	HJ 60 KXF	44
HV 57 TYY	17	YN 08 DFK	21	GX 58 MVF	28	LJ 09 MJF	55	GX 10 HBD	26	HJ 60 KXU	53
HY 57 UMT	50	YN 08 DFL	21	GX 58 MVG	28	MX 09 HJK	14	GX 10 HBE	26	HK 60 NVT	45
HY 57 UMU	50	YN 08 DFO	21	GX 58 MVH	28	MX 09 MHN	14	GX 10 HBF	26	HX 60 EFH	53
LD 57 DKU	52	YN 08 DFP	21	GX 58 MVJ	28	MX 09 MJJ	33	GX 10 HBG	26	HY 60 XRN	41
LK 57 HBP	42	YN 08 DFU	21	GX 58 MVK	28	SJ 09 VXD	56	GX 10 HBH	26	HY 60 XRN	43
RX 57 BSU	54	YN 08 DFV	21	GX 58 MVL	28	SN 09 EMV	56	GX 10 HBJ	26	MX 60 BXE	14
RX 57 BSV	54	YN 08 DFX	21	GX 58 MVM	28	WH 09 SVN	37	GX 10 HBK	26	OO 60 CLC	10
RX 57 BXZ	35	YN 08 DFY	21	GX 58 MVN	28	YD 09 AUE	47	GX 10 HBL	26	RV 60 DKO	49
RX 57 JDO	48	YN 08 DFZ	21	GX 58 MVO	28	YN 09 DXR	24	GX 10 HBN	26	RV 60 DMU	49
RX 57 JHV	57	YN 08 MPX	14	GX 58 MVP	28	YN 09 DXY	24	GX 10 HBO	26	RV 60 DMX	49
RX 57 JHY	57	YN 08 MPY	14	GX 58 MVR	28	YX 09 FNH	14	GX 10 HBP	26	RV 60 DMY	49
RX 57 JHZ	57	YN 08 MMX	36	GX 58 MVS	28			GX 10 HBU	29	RX 60 HPF	43
RX 57 JJE	57	YN 08 OBP	22	GX 58 MVT	28	BX 59 LZD	51	GX 10 HBY	29	SA 60 DLD	19
RX 57 JJK	57	YN 08 OBR	22	GY 58 UOG	52	DY 59 NBM	57	GX 10 HBZ	29	SA 60 DLF	19
RX 57 JJL	57	YN 08 PKV	5	HN 58 LLE	55	EU 59 CAE	43	GX 10 HCD	29	XX 60 CLC	10
RX 57 JJO	57	YP 08 WFF	49	HN 58 ZDJ	55	FJ 59 CCO	36	GX 10 HCE	29	YJ 60 KHG	14
RX 57 JYO	58	YT 08 URO	52	HY 58 PFG	59	GU 59 FYJ	50	GX 10 HCF	29	YN 60 BZY	24
RX 57 MTU	54	YX 08 ATZ	20	KX 58 BHN	6	GU 59 FXR	47	GX 10 HCG	29	YN 60 FMJ	36
SJ 57 GVL	5	YX 08 KNN	45	KX 58 BHO	6	GU 59 GHA	47	GX 10 HCH	29	YP 60 ABN	41
SN 57 DXC	13			KX 58 GUJ	14	GU 59 MYX	50	GX 10 HCJ	29	YP 60 HCU	41
WA 57 CZC	10	AJ 58 JRV	8	KX 58 GUO	5	GV 59 ONP	44	GX 10 HCK	29	YP 60 KJJ	41
YA 57 XCG	54	BK 58 ACV	53	KY 58 FVP	35	GX 59 JYS	26	GX 10 KZA	29	YR 60 WHC	41
YJ 57 YDA	33	BN 58 POU	58	LX 58 DJE	35	HY 59 FPJ	20	GX 10 KZB	29	YT 60 RHY	59
YN 57 BWE	24	BS 58 OKN	45	LX 58 ZXK	43	HY 59 GXS	50	GX 10 KZC	29	YT 60 RRX	59
YN 57 DVC	19	EU 58 EBM	54	LX 58 ZXN	43	LC 59 WEX	48	GX 10 KZE	29		
YN 57 PYJ	24	EY 58 RZR	38	MX 58 AUT	5	LC 59 WFE	48	GX 10 KZF	29	BP 11 JVF	44
		FV 58 LYC	17	MX 58 VGP	14	LC 59 WFG	48	GX 10 KZG	29	BX 11 GWK	36
AE 08 BGO	19	FV 58 MHO	17	MX 58 VGR	14	LC 59 WFO	48	GX 10 KZH	29	BX 11 KXT	47
CN 08 CWA	38	GU 58 CUX	40	NL 58 TZX	35	LC 59 WFX	48	GX 10 KZJ	29	BX 11 KXV	44
CU 08 EZZ	20	GU 58 CZB	56	PO 58 KPU	13	LC 59 WGE	48	GX 10 KZK	29	BX 11 KYN	53
EU 08 KAX	54	GU 58 DBV	5	PO 58 KPV	13	LX 59 BCF	22	GX 10 KZL	29	BX 11 KYR	44
FX 08 YLA	50	GV 58 EFU	57	PO 58 KPX	13	LX 59 BCO	22	GX 10 KZM	29	BX 11 KYS	44
GN 08 VTD	46	GV 58 EFX	57	PO 58 KRD	13	LX 59 EFS	43	GX 10 KZN	29	CV 11 JXD	38
GR 08 AEV	5	GV 58 EHO	57	RV 58 ORO	50	MX 59 PFZ	46	GX 10 KZO	29	FJ 11 DBY	44
GU 08 ACZ	55	GV 58 EKP	57	RX 58 AOK	58	YK 59 WVP	44	GX 10 KZP	29	FJ 11 DFF	53
GU 08 BTO	58	GV 58 ENU	57	RX 58 AOS	43	YT 59 FDN	59	GX 10 KZR	29	GN 11 GFK	59
GV 08 VDD	58	GV 58 EOM	57	RX 58 GWY	5	YT 59 GDO	59	GX 10 KZS	29	GN 11 KKA	49
GV 08 VEF	58	GV 58 EOO	57	RX 58 GXL	5	YT 59 JWA	59	GX 10 KZT	29	GU 11 YPW	45
GX 08 HBJ	33	GV 58 EOX	57	SN 58 BZC	47	YT 59 NZO	36	GX 10 KZU	29	GU 11 YRW	45
GX 08 HBK	33	GV 58 VLH	57	WR 58 ZWL	57	YX 59 BZB	25	GX 10 KZV	29	GX 11 AKF	28
GX 08 HBN	33	GX 58 AOV	17	WR 58 ZWM	57	YX 59 BZC	25	GX 10 KZW	29	GX 11 AKG	28
GX 08 HBO	33	GX 58 GJO	33	WR 58 ZWN	57	YX 59 BZD	25	GX 10 KZY	29	GX 11 AKJ	28
GX 08 HBP	33	GX 58 GJU	33	WR 58 ZWU	57			HJ 10 VMT	43	GX 11 AKK	28
GX 08 HBU	33	GX 58 GJV	33	WR 58 ZWW	57	AD 10 DYY	6	HN 10 ZYZ	55	GX 11 AKN	28
GX 08 HBY	33	GX 58 GJY	33	WR 58 ZXL	57	AE 10 GGV	57	KX 10 DVH	6	GX 11 AKO	28
GX 08 HBZ	33	GX 58 GJZ	33	WR 58 ZXM	57	AK 10 CCU	49	LR 10 NRL	38	GX 11 AKT	28
HY 08 WLN	51	GX 58 GKZ	31	YG 58 SVZ	51	BK 10 EHT	5	MW 10 DWG	44	GX 11 AKU	29
KC 08 KTC	19			YH 58 EZN	50			MX 10 DVH	53	GX 11 AKV	29

WEST SUSSEX – REGISTRATION / PAGE NUMBER INDEX (continued)

Reg	Pg	Reg	Pg	Reg	Pg	Reg	Pg	Reg	Pg	Reg	Pg
GX 11 AKY	29	OU 12 DMO	42	GY 62 LGL	46	GX 13 FSV	14	YX 63 ZXD	22	YN 14 PLF	36
GX 11 AKZ	29	OU 12 DNO	42	GY 62 XPS	56	GX 13 UWH	49	YX 63 ZXE	22	YT 14 UUD	51
GY 11 EFK	54	OU 12 DNX	42	LJ 62 GKY	49	GY 13 VEM	46	YX 63 ZXF	22	YT 14 UVH	51
HV 11 TLY	51	OU 12 DVT	42	LJ 62 JFO	50	HK 13 KNM	43	YX 63 ZXG	22	YY 14 WGD	33
HY 11 PXF	59	OU 12 DVW	42	LJ 62 JGV	52	HK 13 KNO	43	YY 63 KUB	20	YY 14 WGE	33
LV 11 ORX	43	SN 12 AAE	21	LN 62 TXU	53	NL 13 XNZ	35				
MC 11 CLC	10	SN 12 AAF	21	MX 62 AWU	14	RE 13 CJZ	22	BN 14 CUC	20	LJ 64 BHZ	58
PO 11 LNC	36	SN 12 AAJ	21	MX 62 AWZ	14	RX 13 FSD	46	BN 14 CUG	20	LJ 64 BJF	58
RE 11 YZK	46	SN 12 AAK	21	NL 62 BUP	35	VK 13 BJE	45	BN 14 CUH	20	LJ 64 BJO	58
SF 11 LBE	28	SN 12 AAO	22	SN 62 APY	24	YJ 13 GVP	35	BN 14 CUJ	20	LJ 64 BJU	58
SN 11 CTO	36	SN 12 AAU	22	WA 62 FHV	45	YJ 13 GXS	35	BN 14 CUK	20	LJ 64 BJX	58
YJ 11 GJV	35	VN 12 GNP	48	WA 62 FJY	45	YJ 13 GXT	35	BN 14 CUO	20	LJ 64 BKK	58
YT 11 LPO	35	WA 12 HUV	48	YM 62 CZC	57	YN 13 XYT	39	BN 14 CUU	20	LJ 64 BKL	58
YT 11 YZN	41	YJ 12 CJX	35	YN 62 CLF	21	YP 13 KLC	50	BN 14 CUV	20	LJ 64 BKO	58
		YJ 12 PLX	14	YR 62 CNV	52	YR 13 OEB	45	BN 14 CUW	20	LJ 64 BKV	58
BF 61 HBH	24	YJ 12 PLZ	14	YR 62 EAF	39	YT 13 AMX	36	BN 14 CUX	20	SL 64 HWU	32
FJ 61 BVS	53	YJ 12 PMU	14	YS 62 CPV	57	YT 13 AOG	36	BN 14 CUY	20	SL 64 HWV	32
FJ 61 BVT	53	YJ 12 PMV	14	YS 62 CVR	57	YT 13 HXA	57	BN 14 CVA	20	SL 64 HWX	32
GX 61 AYJ	32	YJ 12 PMX	14	YS 62 HWZ	57	YT 13 KHF	58	BN 14 CVB	20	SL 64 HWY	32
GX 61 AYL	32	YJ 12 PMY	14	YS 62 LNC	57	YT 13 KKL	58	BN 14 CVC	20	SL 64 HWZ	32
GX 61 AYM	32	YS 12 ELO	51	YS 62 RVJ	57	YT 13 KKU	58	BU 14 EFS	20	SL 64 HXA	32
GX 61 AYN	32			YS 62 WGZ	57	YT 13 KWD	58	BU 14 EFT	20	SL 64 HXB	32
GX 61 AYO	32	FN 62 CAO	39	YT 62 JAO	36	YT 13 KWG	58	BU 14 EHK	20	SL 64 HXC	32
GX 61 AYP	32	FN 62 CBV	39			YT 13 KWK	58	BU 14 EHL	20	SL 64 HXD	32
GX 61 AYS	32	FN 62 CDX	39	BX 13 BYF	37	YT 13 KWO	58	BX 14 ONO	10	SL 64 HXE	32
GX 61 AYT	32	FN 62 CEY	39	BX 13 BYG	37	YT 13 LOJ	58	GN 14 DVW	52	SL 64 HXF	32
GX 61 AYU	32	FN 62 CFG	39	GN 13 AKP	59	YT 13 MFA	58	GX 14 LHZ	53	SL 64 HXG	32
GX 61 AYV	32	FN 62 CFX	39	GU 13 FPG	49	YT 13 NYO	58	GX 14 LJZ	53	SL 64 HXH	32
GX 61 AYW	32	FN 62 CGE	39	GU 13 KAA	54	YT 13 OFY	58	GX 14 LNO	53	SL 64 HXJ	32
GX 61 AYY	32	GU 62 EXK	53	GX 13 ANF	33	YT 13 POU	58	GX 14 LOA	53	SL 64 HXK	32
GX 61 AYZ	32	GU 62 PJX	56	GX 13 ANP	33			GX 14 LSV	53	SL 64 HXM	32
GX 61 AZF	48	GV 62 KCG	48	GX 13 ANR	33	GK 63 LXU	47	GX 14 LSY	53	SL 64 HXN	32
GY 61 VYX	56	GX 62 BAO	32	GX 13 ANU	30	GK 63 OTB	52	GX 14 LTN	53	SL 64 HXO	32
HN 61 CHD	42	GX 62 BAV	32	GX 13 ANV	30	GX 63 DFE	56	GX 14 LTK	48	SL 64 HXP	33
HN 61 CJO	42	GX 62 BBK	32	GX 13 AOA	30	GX 63 HJZ	46	LC 14 WPZ	44	WA 64 CVV	39
HX 61 HCA	50	GX 62 BBN	32	GX 13 AOB	29	GX 63 YKD	42	LJ 14 BGO	58	YN 64 XSJ	26
HY 61 NXM	60	GX 62 BCU	32	GX 13 AOC	29	HX 63 EZU	35	LJ 14 BGV	58	YN 64 XSK	26
HY 61 NXO	60	GX 62 BDV	32	GX 13 AOD	29	HX 63 EZV	35	LJ 14 BHA	58	YN 64 XSL	26
LJ 61 BZL	55	GX 62 BDZ	32	GX 13 AOE	30	MK 63 WZX	14	LJ 14 BHD	58	YN 64 XSM	26
LR 61 NKJ	48	GX 62 BFK	32	GX 13 AOF	30	PE 63 PZZ	36	LJ 14 BKV	58	YN 64 XSO	26
LR 61 NKL	48	GX 62 BFV	32	GX 13 AOG	30	SN 63 YPU	30	LJ 14 BKX	58	YN 64 XSP	26
LX 61 BFE	51	GX 62 BGE	32	GX 13 AOH	30	WF 63 JYX	52	LJ 14 BKY	58	YN 64 XSR	26
ND 61 HFK	35	GX 62 BGF	32	GX 13 AOJ	30	WN 63 BKL	35	LJ 14 BLV	58	YN 64 XST	26
NJ 61 GHH	35	GX 62 BHL	32	GX 13 AOK	30	YD 63 VCJ	6	LJ 14 BPE	58	YN 64 XSU	27
PO 61 LUT	36	GX 62 BHZ	32	GX 13 AOL	30	YD 63 VCK	6	LJ 14 BPF	58	YN 64 XSV	27
SN 61 CXJ	35	GX 62 BKG	32	GX 13 AOM	30	YD 63 VCL	6	LJ 14 BPU	58	YN 64 XSW	27
VA 61 BFN	14	GX 62 BMZ	32	GX 13 AON	30	YN 63 BYY	19	LJ 14 BPY	58	YN 64 XSX	27
YD 61 GWM	60	GX 62 BNL	32	GX 13 AOO	30	YN 63 BYZ	19	LJ 14 BTF	58	YS 64 UJP	45
YJ 61 CKE	6	GX 62 BNZ	32	GX 13 AOP	30	YS 63 NMX	53	LJ 14 BTU	58		
YJ 61 CKF	6	GX 62 BPV	29	GX 13 AOR	30	YT 63 PMU	59	LJ 14 BUA	58	BN 15 LGX	47
YJ 61 CKG	6	GX 62 BPZ	29	GX 13 AOS	30	YT 63 RKE	59	LJ 14 BUE	58	SK 15 HBC	14
YS 61 RXW	59	GX 62 BTV	29	GX 13 AOT	30	YX 63 GYA	32	LJ 14 BXC	58	SK 15 HBD	14
YS 61 UYL	59	GX 62 BUJ	29	GX 13 AOU	30	YX 63 GYB	32	LJ 14 BXH	58	SK 15 HBE	14
		GX 62 BUU	29	GX 13 AOV	30	YX 63 GYC	32	NL 14 UZO	35	YY 15 GBZ	22
BJ 12 YBM	54	GX 62 BUV	29	GX 13 AOW	30	YX 63 GYD	32	YJ 14 BVG	33	YY 15 GCF	22
GN 12 GYS	50	GX 62 BVA	29	GX 13 AOY	30	YX 63 GYE	32	YJ 14 BVH	33	YY 15 GCK	22
GU 12 ZHG	50	GX 62 BVV	29	GX 13 AOZ	30	YX 63 GYF	32	YJ 14 BVK	33	YY 15 GCO	22
GX 12 DXM	26	GX 62 BVW	29	GX 13 APF	32	YX 63 GYH	32	YJ 14 BVS	33	YY 15 GCU	22
GX 12 DXP	26	GX 62 BWJ	29	GX 13 APK	32	YX 63 GYJ	32	YJ 14 BVT	33	YY 15 GCV	22
GX 12 DXR	26	GX 62 CJO	14	GX 13 APO	32	YX 63 KFD	32	YJ 14 BVU	33	YY 15 GCX	22
GX 12 DXS	26	GX 62 CJU	14	GX 13 APU	32	YX 63 KFE	32	YJ 14 BVV	33	YY 15 GCZ	22
GX 12 DXT	26	GX 62 CKP	14	GX 13 APV	32	YX 63 KFF	32	YJ 14 BVW	33	YY 15 GDA	22
GX 12 DXU	26	GX 62 CMU	14	GX 13 FSL	14	YX 63 ZWW	22	YJ 14 BVX	33	YY 15 GDE	22
GY 12 OCS	56	GX 62 CMY	14	GX 13 FSN	14	YX 63 ZWY	22	YJ 14 BVZ	33		
HV 12 XRG	43	GX 62 CNN	14	GX 13 FSO	14	YX 63 ZWZ	22	YJ 14 CAO	35		
HY 12 KCO	49	GX 62 COA	14	GX 13 FSP	14	YX 63 ZXA	22	YJ 14 CAX	35		
LX 12 BGV	51	GX 62 CSF	14	GX 13 FSS	14	YX 63 ZXB	22	YJ 14 CDY	35		
OU 12 DJF	42			GX 13 FSU	14	YX 63 ZXC	22	YN 14 NRE	24		

OPERATING NAMES AND FLEET NAMES

The following is a list of operating names and fleet names for all operators in the county of West Sussex (WS) who display a name other than their official one.   This list is correct to the PSV Circle News Sheet 905 (June 2015).

Name	Operator's Title
1st Class Travel	Johnson, Woodingdean
A & M Transport	Ahouchi, Crawley
Ace Taxis (Worthing)	Hunnisett, Worthing
Airport Shuttle	Lewis, Haywards Heath
Arun Coaches	Miller, Horsham
B C D	Brotheridge, Horsham
Benjamin's Travel	Ephgrave, Lancing
Black Tie Limo	Howell, Worthing
Breaks-A-Way Travel	Slack, Worthing
Brighton Travel	Williams & Johnson, Beeding
Brightonian	Walker, Beeding
Bunn Leisure	White Horse, Selsey
Channel Travel	Collins, Castle Goring
Crawley Luxury Coaches	Brown, Crawley
D J Services	Jell, East Preston
Davids Travel	Burditt, Haywards Heath
Door 2 Door Shuttle Bus	Hove, Burgess Hill
First Choice Taxis	Roadley, Horsham
Forestburn Enterprises	Kirkwood, Bognor Regis
Gatwick Worth Hotel	Pearl Hotel, Crawley
Goldline	Stagecoach (South)
Hello Travel	Sweetman, Copthorne
Heritage Travel	Coach Hire, Colgate
Horsham Mini Travel	Cable, Horsham
I C C Tours	Collins, Castle Goring
I C P Travel	Pullen, Worthing
Midhurst & Rogate Cars	Farren, Rogate
Normans Travel	Hudson, Bosham
Ocean Coaches	Woodcock, Beeding
Park Limos	Thomas, Faygate
Pavilion Coaches	Hammer, Beeding
Premier Transport	Storbrook, Crawley
Prestige Cars	Malik, Crawley
Richards Minibuses	Brighton Minibus, Worthing
Roadrunner Sussex	Francis & Galton, Lancing
Route 1	Ames, Worthing
Rutherfords Travel	Bell, Eastergate
South East Provincial	Storbrook, Crawley
Southern Transit	Bird, Beeding
Stagecoach in Hants & Surrey	Stagecoach (South)
SussexBus.com (The)	City of Chichester Coaches, Colgate
Sussex Coaches	Ayling, Shipley
Tarring Coaches	Silverton, West Worthing
Taxibus.com (The)	Browning, West Chiltington
United Hire	Khan, Crawley
Westrings	Buckland, East Wittering
Ward Air Travel	Cooksley, Worthing
Yourstaff	Garcia, Bognor Regis

CURRENT AREA/COUNTY CODE to NEWS SHEET INDEX

BD	5	Bedfordshire	HA	2	Hampshire	Qd	BJ	Dealer/Manufacturer
BE	3	Berkshire	HR	4	Herefordshire			demonstrator
BK	5	Buckinghamshire	HT	5	Hertfordshire	SE	9	Scotland East
CA	6	Cumbria	HW	4	Herefordshire &	SH	4	Shropshire
CC	8	Cymru South Central			Worcestershire	SK	5	Suffolk
CD	7	Cleveland	IM	6	Isle of Man	SN	9	Scotland North
CH	6	Cheshire	IS	3	Isles of Scilly	SO	3	Somerset
CI	3	Channel Islands	IW	2	Isle of Wight	SR	2	Surrey
CM	5	Cambridgeshire	KT	2	Kent	SS	9	Scotland South
CN	8	Cymru North	LA	6	Lancashire	ST	4	Staffordshire
CO	3	Cornwall	LE	4	Leicestershire	SW	9	Scotland West
CS	8	Cymru South East	LI	5	Lincolnshire	SY	7	South Yorkshire
CW	8	Cymru Mid & West	LN	1	Greater London	TW	7	Tyne & Wear
DE	4	Derbyshire	MY	6	Merseyside	WI	3	Wiltshire
DM	7	Durham	NG	4	Nottinghamshire	WK	4	Warwickshire
DN	3	Devon	ND	7	Northumberland	WM	4	West Midlands
DT	3	Dorset	NI	9	Northern Ireland	WO	4	Worcestershire
EI	8	Irish Republic	NK	5	Norfolk	WS	2	West Sussex
ES	2	East Sussex	NO	5	Northamptonshire	WY	7	West Yorkshire
EX	2	Essex	NY	7	North Yorkshire	X	BJ	National non-PSV
EY	7	East Yorkshire	O	OJ	Overseas	Y	MB	Non-PSV Minibuses
GL	3	Gloucestershire	OX	3	Oxfordshire			
GM	6	Greater Manchester						

Discovered a mistake ? A missing vehicle ? A withdrawn vehicle ? Know of an Operating Centre
that is not given ? These lists are only as up to date as readers' reports.
If you can add anything on any operator covered in this publication
please send your comments to:-

**The PSV Circle, Unit GK Leroy House, 436 Essex Road, LONDON, N1 3QP
or by e-mail to: reports@psv-circle.org.uk**

KMK 290515   www.psv-circle.org.uk